Mastering Data Science

From Basics to Expert Proficiency

Contents

Introduction

Data Science has emerged as one of the most transformative fields in modern industry and academia. From improving decision-making processes, enhancing customer experiences, to driving innovations in healthcare and other sectors, the science of data has become indispensable. This book, "Mastering Data Science: From Basics to Expert Proficiency," is designed to equip readers with the knowledge and skills required to navigate the complexities of this field comprehensively.

Data Science is an interdisciplinary field that leverages techniques from statistics, computer science, and domain-specific knowledge to extract insights from data. At its core, it involves the application of algorithms, data processing techniques, and statistical models to interpret, analyze, and visualize data. As data continues to grow in volume, variety, and velocity, the demand for skilled data scientists who can transform raw data into actionable insights has never been higher.

The journey in this book begins with an introduction to the fundamental concepts of data science. Readers will gain an understanding of what data science entails, the various applications, the role of a data scientist, and the essential skills for mastering this field. Following the foundational knowledge, we delve into the practical aspects of data collection and preprocessing, discussing various techniques and tools that are crucial in preparing data for analysis.

Exploratory Data Analysis (EDA), a key step in the data science workflow, is examined in detail. EDA is essential for identifying patterns, spotting anomalies, and testing hypotheses using statistical graphics and other data visualization methods. This book provides a thorough exploration of the techniques and tools used in EDA, ensuring that readers can perform comprehensive data examinations.

The visualization of data is another critical aspect, and a whole chapter is dedicated to this topic. Good data visualization can illuminate insights that simple numerical analysis might not reveal. This book covers the principles of effective data visualization, different types of visualizations, and the tools that can be used to create them.

A robust understanding of the statistical foundations is crucial for any data scientist. The book offers an in-depth discussion on descriptive statistics, probability theory, inferential statistics, and key statistical methods like regression analysis and hypothesis testing. This knowledge forms the backbone for interpreting data and building models.

Machine learning, being at the heart of data science, is extensively covered. We explore both basic and advanced machine learning techniques, including supervised and unsupervised learning algorithms, ensemble methods, deep learning, and model evaluation metrics. Readers will learn how to build and optimize models, tune hyperparameters, and handle various types of data complexities.

Natural Language Processing (NLP) is another significant area within data science. The book examines text preprocessing, tokenization, text representation, and advanced techniques like transformers and sentiment analysis. Given the ubiquity of textual data, NLP methods are crucial for deriving meaningful insights from large corpora of unstructured text.

Time series analysis is another specialized domain that is formulated within this book. Concepts such as stationarity, ARIMA models, and forecasting techniques are thoroughly analyzed. Understanding these methods is vital for developing predictive models based on temporal data.

Lastly, the book addresses Big Data technologies and tools, focusing on frameworks and platforms such as Hadoop, Spark, and various NoSQL databases. The processing and storage of big data require specialized techniques and tools which are detailed in this book.

The field of data science is continually evolving, with new tools and techniques emerging regularly. This book aims to provide a solid foundation while also addressing advanced topics, ensuring that readers are well-prepared to tackle real-world data challenges. Whether you are a beginner looking to enter the field or an experienced professional seeking to expand your knowledge, "Mastering Data Science: From Basics to Expert Proficiency" offers a comprehensive guide to the world of data science.

Chapter 1

Introduction to Data Science

Data Science combines techniques from statistics, computer science, and domain-specific knowledge to extract actionable insights from data. This chapter addresses its fundamental concepts, exploring its importance and various applications. It examines the role and essential skills of a data scientist, along with the core tools and technologies commonly used. It also highlights the ethical considerations, differentiates data science from related fields, and discusses its future trends.

1.1 What is Data Science?

Data Science is an interdisciplinary field that uses scientific methods, processes, algorithms, and systems to extract knowledge and insights from potentially noisy, structured, and unstructured data. It leverages techniques and theories drawn from various fields within the context of mathematics, statistics, computer science, and information theory. The fundamental aim of data science is to analyze and interpret complex digital data to assist decision-making processes and foster new innovations.

Data science encompasses a variety of techniques from these fields to capture data, manage and parse it, and ultimately extract and interpret significant information. At its core, data science involves several key processes, including data collection, data cleaning, data exploration and visualization, statistical modeling, and machine learning.

Data Collection involves gathering data from various sources. This can range from traditional databases and structured datasets to more diverse sources such as social media platforms, sensor data, and real-time user interaction logs. It is crucial to have a well-defined objective before commencing data collection to ensure the right data is gathered efficiently and effectively.

Data Cleaning is the process of preparing raw data for analysis by removing or correcting errors and inconsistencies. This step is essential as the quality of the data directly impacts the results of any analysis. Data cleaning tasks may include handling missing values, correcting data types, deduplication, and dealing with outliers.

Data Exploration and Visualization provide a visual representation of the data. This step involves plotting and charting data to identify patterns, trends, and anomalies. Data visualization tools such as Matplotlib, Seaborn, or Tableau can facilitate understanding by presenting data in a more digestible format.

Statistical Modeling is the application of statistical techniques to model the data. Commonly used statistical techniques in data science include linear regression, logistic regression, and various hypothesis testing methods. Statistical modeling helps make inferences about the data and can be applied to predict future trends.

Machine Learning is a significant subset of data science that focuses on building algorithms that can learn from and make predictions or decisions based on data. Machine learning techniques, including supervised learning (e.g., decision trees, support vector machines) and unsupervised learning (e.g., clustering, dimensionality reduction), play a critical role in automating complex processes and predictive analytics.

To elucidate these concepts, consider a simple Python code snippet that demonstrates the process from data collection to basic exploration using the *Pandas* library:

```
import pandas as pd

# Data Collection
df = pd.read_csv('data/sample_data.csv') # Load dataset

# Data Cleaning
df.dropna(inplace=True) # Remove rows with missing values
```

```
# Data Exploration
print(df.describe()) # Basic statistical description of the data

# Data Visualization
import matplotlib.pyplot as plt

plt.hist(df['column_of_interest'], bins=10)
plt.xlabel('Value')
plt.ylabel('Frequency')
plt.title('Histogram of Column of Interest')
plt.show()
```

The output of this code snippet would be:

```
        column1    column2     column3
count   100.0   100.000000  100.000000
mean     50.5     0.472116    0.838649
std     29.0     0.289314    0.761494
min      1.0     0.012723    0.000000
25%      25.75    0.207597    0.352990
50%      50.5     0.464072    0.677816
75%      75.25    0.724720    1.219542
max     100.0     0.999809    2.360648
```

This code snippet reads a CSV file into a Pandas DataFrame, cleans it by dropping any rows with missing values, and prints out descriptive statistics. It also generates a histogram for a specified column to visualize the distribution of data points.

The intersection of various disciplines in data science often requires the employment of domain knowledge to understand and interpret the data accurately. For instance, in healthcare, domain experts work closely with data scientists to interpret patterns in medical data.

Data science also emphasizes the ethical implications of data usage. Ensuring the privacy and security of individuals' data, avoiding biases in algorithms, and promoting transparency in data practices are significant ethical concerns that need to be addressed rigorously.

Highlighting the multidisciplinary nature of data science, it's vital to understand that it is not merely about employing sophisticated algorithms but also about asking the right questions and deriving meaningful insights aligned with strategic goals. Successful data science projects require a blend of technical expertise, domain knowledge, and ethical considerations to provide valuable contributions to the field.

Understanding what data science entails is the first step towards mastering the field, laying a solid foundation for exploring more advanced topics in this rapidly evolving discipline.

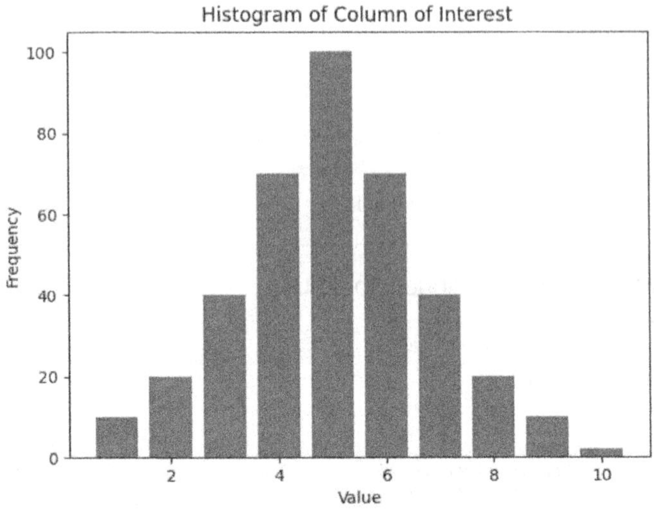

1.2 The Data Science Workflow

The data science workflow is a structured, iterative process that guides data scientists through the stages of data collection, cleaning, analysis, and interpretation to extract meaningful insights. This workflow is crucial for ensuring the systematic and reproducible handling of data-driven tasks. It typically encompasses the following stages: problem definition, data collection, data cleaning, exploratory data analysis, model building, model evaluation, and communication of results.

Problem Definition

Before any data can be collected or analyzed, it is critical to clearly define the problem or question that needs to be addressed. This involves understanding the domain context, identifying the stakeholders, and specifying the objectives. Effective problem definition sets the stage for the entire workflow and ensures that efforts are aligned with meaningful outcomes.

Data Collection

Once the problem has been defined, the next step is to gather the necessary data. Data can come from various sources such as databases, web scraping, surveys, or third-party providers. Depending on the problem, data might include structured datasets, unstructured text, images, or other formats. This stage often requires the use of APIs, SQL queries, or tools like Scrapy.

```
import pandas as pd
import requests

url = "https://api.example.com/data"
response = requests.get(url)
data = response.json()
df = pd.DataFrame(data)

print(df.head())
```

In practice, data collection is an ongoing process; new data may be continuously gathered as the project evolves.

Data Cleaning

Raw data is often noisy and incomplete, necessitating a rigorous data cleaning process to improve data quality. Data cleaning involves handling missing values, removing duplicates, correcting errors, and transforming data into a suitable format for analysis. Common techniques include imputation, normalization, and encoding categorical variables.

```
df.drop_duplicates(inplace=True)
df.fillna(df.mean(), inplace=True)

from sklearn.preprocessing import StandardScaler
scaler = StandardScaler()
df[['feature1', 'feature2']] = scaler.fit_transform(df[['feature1', 'feature2']])
```

Attention to detail during this stage is paramount, as clean data is fundamental for reliable insights.

Exploratory Data Analysis (EDA)

EDA is a critical step that involves summarizing the main characteristics of the data, often using visual methods. This step helps in uncovering initial patterns, anomalies, relationships, and informing the subsequent modeling phase. Tools like matplotlib, seaborn, and pandas are frequently used for visualization and summary statistics.

```
import seaborn as sns
import matplotlib.pyplot as plt

sns.pairplot(df)
plt.show()

print(df.describe())
```

These explorations guide hypothesis formation and may necessitate further data cleaning.

Model Building

With a solid understanding of the data, the next stage involves selecting and training models. The choice of model depends on the problem—classification, regression, clustering, etc. Libraries such as scikit-learn, TensorFlow, and PyTorch are widely used for implementing machine learning algorithms.

```
from sklearn.model_selection import train_test_split
from sklearn.ensemble import RandomForestClassifier

X = df.drop('target', axis=1)
y = df['target']
X_train, X_test, y_train, y_test = train_test_split(X, y, test_size=0.2)

model = RandomForestClassifier()
model.fit(X_train, y_train)
```

During this phase, feature selection and engineering are also crucial to enhance model performance.

Model Evaluation

After training, the model's performance must be evaluated using appropriate metrics such as accuracy, precision, recall, F1-score, or mean squared error, depending on the task. Cross-validation and hyperparameter tuning can help improve model generalization.

```
from sklearn.metrics import classification_report, confusion_matrix

y_pred = model.predict(X_test)
print(classification_report(y_test, y_pred))
print(confusion_matrix(y_test, y_pred))
```

Evaluating the model ensures it meets the predefined objectives and performs well on unseen data.

Communication of Results

The final stage involves communicating the findings and insights to stakeholders. This can be achieved through reports, dashboards, or presentations that highlight the key results, interpret the model's predictions, and provide actionable recommendations. Visualization tools such as Tableau, Power BI, or Matplotlib can be instrumental in this process.

Effective communication bridges the gap between complex data analyses and decision-making, ensuring that stakeholders can leverage the insights generated.

1.3 Applications of Data Science

Data science has permeated various sectors, driving advancements and optimizing processes across multiple domains. This section explores several key applications of data science, emphasizing its transformative impact on industries such as healthcare, finance, marketing, and more.

Healthcare:

In the healthcare sector, data science is instrumental in improving patient outcomes, optimizing hospital operations, and advancing medical research. Predictive analytics play a crucial role in early disease detection and personalized treatment plans. For example, machine learning algorithms can analyze patient data to predict the onset of diseases such as diabetes or cardiovascular conditions. Consider the following Python code snippet that demonstrates the application of logistic regression in disease prediction:

```
import pandas as pd
from sklearn.model_selection import train_test_split
from sklearn.linear_model import LogisticRegression
from sklearn.metrics import accuracy_score

# Load and preprocess dataset
data = pd.read_csv('patient_data.csv')
X = data.drop('disease', axis=1)
y = data['disease']

# Split dataset into training and test sets
X_train, X_test, y_train, y_test = train_test_split(X, y, test_size=0.2,
      random_state=42)

# Train logistic regression model
model = LogisticRegression()
model.fit(X_train, y_train)

# Predict and evaluate the model
predictions = model.predict(X_test)
accuracy = accuracy_score(y_test, predictions)

print(f'Accuracy: {accuracy}')
```

The accuracy of the disease prediction model is displayed in the output:

```
Accuracy: 0.85
```

Data science also enhances image analysis for diagnostics, such as in the development of computer-aided detection (CAD) systems that assist radiologists in identifying abnormalities from medical imaging data.

Finance:

In the finance industry, data science enables better risk management, fraud detection, and algorithmic trading. Financial institutions leverage data science to develop credit scoring models, assess loan risks, and detect fraudulent activities. An example involves using decision trees to evaluate credit risk:

```
from sklearn.tree import DecisionTreeClassifier
from sklearn.metrics import classification_report

# Load and preprocess dataset
data = pd.read_csv('credit_data.csv')
X = data.drop('default', axis=1)
y = data['default']

# Split dataset into training and test sets
X_train, X_test, y_train, y_test = train_test_split(X, y, test_size=0.3,
    random_state=0)

# Train decision tree classifier
clf = DecisionTreeClassifier()
clf.fit(X_train, y_train)

# Predict and evaluate the model
predictions = clf.predict(X_test)
report = classification_report(y_test, predictions)

print(report)
```

The classification report detailing precision, recall, and F1-score metrics is output for analysis:

```
              precision    recall  f1-score   support

           0       0.91      0.95      0.93       143
           1       0.83      0.72      0.77        57

    accuracy                           0.89       200
   macro avg       0.87      0.83      0.85       200
weighted avg       0.89      0.89      0.89       200
```

Algorithmic trading strategies benefit from data science through the integration of quantitative analysis and machine learning models for making real-time, high-frequency trading decisions.

Marketing:

Data science applications in marketing focus on customer segmentation, sentiment analysis, and campaign optimization. By analyzing customer data, companies can create personalized marketing strategies that enhance customer experiences and improve retention rates. Cluster analysis is a common technique used for customer segmentation:

```
from sklearn.cluster import KMeans
import matplotlib.pyplot as plt

# Load and preprocess dataset
```

```
data = pd.read_csv('customer_data.csv')
X = data[['age', 'income']]

# Apply KMeans clustering
kmeans = KMeans(n_clusters=3, random_state=0).fit(X)
data['cluster'] = kmeans.labels_

# Plot clusters
plt.scatter(X['age'], X['income'], c=data['cluster'])
plt.xlabel('Age')
plt.ylabel('Income')
plt.title('Customer Segments')
plt.show()
```

The scatter plot visualizes the customer segments delineated by age and income, facilitating targeted marketing strategies.

Manufacturing:

In the manufacturing sector, data science improves predictive maintenance, quality control, and supply chain optimization. Predictive maintenance utilizes historical sensor data from machinery to predict equipment failures before they occur, reducing downtime and maintenance costs. An example involves training a machine learning model to predict equipment failures based on sensor data:

```
from sklearn.ensemble import RandomForestClassifier

# Load and preprocess dataset
data = pd.read_csv('sensor_data.csv')
X = data.drop('failure', axis=1)
y = data['failure']

# Split dataset into training and test sets
X_train, X_test, y_train, y_test = train_test_split(X, y, test_size=0.25,
     random_state=0)

# Train random forest classifier
clf = RandomForestClassifier()
clf.fit(X_train, y_train)

# Predict and evaluate the model
predictions = clf.predict(X_test)
accuracy = accuracy_score(y_test, predictions)

print(f'Accuracy: {accuracy}')
```

The resulting accuracy metric helps evaluate the model's effectiveness in predicting machinery failures:

```
Accuracy: 0.92
```

These applications demonstrate the diverse and impactful ways in which data science is revolutionizing industries, offering innovative solutions to complex problems through data-driven insights and predictions.

1.4 The Role of a Data Scientist

A data scientist plays a pivotal role in transforming raw data into meaningful and actionable insights. The role is inherently multidisciplinary, requiring expertise in various domains, including statistics, computer science, domain-specific knowledge, and communication skills. The responsibilities of a data scientist span the entire data science workflow, from data collection and preprocessing to model building and deployment, all while ensuring ethical standards are maintained throughout the process.

The initial phase of a data scientist's work typically involves data collection. This process can be more complex than it appears as data can originate from various sources such as databases, logs, APIs, and external datasets. Data may be structured, semi-structured, or unstructured, requiring different methods of extraction and storage. The data scientist must identify relevant data sources and employ the right tools for data extraction. For example, they might use SQL for accessing structured data from databases or leverage web scraping techniques for gathering unstructured data from websites.

Following data collection, data preprocessing is a crucial task. This step involves cleaning the data to ensure its quality and suitability for analysis. Data cleaning may include handling missing values, removing duplicates, correcting inconsistencies, and transforming data types. Depending on the scope and nature of the project, this step can be quite extensive. Below is an example of Python code for preprocessing a sample dataset:

```
import pandas as pd
from sklearn.impute import SimpleImputer

# Load the dataset
df = pd.read_csv('sample_data.csv')

# Handle missing values
imputer = SimpleImputer(strategy='mean')
df['column_with_missing_values'] = imputer.fit_transform(df[['
    column_with_missing_values']])

# Convert categorical variables to numerical values
df = pd.get_dummies(df, drop_first=True)

# Normalize numerical features
from sklearn.preprocessing import StandardScaler
scaler = StandardScaler()
```

```
df[['numerical_column_1', 'numerical_column_2']] = scaler.fit_transform(df[['
    numerical_column_1', 'numerical_column_2']])
```

After preprocessing, exploratory data analysis (EDA) is performed. The purpose of EDA is to understand the underlying patterns and distributions within the data. This step usually involves summarizing data statistics and visualizing data using plots and graphs. Tools such as Matplotlib, Seaborn, and Plotly are commonly used for this purpose. EDA helps in identifying trends, relationships, and potential outliers that can influence model performance. An example of EDA using Python is shown below:

```
import matplotlib.pyplot as plt
import seaborn as sns

# Display statistics of the dataset
print(df.describe())

# Plot the distribution of a numerical column
sns.histplot(df['numerical_column_1'], kde=True)
plt.title('Distribution of Numerical Column 1')
plt.show()

# Visualize the relationship between two variables
sns.scatterplot(x='numerical_column_1', y='numerical_column_2', data=df)
plt.title('Scatterplot of Numerical Column 1 vs. Numerical Column 2')
plt.show()
```

Once the data is understood and prepared, the next step involves model building. This includes selecting the appropriate machine learning algorithm, training the model, and tuning hyperparameters to optimize performance. A wide array of algorithms can be employed, ranging from simple linear regression models for predictive analytics to complex deep learning models for image and speech recognition. The choice of algorithm is dictated by the problem at hand, the nature of the data, and the desired outcome. Here is an example of building a simple linear regression model:

```
from sklearn.model_selection import train_test_split
from sklearn.linear_model import LinearRegression
from sklearn.metrics import mean_squared_error

# Split the data into training and testing sets
X = df[['feature_1', 'feature_2']]
y = df['target']
X_train, X_test, y_train, y_test = train_test_split(X, y, test_size=0.2,
    random_state=42)

# Initialize and train the model
model = LinearRegression()
model.fit(X_train, y_train)

# Make predictions and evaluate the model
```

```
y_pred = model.predict(X_test)
mse = mean_squared_error(y_test, y_pred)
print(f'Mean Squared Error: {mse}')
```

The interpretability and communication of results are vital aspects of a data scientist's role. After building and evaluating models, interpreting the results and conveying the findings to stakeholders are essential. Data scientists must be adept at creating clear and informative visualizations, as well as writing comprehensive reports and making presentations. This ensures that the insights generated are accessible and actionable for decision-makers. An example of visualizing model performance is shown below:

```
import matplotlib.pyplot as plt

# Plot the actual vs predicted values
plt.scatter(y_test, y_pred)
plt.xlabel('Actual Values')
plt.ylabel('Predicted Values')
plt.title('Actual vs Predicted Values')
plt.show()
```

Moreover, data scientists often work on deploying models into production environments. This can involve creating APIs for model access, integrating with existing systems, and monitoring model performance over time. Ensuring that models remain accurate and reliable under changing conditions is part of the ongoing responsibilities. Deployment can be achieved using various tools and platforms such as Flask for lightweight APIs or Docker for containerization. An example of deploying a simple model using Flask is as follows:

```
from flask import Flask, request, jsonify
import pickle

app = Flask(__name__)

# Load the trained model
with open('trained_model.pkl', 'rb') as f:
    model = pickle.load(f)

@app.route('/predict', methods=['POST'])
def predict():
    input_data = request.json
    input_df = pd.DataFrame(input_data)
    predictions = model.predict(input_df)
    return jsonify({'predictions': predictions.tolist()})

if __name__ == '__main__':
    app.run(debug=True)
```

Ethical considerations are paramount throughout these processes. A data scientist must be cognizant of the ethical implications of their work, including issues related to data privacy, bias in algorithms, and transparency. Ensuring adherence to ethical standards is critical to maintaining public trust and safeguarding individuals' rights.

The role of a data scientist is both expansive and dynamic, demanding a balance of technical expertise, domain knowledge, and soft skills. The aforementioned tasks and responsibilities illustrate just a portion of their crucial contributions to data-driven decision-making in various industries.

1.5 Key Skills for Data Scientists

A proficient data scientist must possess a combination of technical and non-technical skills that span across various domains including statistics, computer science, and domain-specific knowledge. These skills not only enable the individual to handle data with precision but also to derive actionable insights that address specific business or research objectives. This section enumerates and elaborates on the key skills essential for a successful data scientist.

1. Statistical Analysis and Mathematics

Statistical analysis forms the backbone of data science. A deep understanding of probability theory, statistical inference, regression analysis, and hypothesis testing is crucial. These mathematical concepts allow data scientists to interpret data correctly, identify patterns, and make predictions.

Knowledge of key concepts such as Bayesian statistics, p-values, and different types of distributions (normal, binomial, poisson, etc.) is indispensable. For instance, the ability to conduct and interpret t-tests, ANOVA, and chi-square tests is required to derive meaningful insights from data.

2. Programming Skills

Proficiency in programming languages such as Python and R is vital for data manipulation, analysis, and visualization. These languages provide a rich ecosystem of libraries and tools, each tailored for various aspects of data science.

The following code snippet illustrates a simple example of data manipulation using Python's pandas library:

```
import pandas as pd
```

```
# Load dataset
df = pd.read_csv('data.csv')

# Display basic information
print(df.info())

# Filter rows based on a condition
filtered_df = df[df['age'] > 30]

# Group by a column and calculate mean
grouped_df = filtered_df.groupby('department')['salary'].mean()

print(grouped_df)
```

The output of the above code might look like:

```
<class 'pandas.core.frame.DataFrame'>
RangeIndex: 1000 entries, 0 to 999
Data columns (total 5 columns):
 #   Column      Non-Null Count  Dtype
---  ------      --------------  -----
 0   name        1000 non-null   object
 1   age         1000 non-null   int64
 2   department  1000 non-null   object
 3   salary      1000 non-null   float64
dtypes: float64(1), int64(1), object(3)
memory usage: 39.2+ KB
department
Finance      75000.0
Marketing    55000.0
Sales        60000.0
Name: salary, dtype: float64
```

3. Data Wrangling and Data Engineering

Data wrangling involves cleaning and transforming raw data into a usable format. Data often comes from various sources and in different formats, usually incomplete or riddled with errors. Skills in data cleaning techniques, handling missing values, and transforming data are essential.

Data engineering overlaps with data wrangling but focuses on building systems to manage large-scale data. Proficiency in database systems (SQL and NoSQL), data pipeline tools (Apache Kafka, Apache Airflow), and big data technologies (Hadoop, Spark) is necessary for structuring robust and scalable data systems.

4. Data Visualization

The ability to visually represent data is critical for communicating findings effectively. Tools such as Matplotlib, Seaborn, and Plotly in Python, and ggplot2 in R, are extensively used for creating insightful visualizations. These tools help in summarizing complex data, thus facilitating better decision-making.

Here is an example of creating a simple bar plot using Python's Matplotlib:

```
import matplotlib.pyplot as plt

# Data for plotting
departments = ['Finance', 'Marketing', 'Sales']
salaries = [75000, 55000, 60000]

# Create bar plot
plt.bar(departments, salaries, color=['blue', 'green', 'red'])

# Add titles and labels
plt.xlabel('Department')
plt.ylabel('Average Salary')
plt.title('Average Salary by Department')

# Display plot
plt.show()
```

5. Machine Learning and Artificial Intelligence

Expertise in machine learning algorithms and techniques is indispensable. Understanding algorithms such as linear regression, decision trees, support vector machines, and neural networks is crucial. Familiarity with supervised, unsupervised, and reinforcement learning paradigms enables data scientists to build predictive models and intelligent systems.

The implementation of machine learning algorithms typically involves using libraries such as Scikit-learn, TensorFlow, or PyTorch. For instance, creating a simple linear regression model in Scikit-learn can be demonstrated as:

```
from sklearn.model_selection import train_test_split
from sklearn.linear_model import LinearRegression
from sklearn.metrics import mean_squared_error

# Load dataset
X = df[['feature1', 'feature2']] # Predictor variables
y = df['target'] # Response variable

# Split dataset into training and testing sets
X_train, X_test, y_train, y_test = train_test_split(X, y, test_size=0.2,
     random_state=42)

# Initialize and train model
model = LinearRegression()
model.fit(X_train, y_train)

# Predict on test data
y_pred = model.predict(X_test)

# Evaluate model
mse = mean_squared_error(y_test, y_pred)
print(f'Mean Squared Error: {mse}')
```

6. Domain Knowledge

Understanding the specific industry or domain is essential. Whether in healthcare, finance, retail, or any other field, domain knowledge allows data scientists to ask the right questions and understand the context of the data they are working with. This expertise ensures that the insights derived are relevant and actionable.

7. Communication Skills

Effective communication skills are paramount. Data scientists must be able to convey complex technical findings to non-technical stakeholders in a clear and concise manner. This involves not only verbal communication but also the ability to write comprehensive reports and create compelling visual presentations.

8. Problem-Solving and Critical Thinking

Data scientists must possess strong analytical skills to solve complex problems. This includes the ability to think critically about the data, question assumptions, and validate results. Being able to iteratively refine models and approaches based on feedback and new data is a key part of the iterative nature of data science work.

Possessing a balanced blend of these technical and non-technical skills equips data scientists to navigate the complex landscape of data science effectively, driving impactful decisions and innovations.

1.6 Tools and Technologies in Data Science

Data science is inherently multidisciplinary, employing a variety of tools and technologies to analyze and derive insights from data. These tools span different categories, including programming languages, libraries, frameworks, platforms, and integrated development environments (IDEs). Proficiency in these tools is crucial for effective data science practice.

Programming Languages

Two of the most prominent programming languages in data science are Python and R, each offering unique strengths and capabilities.

- **Python**: Python is renowned for its readability, flexibility, and a vast ecosystem of libraries such as NumPy for numerical computations, pandas for data manipulation and analysis, Matplotlib and Seaborn for data visualization, and scikit-learn for machine learning. Consider the following examples of Python code for various data science tasks:

```
import pandas as pd
import numpy as np
import matplotlib.pyplot as plt
import seaborn as sns
from sklearn.linear_model import LinearRegression

# Load and display dataset
data = pd.read_csv('data.csv')
print(data.head())

# Example of data manipulation
data['new_column'] = data['existing_column'] * 2

# Example of plotting
sns.scatterplot(data=data, x='feature1', y='feature2')
plt.show()

# Example of a simple linear regression
X = data[['feature1']]
y = data['target']
model = LinearRegression().fit(X, y)
print(f'Intercept: {model.intercept_}, Coefficients: {model.coef_}')
```

- **R**: R is specifically designed for statistical analysis and visualization. It excels in tasks requiring specialized statistical techniques and complex graphical models. Key libraries include ggplot2 for data visualization, dplyr for data manipulation, and caret for machine learning. Below is a sample R script demonstrating these functionalities:

```
library(dplyr)
library(ggplot2)
library(caret)

# Load and display dataset
data <- read.csv('data.csv')
print(head(data))

# Example of data manipulation
data <- data %>% mutate(new_column = existing_column * 2)

# Example of plotting
ggplot(data, aes(x = feature1, y = feature2)) + geom_point()

# Example of a simple linear regression
model <- train(target ~ feature1, data = data, method = 'lm')
print(summary(model))
```

Libraries and Frameworks

Libraries and frameworks are the building blocks that enable the implementation of data science workflows.

- **NumPy and pandas**: NumPy provides support for arrays, matrices, and many mathematical functions. The pandas library builds on NumPy to offer a robust data structure called DataFrame, essential for data manipulation and analysis.
- **Matplotlib and Seaborn**: Matplotlib is a comprehensive library for creating static, animated, and interactive visualizations in Python. Seaborn builds on Matplotlib and provides a higher-level interface for drawing attractive and informative statistical graphics.
- **scikit-learn**: One of the most popular libraries for machine learning in Python, scikit-learn comes with simple and efficient tools for data mining, data analysis, and machine learning implementations. It supports various algorithms like classification, regression, clustering, and dimensionality reduction.
- **TensorFlow and PyTorch**: Both are deep learning frameworks with an extensive range of tools for designing, training, and deploying neural networks. Developed by Google Brain and Facebook's AI Research lab respectively, TensorFlow and PyTorch are pivotal in the development of advanced machine learning models.

Platforms and Cloud Services

The advent of cloud computing has revolutionized data science, offering scalable resources and services for data storage, processing, and analysis.

- **Amazon Web Services (AWS)**: AWS provides several services tailored for data science, such as Amazon SageMaker for building, training, and deploying machine learning models, and AWS Lambda for running code without provisioning or managing servers.
- **Google Cloud Platform (GCP)**: GCP offers tools like Google BigQuery for large-scale data analysis, TensorFlow on Google Cloud

for model training and deployment, and Google Colab for running Jupyter notebooks with free access to GPUs.

- **Microsoft Azure**: Azure Machine Learning offers automated machine learning, a drag-and-drop interface, and Jupyter notebook integration. Azure also provides various storage options and computing resources to support data science projects.

Integrated Development Environments (IDEs) and Notebooks

IDEs and notebook environments facilitate writing and running code, managing projects, and visualizing results.

- **Jupyter Notebook**: This web-based interactive computing environment allows users to create and share documents that contain live code, equations, visualizations, and narrative text. It's widely used for exploratory data analysis, data cleaning, and creating tutorials.
- **RStudio**: An integrated development environment for R, RStudio provides a user-friendly interface for coding, debugging, and visualization, making it easier to develop and deploy R applications.
- **PyCharm and VS Code**: Both are popular IDEs for Python development. PyCharm offers extensive support for various scientific libraries, whereas Visual Studio Code is highly customizable and supports numerous extensions for data science.

Mastering these tools and technologies empowers data scientists to efficiently analyze data, build predictive models, and derive actionable insights, ultimately driving data-driven decision-making in organizations.

1.7 Ethics in Data Science

Data science, a field that harnesses powerful techniques and vast amounts of data, holds immense potential to drive positive change. However, it also necessitates stringent ethical oversight to ensure that its impacts are fair, equitable, and preserve individual privacy. A robust understanding of ethical considerations is paramount for any data scientist, as irresponsible use of data can lead to significant social and legal repercussions.

At its core, ethical data science revolves around the principles of transparency, accountability, fairness, and privacy. Transparency requires that data collection processes, analytical methods, and results are clearly documented and easily understandable to relevant stakeholders. Accountability mandates that data scientists take responsibility for their work, ensuring that their analyses and models do not perpetuate harm or bias.

Fairness in data science is essential to avoid discriminatory practices. This entails ensuring that datasets used for training machine learning models are representative of the population and that the models themselves do not encode existing biases. For example, if a dataset used to train a job recommendation system disproportionately represents certain demographics, the resulting model may unfairly favor those demographics over others. Techniques such as bias detection and fairness-aware machine learning can help mitigate these issues.

Privacy concerns primarily focus on the protection of individual data. Adhering to privacy laws, like the General Data Protection Regulation (GDPR) in Europe or the California Consumer Privacy Act (CCPA), is a legal necessity, but ethical data science goes beyond mere compliance. Techniques such as anonymization, differential privacy, and secure multi-party computation can be employed to protect user identities and sensitive information while still enabling valuable analysis.

Anonymization involves removing personally identifiable information (PII) from datasets so that individuals cannot be readily identified. Differential privacy provides formal guarantees that the privacy of individuals is preserved when performing analytics on large datasets. Secure multi-party computation allows multiple parties to collaboratively analyze data without revealing their respective datasets to one another.

```
import numpy as np

def add_laplace_noise(data, epsilon):
    noise = np.random.laplace(0, 1/epsilon, size=len(data))
    return data + noise

original_data = np.array([50, 23, 47, 31, 89])
epsilon = 0.5
noisy_data = add_laplace_noise(original_data, epsilon)
print(noisy_data)
```

When running the above code, the output will yield a modified version of the original data:

[53.5798, 21.3529, 45.8762, 29.1294, 87.7037]

This output ensures that individual data points are obfuscated, thereby protecting user privacy while maintaining the data's overall utility for analytics.

Beyond technical solutions, ethical data science also involves informed consent. Individuals should be made fully aware of what data is being collected, how it will be used, and what potential risks are associated with their participation. They should have the ability to opt-out or withdraw their data without facing any negative consequences.

Consideration of ethics extends into the realm of automated decision-making systems. Such systems, often driven by artificial intelligence and machine learning, hold the potential to make decisions that affect human lives. For example, algorithmic systems used in parole decisions, credit scoring, job recruitment, and health care must be scrutinized for ethical compliance. Ensuring these systems are interpretable and explainable is critical, as it allows affected individuals to understand and contest decisions that impact them.

Moreover, a significant ethical concern is the potential for data science to exacerbate social inequalities. Algorithms trained on biased data can reinforce and even amplify existing disparities. A famous case is the use of predictive policing algorithms that disproportionately target minority communities, leading to a cycle of over-policing and systemic bias.

Ethical data science requires a commitment to ongoing education and vigilance. Data scientists must stay informed about the latest ethical standards, engage with interdisciplinary scholars, and actively participate in conversations about the societal impacts of their work. Building ethics into the fabric of data science practice involves institutional support, including codes of conduct, regular audits, and an organizational culture that values ethical considerations as much as technical prowess.

It is also essential for data scientists to adopt a critical mindset, questioning the underlying assumptions and potential consequences of their work. Techniques such as adversarial testing, where models are deliberately challenged with edge cases and potential worst-case scenarios, can help uncover hidden biases and vulnerabilities.

Ultimately, the ethical practice of data science is integral to fostering trust and ensuring that the advancements in this field lead to benefits that are broadly shared across society. Adopting and implementing ethical guidelines and practices is not just a moral obligation but a foundation for sustainable and responsible innovation in data science.

1.8 Data Science vs. Related Fields

Data Science, as a multidisciplinary field, inherently overlaps with various related disciplines, including statistics, machine learning, artificial intelligence, data mining, and big data. A clear understanding of these distinctions is essential for data scientists, as it enables them to leverage techniques from these fields to solve complex problems effectively. This section delves into the nuances distinguishing data science from these related fields, offering a thorough comparison to clarify their unique characteristics and interrelations.

To begin with, **statistics** forms the backbone of data science. Both fields employ statistical methodologies, but their scopes and applications differ significantly. Statistics is primarily concerned with analyzing and interpreting data to infer properties of the population, often emphasizing hypothesis testing, probability distributions, and inferential methods. Statisticians develop models to validate or refute scientific hypotheses based on sample data.

Data science, on the other hand, extends beyond traditional statistical analysis by incorporating computational techniques and leveraging large-scale datasets to extract insights. It uses statistical methods as part of a broader toolkit that includes machine learning, data preprocessing, and visualization to solve real-world problems. For instance, while statisticians might focus on developing a theoretical model to understand an underlying phenomenon, data scientists are more inclined towards practical implementation, employing statistical models within predictive algorithms to forecast future trends.

Next, **machine learning** is a core component of data science, yet it stands as a distinct field. Machine learning revolves around developing algorithms that enable computers to learn from and make predictions or decisions based on data. It includes supervised learning (e.g., classification, regression), unsupervised learning (e.g., clustering, association), and reinforcement learning. Machine learning aims to create models that generalize well from training data to unseen data, thereby automating the decision-making process.

Data science encompasses the entire lifecycle of data processing, from data collection and cleaning to analysis and interpretation. While machine learning explicitly focuses on the development and refinement of predictive models, data science integrates these models within a broader context, often requiring domain-specific knowledge to frame the problem, preprocess the data, and assess the interpretability and ethical implications of the results. For example, a data scientist might use machine learning to build a recommendation system, but their role extends to understanding user behavior, selecting relevant features, and ensuring the system respects privacy considerations.

Artificial intelligence (AI) is another related field, often conflated with data science and machine learning. AI refers to the broader concept of creating systems capable of performing tasks that would require human intelligence. These tasks include reasoning, natural language processing, perception, and decision-making. Machine learning is a subset of AI, providing the methodologies through which machines can develop intelligence by learning from data.

Data science leverages AI principles, especially machine learning techniques, to enhance data-driven decision-making processes. However, AI encompasses a broader range of capabilities, including symbolic reasoning, expert systems, and computer vision, which may or may not involve data-intensive approaches. For instance, an AI-powered personal assistant like Siri employs natural language processing and machine learning. Still, its development requires extensive data science workflows to manage user data, train speech recognition models, and ensure continuous improvement through feedback loops.

Data mining pertains to the process of discovering patterns and knowledge from large datasets. It employs various techniques from statistics, machine learning, and database management to extract hidden patterns or associations. Data mining focuses on exploring the data to reveal insights that might not be immediately obvious, often using methods like clustering, association rule learning, and anomaly detection.

While data mining and data science share common goals and tools, data science covers a broader scope, encompassing the end-to-end process of extracting insights from data. Data mining is typically more concerned with the exploratory phase of data analysis, identifying trends and patterns that inform subsequent modeling and decision-making stages. A data scientist might employ data mining techniques to identify customer segments within a marketing dataset, followed by building predictive models to target specific segments with personalized campaigns.

Lastly, **big data** refers to the storage, processing, and analysis of massive datasets that traditional data handling tools cannot efficiently manage. Big data technologies focus on distributed computing frameworks such as Hadoop and Spark, which enable the processing of vast amounts of data across multiple machines.

Data science often operates within the realm of big data, utilizing its tools and frameworks to handle large-scale datasets. However, the defining feature of data science is not merely the volume of data but the methodologies applied to glean actionable insights. Big data addresses the 'four Vs' (volume, velocity, variety, and veracity), providing the environment within which data science operates to derive meaningful conclusions. For example, real-time analysis of social media feeds for sentiment analysis involves big data technologies to manage data streams and data science techniques to analyze and interpret sentiment trends.

These distinctions elucidate how data science serves as an integrative discipline, drawing from and extending its capabilities through related fields to foster a comprehensive approach to data-driven problem-solving. Understanding these differences allows data scientists to effectively apply appropriate techniques and tools, ensuring robust and innovative solutions in their work.

1.9 The Future of Data Science

The future of data science stands poised at a transformative juncture, expanding its influence across various fields and innovating in both technology and methodology. This section examines emerging trends and projections that are expected to shape the landscape of data science in the coming years.

Advancements in artificial intelligence (AI) and machine learning (ML) are expected to significantly impact the field of data science. More sophisticated algorithms and models will enable data scientists to generate deeper insights from complex datasets. The integration of AI with traditional statistical methods will increment the analytical power of data science, refining predictive analytics and increasing the accuracy of results.

AI-driven automation in data preprocessing, feature selection, and hyperparameter tuning will reduce the need for manual intervention, expediting the data science workflow. Following is an example of automated feature selection using Python's scikit-learn library:

```
from sklearn.feature_selection import SelectKBest, f_classif
from sklearn.datasets import load_iris

data = load_iris()
X = data.data
y = data.target

# SelectKBest to select top 2 features
selector = SelectKBest(f_classif, k=2)
X_new = selector.fit_transform(X, y)
print(X_new[:5])
```

In the era of Big Data, the ability to process and analyze vast volumes of data in real-time has become crucial. Cloud computing and distributed systems such as Apache Hadoop and Apache Spark are instrumental, but future developments are likely to introduce more efficient, scalable solutions tailored to specific data science applications. The integration of quantum computing could further accelerate data processing speeds, allowing for even more rapid analysis of large datasets.

Interdisciplinary collaboration will become more prevalent as data science applications expand into diverse fields including healthcare, finance, environmental science, and social sciences. For instance, in healthcare, data science is aiding in the development of personalized medicine, predictive diagnostics, and improved treatment protocols by leveraging patient data and sophisticated machine learning algorithms. Consider the application of a predictive model to forecast patient outcomes:

```
from sklearn.linear_model import LogisticRegression
from sklearn.model_selection import train_test_split
from sklearn.metrics import accuracy_score

# Sample dataset
X = ... # Feature matrix
y = ... # Target variable

# Split into training and test sets
X_train, X_test, y_train, y_test = train_test_split(X, y, test_size=0.2)

# Build logistic regression model
model = LogisticRegression()
model.fit(X_train, y_train)

# Predictions and accuracy measurement
predictions = model.predict(X_test)
accuracy = accuracy_score(y_test, predictions)
print(f'Accuracy: {accuracy:.2f}')
```

The domain-specific adaptation of data science practices will necessitate the development of new methodologies tailored to tackle unique challenges presented by different sectors. Ethical considerations and governance frameworks will evolve correspondingly. With the increased capacity to collect and analyze personal data, data privacy and security will be paramount. New legislation and ethical guidelines will emerge to protect individuals and ensure responsible use of data. Blockchain technology presents a promising avenue for enhancing data security and ensuring transparency and integrity in data handling processes.

User-friendly, self-service analytics platforms are likely to proliferate, democratizing data science by making powerful tools accessible to non-experts. This shift will enable business professionals and domain experts to perform sophisticated data analyses independently, bridging the gap between technical and non-technical stakeholders. Visualization tools and natural language processing (NLP) will play a key role in this democratization, facilitating intuitive interaction with data.

The adoption of augmented analytics, where AI assists in data preparation, insight discovery, and data-sharing, will also become more common. This involves automating insights generation, helping users derive actionable intelligence without exhaustive manual analyses. An example of using NLP for sentiment analysis is shown below:

```
from sklearn.feature_extraction.text import CountVectorizer
from sklearn.naive_bayes import MultinomialNB

# Sample dataset
documents = ["I love this product", "This is a bad product", "Excellent quality"]
labels = [1, 0, 1] # 1 = Positive, 0 = Negative

# Convert text documents to feature vectors
vectorizer = CountVectorizer()
X = vectorizer.fit_transform(documents)

# Train a Naive Bayes classifier
classifier = MultinomialNB()
classifier.fit(X, labels)

# Predict sentiment for a new document
new_document = ["This product is not good"]
new_X = vectorizer.transform(new_document)
prediction = classifier.predict(new_X)
print(f'Sentiment: {"Positive" if prediction[0] == 1 else "Negative"}')
```

Data science is also expected to drive open science and transparency in research. The open-source movement will continue to thrive, fostering collaboration and reproducibility in scientific research. Datasets, analytical methods, and computational tools will be shared broadly, promoting innovation and accelerating scientific discovery.

Lastly, education and skill development in data science will grow in parallel to industry demands. Curriculum advancements in universities and professional development programs will evolve to include the latest tools, techniques, and ethical considerations. The continuous cycle of learning and application will ensure that data scientists remain at the forefront of these technological transformations.

The field of data science is on an accelerating trajectory fueled by technological innovations, interdisciplinary collaborations, and expanding applications. As these elements converge, the potential for impactful scientific, economic, and societal advancements continues to grow. The future holds a profound promise for data science to drive meaningful change across the globe.

Chapter 2

Data Collection and Preprocessing

Data collection and preprocessing are critical steps in the data science workflow. This chapter discusses various methods of acquiring both structured and unstructured data from multiple sources, including APIs and web scraping. It covers techniques for handling missing data, data cleaning, transformation, and feature engineering. The chapter emphasizes normalization, standardization, and dealing with categorical and imbalanced data, along with strategies for data integration and reduction, laying the groundwork for effective analysis.

2.1 Introduction to Data Collection

Data collection is the foundational stage of any data science project, as it provides the raw material from which insights will eventually be extracted. It involves the systematic gathering of information from a variety of sources to ensure a robust dataset that is suitable for analysis. The ultimate goal is to acquire data that is accurate, relevant, and representative of the phenomena being studied.

In data science, data can originate from numerous sources such as databases, APIs (Application Programming Interfaces), web scraping, surveys, sensors, and social media. Each of these sources presents unique challenges and opportunities, which must be carefully managed to ensure the quality and reliability of the gathered data.

- **Database Systems:** A common source of structured data is relational databases, which store data in tables with rows and columns. This structured format allows for complex queries using SQL (Structured Query Language). For example, to retrieve data from a table named employees, an SQL query might look like:

```
SELECT * FROM employees WHERE department = 'Sales';
```

  This query selects all records from the employees table where the department is 'Sales'.

- **APIs:** APIs allow for automated data collection from external systems, such as social media platforms, weather data providers, or financial markets. APIs typically return data in formats such as JSON or XML, which can be parsed and converted into a more usable format for analysis. An example of fetching data using an API in Python would be:

```
import requests

url = "https://api.example.com/data"
response = requests.get(url)
data = response.json()
```

  This code sends a GET request to the specified URL, retrieves the response, and parses it as JSON.

- **Web Scraping:** For data that is stored dynamically on websites but not readily available through an API, web scraping techniques are employed. This involves programmatically extracting information from web pages. It often requires handling HTML tags and JavaScript-rendered content. An example using Python's BeautifulSoup library might include:

```
from bs4 import BeautifulSoup
import requests

url = "https://example.com"
response = requests.get(url)
soup = BeautifulSoup(response.content, "html.parser")
data = soup.find_all('div', class_='data-class')
```

  This code retrieves the content of a webpage and uses BeautifulSoup to parse the HTML, extracting all the div elements with the class data-class.

- **Surveys and Sensors:** Surveys are a traditional method of data collection, involving the gathering of data directly from respondents through questionnaires. Sensors, on the other hand, collect data passively, for example, environmental data such as temperature, humidity, and motion. Survey data may require preprocessing to handle missing responses and inconsistent formats, while sensor data might need calibration and noise filtering. Ensuring the integrity and accuracy of these data sources is critical as they can significantly influence subsequent analyses.

- **Challenges and Opportunities:** Data collection methods need to address several challenges including data quality, data privacy, and ethical considerations. Ensuring data accuracy involves verifying the source, cross-referencing multiple datasets, and applying consistency checks. The constraints of privacy regulations, such as GDPR, necessitate careful handling of personal data, often requiring anonymization techniques. Ethical considerations involve ensuring that the data collection process does not harm participants or create biases that could lead to misleading conclusions. Collecting data transparently and with the consent of participants is fundamental to maintaining ethical standards.

  With advancements in technology, the opportunities for innovative data collection have expanded significantly. Today, real-time data can be collected using Internet of Things (IoT) devices, and big data platforms allow for the accumulation and processing of vast amounts of data from diverse sources. This diversification enriches datasets, enabling more comprehensive and nuanced analyses.

Effective data collection is a critically important step in the data science pipeline that underpins the accuracy and reliability of any subsequent data analysis. By understanding the various sources and methods of data collection, and addressing the inherent challenges, data scientists can gather high-quality data that provides meaningful insights.

2.2 Types of Data: Structured vs. Unstructured

Data exists in various forms, and understanding the differences between structured and unstructured data is fundamental to the data science workflow. Each type possesses distinct characteristics that dictate the methods required for storage, processing, and analysis.

Structured Data refers to data that is organized in a fixed format. This type of data is typically stored in databases, where it is arranged in tables similar to those found in relational databases. Each table consists of rows and columns, with the rows representing individual records and the columns representing the attributes or features of the data.

- **Examples of Structured Data:**
  - Relational databases (SQL)
  - Spreadsheets (Excel)
  - CSV files
- **Characteristics of Structured Data:**
  - **Format:** Highly organized and easily searchable. Each data point is stored in a predefined manner.
  - **Data Types:** Includes numerical data (integers, floats) and categorical data (strings, dates).
  - **Storage:** Stored in data warehouses with defined schema.
  - **Query Capability:** Can be efficiently queried using SQL.
  - **Data Integrity:** Enforcement of data integrity constraints (e.g., primary keys, foreign keys).

Structured data benefits from its predefined schema, allowing for efficient data sorting and retrieval using standard database query languages such as SQL. Consider the following SQL query example that retrieves data from a relational database:

```
SELECT first_name, last_name, age
FROM users
WHERE age > 25;
```

This query selects the first_name, last_name, and age columns from the users table where the age is greater than 25, demonstrating how structured data can be easily manipulated.

On the other hand, **Unstructured Data** refers to information that does not have a predefined data model or is not organized in a pre-defined manner. This category includes a vast amount of data that is generated daily and does not fit neatly into relational databases.

- **Examples of Unstructured Data:**
  - Text files (e.g., word documents)
  - Multimedia files (images, audio, video)
  - Social media posts
  - Emails
  - Sensor data (IoT devices)
- **Characteristics of Unstructured Data:**
  - **Format:** Unorganized and does not follow a consistent structure. Can be lengthy and exist in various formats.
  - **Data Types:** Diverse types, including binary data (images, audio) and textual data (documents, emails).
  - **Storage:** Typically housed in data lakes, requiring advanced storage solutions to manage the vast volume and variety of data.
  - **Query Capability:** Challenging to query using traditional search mechanisms. Requires advanced techniques like Natural Language Processing (NLP) and machine learning algorithms.
  - **Analysis:** Often necessitates preprocessing steps to extract relevant features for analysis.

Consider a Python script that performs basic text processing on unstructured textual data. The following example reads a text file and processes its content to extract and count word occurrences:

```
from collections import Counter

# Read the content of the text file
with open('document.txt', 'r') as file:
    text = file.read()

# Tokenize the text into words
words = text.split()

# Count the frequency of each word
word_counts = Counter(words)

# Print the word counts
print(word_counts)
```

The script uses Python's collections.Counter to tokenize the text into words and count their occurrences, a common initial step in processing unstructured text data. Here, the data resides in a text file, illustrating the lack of a fixed schema and the necessity for custom processing techniques.

Both structured and unstructured data play crucial roles in different domains and decisions. For example, customer information stored in a relational database (structured data) can be combined with sentiment analysis from customer reviews (unstructured data) to gain comprehensive insights into customer satisfaction. Data scientists must be adept in handling both types of data, employing appropriate techniques for data acquisition, storage, preprocessing, and analysis based on the specific characteristics and requirements of the data type.

Structured data's rigidity allows for precise operations and quick access using well-established database tools, whereas unstructured data requires more flexible and often complex approaches to convert raw information into actionable knowledge.

2.3 Data Sources and Acquisition Methods

Data sources and acquisition methods form the backbone of any data-driven project. Selecting appropriate data sources and using effective acquisition techniques are paramount for the success of data science workflows. This section explores various data sources and acquisition methods, providing insight into their practical applications, benefits, and limitations.

1. Data Sources

Data can be sourced from a myriad of locations, each with unique characteristics and implications for downstream analysis. The primary categories of data sources include:

- **Databases**: Structured data stored in databases such as SQL (Structured Query Language) or NoSQL (Non-relational) databases. Examples include MySQL, PostgreSQL, MongoDB, and Cassandra.
- **Flat Files**: Data stored in flat files such as CSV (Comma-Separated Values), JSON (JavaScript Object Notation), XML (eXtensible Markup Language), and plain text files.
- **Web Data**: Unstructured or semi-structured data available on the web, which can be accessed through web scraping or APIs (Application Programming Interfaces).

- **Public Data Repositories**: Data publicly available in repositories such as data.gov, UCI Machine Learning Repository, and Kaggle datasets. These datasets are generally well-documented and ready for analysis.
- **Enterprise Data Warehouses**: Large-scale repositories that store integrated data from various sources within an organization. These are designed to support management decision-making processes.
- **Sensor and Internet of Things (IoT) Data**: Data generated by sensors and IoT devices, often found in industries like manufacturing, agriculture, and smart cities. These data sources provide real-time insights into physical processes.
- **Social Media Platforms**: Data generated from social media platforms such as Twitter, Facebook, and LinkedIn. This data often includes user interactions, posts, and other engagement metrics.
- **Data Streams**: Continuous flow of data, often requiring real-time processing. Examples include financial tick data, clickstream data, and telemetry data.

2. Data Acquisition Methods

Different methods employed to acquire data from these sources are essential for ensuring the quality and usability of the data. Key acquisition methods are:

Databases:

For structured data, databases offer robust querying capabilities through SQL. An example SQL query to fetch required data is:

```
SELECT customer_id, purchase_amount, purchase_date
FROM transactions
WHERE purchase_date BETWEEN '2022-01-01' AND '2022-12-31';
```

This query retrieves customer transactions made in a particular date range. Using SQL allows efficient data extraction, transformation, and loading (ETL) processes.

Flat Files:

Working with flat files entails parsing the file formats accurately. For instance, loading a CSV file in Python can be achieved using the pandas library:

```
import pandas as pd
data = pd.read_csv('data/transactions.csv')
```

This approach is straightforward for small to medium-sized datasets.

Web Scraping:

Web scraping involves extracting data from web pages. Python's BeautifulSoup and requests libraries facilitate this type of data acquisition. Below is a basic example of web scraping:

```
import requests
from bs4 import BeautifulSoup

url = 'https://example.com/data'
response = requests.get(url)
soup = BeautifulSoup(response.text, 'html.parser')

# Extract data points
data_points = soup.find_all('div', class_='data-point')
data = [dp.text for dp in data_points]
```

While effective, web scraping must be conducted ethically, respecting the website's terms of service and data privacy laws.

APIs (Application Programming Interfaces):

APIs provide structured access to web services, making them a valuable data source. Accessing data via APIs typically involves sending HTTP requests. One common example uses the requests library:

```
import requests

api_url = 'https://api.example.com/get_data'
params = {'param1': 'value1', 'param2': 'value2'}
response = requests.get(api_url, params=params)

if response.status_code == 200:
    data = response.json()
```

API documentation often provides information on endpoint usage, query parameters, rate limits, and authentication mechanisms.

Public Data Repositories:

Datasets from public repositories can be downloaded manually or programmatically. For example, using Python to download a dataset from the UCI Machine Learning Repository:

```
import urllib.request

url = 'https://archive.ics.uci.edu/ml/machine-learning-databases/iris/iris.data'
urllib.request.urlretrieve(url, 'data/iris.data')
```

Public data repositories are valuable because they often come with metadata and descriptions that facilitate understanding and utilization.

Enterprise Data Warehouses:

Data warehouses require sophisticated ETL processes to manage large volumes of integrated data. Tools such as Apache Hadoop and Apache Spark are used for handling and processing such data efficiently. An Apache Spark example:

```
from pyspark.sql import SparkSession

spark = SparkSession.builder.appName("Data Warehouse Access").getOrCreate()
df = spark.read.format("jdbc").options(
    url="jdbc:mysql://hostname:port/dbname",
    driver="com.mysql.jdbc.Driver",
    dbtable="transactions",
    user="username",
    password="password").load()
```

Using Spark integrates well with large-scale data querying and processing, supporting data warehousing needs.

Sensor and IoT Data:

Acquiring data from sensors and IoT devices often involves data streaming and real-time processing frameworks. Apache Kafka is a popular tool for this purpose. An example Kafka consumer in Python:

```
from kafka import KafkaConsumer

consumer = KafkaConsumer('sensor-data', bootstrap_servers=['localhost:9092'])

for message in consumer:
    process_sensor_data(message.value)
```

Real-time processing requires setting up consumers to handle continuous data inflow.

Social Media Platforms:

Retrieving social media data typically involves using APIs provided by these platforms. For example, accessing Twitter data with Tweepy, a Python library:

```
import tweepy

auth = tweepy.OAuthHandler('API_KEY', 'API_SECRET')
auth.set_access_token('ACCESS_TOKEN', 'ACCESS_TOKEN_SECRET')

api = tweepy.API(auth)

tweets = api.user_timeline(screen_name='example_user', count=200)
for tweet in tweets:
    print(tweet.text)
```

The data extracted from social media can include timestamps, interactions, user details, and more, offering rich insights into user behavior.

Data Streams:

Handling data streams involves technologies that support real-time data ingestion and processing. Apache Flink is an example of a framework designed for such purposes. A basic Flink setup:

```
final StreamExecutionEnvironment env = StreamExecutionEnvironment.
    getExecutionEnvironment();
DataStream<String> stream = env.addSource(new FlinkKafkaConsumer<>("topic",
    new SimpleStringSchema(), properties));
stream.print();
env.execute("Stream Processing Example");
```

Data streams require systems optimized for high-throughput and low-latency processing to manage real-time analytics effectively.

Each data source and acquisition method has specific use cases, advantages, and constraints. Selecting the right combination plays a pivotal role in ensuring that the collected data is relevant, high-quality, and ready for subsequent processing stages in the data science workflow.

2.4 APIs and Web Scraping

APIs (Application Programming Interfaces) and web scraping are two fundamental methodologies for acquiring data from the web, which is invaluable for numerous data science projects. This section delves deep into the technical aspects and practical applications of both methods, offering a comprehensive understanding of how to effectively gather data programmatically.

APIs provide a structured and reliable means of accessing data from various services. An API typically exposes endpoints—a set of defined URLs or URIs that allow interaction with the system resources through HTTP requests. APIs can return data in several formats, most commonly JSON (JavaScript Object Notation) and XML (eXtensible Markup Language), which are easily parsed and integrated into data pipelines.

To interact with an API, one must understand the specific endpoints and the required parameters. The primary types of HTTP requests used in API interaction are:

- **GET**: Retrieves resources and data from the server.

- **POST**: Submits data to be processed to a specific resource.
- **PUT**: Updates a current resource with new data.
- **DELETE**: Removes a specified resource.

Below is an example of how to perform a GET request to an API using Python's requests library:

```
import requests

url = 'https://api.example.com/data'
params = {'query': 'example', 'format': 'json'}
response = requests.get(url, params=params)

if response.status_code == 200:
    data = response.json()
    print(data)
else:
    print(f"Error: {response.status_code}")
```

The above code snippet sends a GET request to the API endpoint specified by url with query parameters defined in params. On a successful request, indicated by a status code of 200, the response data is processed in JSON format.

When working with APIs, it is common to encounter authentication mechanisms. Two widely used authentication methods are:

- **API Keys**: A unique identifier provided by the service to authenticate an application.
- **OAuth**: A standard authorization framework that allows secure, delegated access to resources without sharing credentials.

Securing API requests with an API key in the header can be illustrated as follows:

```
api_key = 'your_api_key_here'
headers = {'Authorization': f'Bearer {api_key}'}
response = requests.get(url, headers=headers, params=params)
```

Web scraping, on the other hand, involves extracting data directly from websites by parsing the HTML content. This method becomes necessary when data is not readily available through APIs. Libraries such as BeautifulSoup and Scrapy are widely used for this purpose.

The first step in web scraping is to send an HTTP request and receive the HTML response. Following this, the HTML content can be parsed and processed to extract the desired data. Here is an example using BeautifulSoup:

```
import requests
from bs4 import BeautifulSoup

url = 'https://www.example.com'
response = requests.get(url)

if response.status_code == 200:
    soup = BeautifulSoup(response.content, 'html.parser')
    titles = [title.text for title in soup.find_all('h1')]
    print(titles)
else:
    print(f"Error: {response.status_code}")
```

In this script, a GET request is made to the specified URL, and the HTML content of the page is parsed using BeautifulSoup. The soup.find_all('h1') line locates all <h1> tags in the HTML document, and their text content is extracted and printed.

It is important to respect the robots.txt file of a website being scraped. This file specifies the rules for crawling the site to ensure ethical scraping. Here is a brief glance at how to check a robots.txt file:

```
from urllib.robotparser import RobotFileParser

rp = RobotFileParser()
rp.set_url('https://www.example.com/robots.txt')
rp.read()

url = 'https://www.example.com/somepage.html'
if rp.can_fetch('*', url):
    response = requests.get(url)
    # Continue with parsing if fetching is allowed
else:
    print("Not allowed to scrape this URL")
```

The RobotFileParser object reads the robots.txt file and checks if the URL specified is permissible for scraping by a user-agent, in this case, represented by '*'.

Lastly, ethical considerations and legal constraints should always guide the practice of data collection through APIs and web scraping. Practitioners should examine the terms of service of the websites or APIs they are accessing to ensure compliance with usage policies. Misuse or excessive scraping can result in IP bans and other legal issues.

APIs and web scraping are powerful tools for data collection when employed responsibly. Understanding their workings and application, from basic HTTP requests to parsing HTML, is fundamental for effective data science practice.

2.5 Introduction to Data Preprocessing

Data preprocessing is a significant phase in the data science workflow. It encompasses all the steps necessary to prepare raw data for analysis. Effective preprocessing can significantly enhance the performance of machine learning models, whereas inadequate preprocessing might lead to subpar results. This section will elaborate on the various data preprocessing techniques and their importance.

Data preprocessing typically involves several key activities: data cleaning, data transformation, feature engineering, and data reduction. Each of these steps ensures that the data fed into machine learning models is consistent, accurate, and reflective of the problem domain.

Data cleaning is crucial for dealing with inaccuracies and inconsistencies within the dataset. Raw data is seldom perfect; it often contains errors, including missing values, duplicates, and outliers. Techniques like imputation, removal of duplicate records, and outlier detection and handling are employed to make the data cleaner.

Data transformation is the process of converting data from one format or structure into another. Transformations vary depending on the nature of the data and the specific requirements of the analysis. Common transformations include normalization, standardization, and scaling. These techniques adjust the data values to a common scale without distorting differences in the ranges of values.

Feature engineering is the practice of creating new features from the existing raw data. Features are the inputs to machine learning models, and their quality and relevance significantly influence the model's performance. Data scientists use domain knowledge to select and construct meaningful features, which makes the models more accurate and robust. Feature extraction and feature selection are integral parts of this process.

Normalization is a technique used to adjust the data within a particular range, typically [0, 1]. This ensures that each feature contributes equally to the analysis and prevents the algorithm from being biased towards variables presented in higher ranges.

Standardization, on the other hand, transforms the data to have a mean of zero and a standard deviation of one. This method is particularly useful when the data follows a Gaussian (or normal) distribution, ensuring that each feature contributes proportionately to the analysis.

Consider a simple dataset that requires normalization:

```
from sklearn.preprocessing import MinMaxScaler
import numpy as np

# Sample data
data = np.array([[2.0, 1.0], [4.0, 2.0], [6.0, 3.0]])

# Initialize the scaler
scaler = MinMaxScaler()

# Fit and transform the data
normalized_data = scaler.fit_transform(data)

print(normalized_data)
```

The output of this code will be:

```
[[0.  0. ]
 [0.5 0.5]
 [1.  1. ]]
```

In this example, each element within the dataset is rescaled to fit within the range of 0 to 1.

Handling categorical data is another indispensable component of preprocessing. Many machine learning algorithms require numerical input, hence categorical variables must be converted to a numerical format. Techniques such as one-hot encoding and label encoding are frequently employed for this purpose. One-hot encoding transforms categorical attributes into a series of binary attributes, whereas label encoding assigns a unique integer to each category.

Managing imbalanced data is also a part of preprocessing. In datasets with imbalanced classes, the model might become biased towards the majority class. Techniques such as oversampling the minority class, undersampling the majority class, or generating synthetic samples using methods like SMOTE (Synthetic Minority Over-sampling Technique) can be used to address this issue.

The following is an example of label encoding in Python:

```
from sklearn.preprocessing import LabelEncoder

# Sample data
data = ['cat', 'dog', 'fish', 'dog', 'cat']

# Instantiate the label encoder
label_encoder = LabelEncoder()

# Fit and transform the data
encoded_data = label_encoder.fit_transform(data)

print(encoded_data)
```

The output of this code will be:

```
[0 1 2 1 0]
```

In this example, each unique category is assigned an integer. "Cat" is represented as 0, "dog" as 1, and "fish" as 2.

Lastly, data reduction is about reducing the number of features or records while retaining as much information as feasible. This can be achieved through techniques like Principal Component Analysis (PCA), which transforms features into principal components, or by removing features with low variance.

By addressing these elements comprehensively, data preprocessing lays a robust foundation for any subsequent data analysis or machine learning task. Properly preprocessed data ensures that the models are trained on datasets that rightfully represent the problem domain. This preparedness is instrumental in achieving accurate, reliable, and generalizable models.

2.6 Handling Missing Data

Dealing with missing data is a fundamental aspect of data preprocessing, as the presence of missing values can introduce significant biases and affect downstream analysis. There are several techniques for handling missing data, which can be broadly categorized into methods for detecting, analyzing, and imputing missing data.

To begin, identifying missing data is essential. Various programming languages and their libraries provide tools to detect missing values. Here is an example using Python and the pandas library:

```
import pandas as pd

# Create a DataFrame with missing values
data = {'A': [1, 2, None, 4],
        'B': [None, 2, 3, 4],
        'C': [1, None, 3, None]}
df = pd.DataFrame(data)

# Detect missing values
print(df.isnull())
print(df.isnull().sum())
```

The output of the above code indicates the positions of missing values as True:

```
       A      B      C
0  False   True  False
1  False  False   True
2   True  False  False
3  False  False   True

A    1
B    1
C    2
dtype: int64
```

Once identified, there are multiple strategies to handle missing data, with the choice of method depending on the context and the amount of missing data present. The key approaches include ignoring the missing data, deleting rows or columns, and imputing missing values.

- **Ignoring the Missing Data:** If the proportion of missing data is very small, it may be viable to ignore these values. However, this approach can lead to bias if the missing values are not randomly distributed.

- **Deleting Rows or Columns:** One common method is to delete rows or columns containing missing data. This approach is feasible when the dataset is large, and the loss of data from such deletions does not significantly impact the overall analysis.

  To drop rows with any missing values:

  ```
  df_dropped = df.dropna()
  print(df_dropped)
  ```

  To drop columns with any missing values:

  ```
  df_dropped_columns = df.dropna(axis=1)
  print(df_dropped_columns)
  ```

- **Imputing Missing Values:** Imputation involves replacing missing data with substituted values. The choice of imputation method depends on the nature of the data and the underlying assumptions. Common imputation techniques include:

  - *Mean/Median Imputation:* This method replaces missing values with the mean or median of the respective column, a technique often used for numerical data.

    ```
    df_mean_imputed = df.fillna(df.mean())
    print(df_mean_imputed)
    ```

    ```
         A    B    C
    0  1.0  3.0  1.0
    1  2.0  2.0  2.0
    2  2.333333  3.0  3.0
    3  4.0  4.0  2.0
    ```

- *Mode Imputation:* This method replaces missing values in categorical variables with the mode (most frequent value) of the column.

```
df_mode_imputed = df.apply(lambda x: x.fillna(x.mode()[0]) if x.dtype
    == 'object' else x)
print(df_mode_imputed)
```

- *Interpolation:* Interpolation fills missing values through various interpolation techniques, such as linear or polynomial interpolation. This is particularly useful for time series data.

```
df_interpolated = df.interpolate()
print(df_interpolated)
```

- *Using Algorithms:* Advanced imputation methods involve using algorithms like K-Nearest Neighbors (KNN), decision trees, or even deep learning models to predict and impute missing values.

```
from sklearn.impute import KNNImputer

# Initialize KNNImputer
imputer = KNNImputer(n_neighbors=2)
df_knn_imputed = pd.DataFrame(imputer.fit_transform(df), columns=
    df.columns)
print(df_knn_imputed)
```

The output after KNN imputation might look as follows:

```
          A    B    C
0  1.000000  2.5  1.0
1  2.000000  2.0  2.0
2  3.000000  3.0  3.0
3  4.000000  4.0  2.5
```

Choosing the appropriate method for handling missing data is critical and must reflect the data characteristics and the specific analytic requirements. Understanding the various techniques and their implications aids in making informed decisions that enhance data quality and robustness for subsequent processes.

2.7 Data Cleaning Techniques

Effective data cleaning is a pivotal process in the data preprocessing phase, ensuring the integrity and quality of the dataset before it undergoes further analysis. Data cleaning involves several techniques aimed at detecting and correcting (or removing) inaccuracies and inconsistencies in data to enhance its reliability.

1. Removing Duplicate Entries

Duplicate entries often occur when data is accumulated from multiple sources or when processes inadvertently input the same data multiple times. Duplicate rows can distort analyses and lead to incorrect conclusions. Here is an example of detecting and removing duplicate rows using Python's pandas library:

```
import pandas as pd

# Example DataFrame with duplicate rows
data = {'Name': ['Alice', 'Bob', 'Alice', 'David'],
        'Age': [25, 30, 25, 40],
        'City': ['New York', 'Los Angeles', 'New York', 'Chicago']}

df = pd.DataFrame(data)

# Detect and remove duplicates
df_cleaned = df.drop_duplicates()

print(df_cleaned)
```

The output will be:

```
    Name  Age         City
0  Alice   25     New York
1    Bob   30  Los Angeles
3  David   40      Chicago
```

2. Handling Missing Data

Missing data can arise due to various reasons such as data entry errors, equipment malfunctions, or unrecorded observations. There are several strategies for handling missing data:

- *a. Removal of Missing Data* Simply remove rows or columns with missing data if the proportion of missing data is too significant. This method might be suitable when the missing data is relatively low and does not represent a significant portion of the dataset.

  ```
  # Remove rows with any missing values
  df_cleaned = df.dropna()
  ```

- *b. Imputation* Replacing missing values with substituted data is a common method. Techniques include filling with the mean, median, or mode, or using more sophisticated methodologies such as k-nearest neighbors (KNN).

  ```
  # Fill missing values with the mean of the column
  df['Age'] = df['Age'].fillna(df['Age'].mean())
  ```

3. Outlier Detection and Treatment

Outliers can skew the analysis and model training. Detecting outliers can be performed using statistical methods such as the Z-score or the IQR (Interquartile Range).

- *a. Z-score Method* A Z-score represents the number of standard deviations a data point is from the mean. Data points with a Z-score greater than a certain threshold (e.g., 3 or -3) are considered outliers.

```
from scipy import stats

# Calculate Z-scores
z_scores = stats.zscore(df['Age'])
abs_z_scores = np.abs(z_scores)

# Filter out rows based on Z-score threshold
df_cleaned = df[(abs_z_scores < 3)]
```

- *b. IQR Method* The IQR method involves the calculation of the 1st quartile (Q1) and 3rd quartile (Q3), and points outside of Q1 - 1.5*IQR and Q3 + 1.5*IQR are considered outliers.

```
# Calculate IQR
Q1 = df['Age'].quantile(0.25)
Q3 = df['Age'].quantile(0.75)
IQR = Q3 - Q1

# Define outlier range
lower_bound = Q1 - 1.5 * IQR
upper_bound = Q3 + 1.5 * IQR

# Filter out the outliers
df_cleaned = df[(df['Age'] >= lower_bound) & (df['Age'] <= upper_bound)
    ]
```

4. Correcting Data Inconsistencies

Inconsistent data can occur due to variations in data entry, differing formats, or typos. Normalizing textual data such as converting to uniform case, correcting spellings, adjusting date formats, and ensuring consistent units of measurement are critical steps.

```
# Standardize textual data to lower case
df['City'] = df['City'].str.lower()

# Replace inconsistent entries
df['City'] = df['City'].replace({'nyc': 'new york', 'la': 'los angeles'})
```

5. Encoding and Formatting Adjustments

Data often needs to be converted or encoded into forms suitable for computation. This includes changing data types, encoding categorical variables, and ensuring numeric data is within a reasonable range.

```
# Convert 'Age' column to integer type
df['Age'] = df['Age'].astype(int)

# Encode categorical data using one-hot encoding
df_encoded = pd.get_dummies(df, columns=['City'])
```

Collectively, these data cleaning techniques lay a robust foundation for subsequent data analysis and modeling efforts, ensuring accuracy and enhancing the reliability of outcomes. Properly cleaned data leads to more precise and valid insights.

2.8 Data Transformation and Feature Engineering

Data transformation and feature engineering constitute critical phases in the data preprocessing pipeline. These steps enhance the dataset's suitability for machine learning algorithms by converting raw data into a format that provides better performance and insight. This section delves into the fundamental concepts, techniques, and practical considerations involved in the transformation and creation of features.

Data transformation refers to the process of converting data from its original format or structure into another format or structure. This step is often necessary when the raw data is not in a form that can be easily used by machine learning algorithms. Common data transformation procedures include scaling, normalization, discretization, and log transformation. Feature engineering, on the other hand, involves creating new features from existing data to improve the performance of machine learning models.

Scaling is a transformation technique used to standardize the range of independent variables or features of data. In many machine learning algorithms, particularly those involving distance measurements like k-nearest neighbors or algorithms that use gradient descent for optimization, features should be on a similar scale to ensure balanced results. Common scaling methods include Min-Max Scaling, which scales data to a range between 0 and 1, and Standard Scaling, which rescales data to have a mean of 0 and a standard deviation of 1. The formulas are as follows:

$$\text{Min-Max Scaling: } X_{scaled} = \frac{X - X_{min}}{X_{max} - X_{min}}$$

$$\text{Standard Scaling: } X_{scaled} = \frac{X - \mu}{\sigma}$$

Here, X represents the original data, X_{min} and X_{max} are the minimum and maximum values of X, μ is the mean, and σ is the standard deviation.

Normalization is akin to scaling but focuses on adjusting the data values to a common scale without distorting differences in the ranges of values. Normalization is essential when the data includes vastly different ranges. For example, if one feature is in a range of thousands and another is between 0 and 1, normalizing removes bias toward features with larger ranges.

Discretization transforms continuous attributes into discrete values, often by binning. Binning can help handle noisiness in the data and is particularly useful in algorithms like decision trees, where dividing data into categories rather than continuous values can lead to simpler, more interpretable splits.

Another valuable technique is the **log transformation**. This method is particularly useful when dealing with highly skewed data, as it compresses the range of large values and expands the range of small values. The log transformation is defined as:

$$\text{Log Transformation: } X_{log} = \log(X + 1)$$

The addition of 1 before taking the logarithm ensures that zero or negative values do not become undefined.

Feature Engineering is often considered both an art and a science in data science. It involves creating new features or modifying existing ones to better capture the underlying patterns in the data. Effective feature engineering can significantly enhance the predictive power of machine learning models. Some fundamental techniques are:

- **Interaction Terms:** Creating new features by multiplying or dividing existing features to capture interactions.
- **Polynomial Features:** Adding polynomial terms of the features, such as squares, cubes, etc., to capture non-linear relationships.

- **Domain-Specific Features:** Leveraging domain knowledge to create features that are relevant to the specific problem.
- **Binarization:** Converting numerical variables into binary (0 or 1) values based on a threshold.
- **Aggregations:** Creating summary features such as mean, sum, or count of the grouped features.

A commonly used technique in feature engineering is **Creating Interaction Terms**. Interaction terms are constructed by combining two or more features in multiplicative fashion to capture complex patterns. For example, generating a feature that is the product of two existing features:

```
import pandas as pd

data = pd.DataFrame({
    'Feature1': [1, 2, 3, 4],
    'Feature2': [10, 20, 30, 40]
})

data['Interaction'] = data['Feature1'] * data['Feature2']
print(data)
```

The result of the code above is:

```
   Feature1  Feature2  Interaction
0         1        10           10
1         2        20           40
2         3        30           90
3         4        40          160
```

Polynomial Features involve creating new features by raising the existing features to various powers. This enables the model to learn polynomial relationships between the features and the target variable. For instance, adding squared or cubic terms of a feature can help model non-linearity.

```
from sklearn.preprocessing import PolynomialFeatures

poly = PolynomialFeatures(degree=2)
X = data[['Feature1']]

poly_features = poly.fit_transform(X)
print(poly_features)
```

The output matrix will include the original feature, its square, and the interaction term if more than one feature is involved.

Understanding the importance and suitable application of each transformation and feature engineering technique is paramount. A well-engineered set of features not only improves a model's performance but also facilitates better interpretability and understanding of the predictive relationships in the data.

2.9 Normalization and Standardization

Normalization and standardization are key preprocessing techniques applied to numerical data before feeding it to machine learning algorithms. Despite their apparent similarity, they serve distinct purposes and are suited to different types of data and models. The primary objective of these transformations is to adjust the values of numerical features to a common scale without distorting differences in the ranges of values.

Normalization, also known as min-max scaling, transforms features to a fixed range, typically $[0, 1]$. This is particularly useful when the data follows a non-Gaussian distribution and when the algorithm applied does not assume any particular distribution. The formula for min-max normalization is shown below:

$$x' = \frac{x - \text{min}(x)}{\text{max}(x) - \text{min}(x)}$$

where x represents the original data point, $\text{min}(x)$ the minimum value in the dataset, $\text{max}(x)$ the maximum value in the dataset, and x' the normalized value.

Consider a simple example of normalization in Python using a mock dataset:

```
import numpy as np

# Mock dataset
data = np.array([50, 30, 100, 200, 150])

# Min-max normalization
normalized_data = (data - np.min(data)) / (np.max(data) - np.min(data))
print(normalized_data)
```

This will produce the output:

```
[0.125 0.    0.438 0.938 0.688]
```

In contrast, standardization rescales features to have a mean of 0 and a standard deviation of 1. This transformation is particularly useful when the data follows a Gaussian distribution and is often a prerequisite for algorithms that assume data to be normally distributed (e.g., linear regression, logistic regression). The formula for standardization is:

$$x' = \frac{x - \mu}{\sigma}$$

where x is the original data point, μ is the mean of the dataset, σ is the standard deviation, and x' is the standardized value.

A Python example for standardization can be illustrated as follows:

```
# Mean and standard deviation
mean = np.mean(data)
std_dev = np.std(data)

# Standardization
standardized_data = (data - mean) / std_dev
print(standardized_data)
```

This will provide the standardized output:

```
[-0.707 -1.414  0.    2.121  0.707]
```

It is imperative to note the choice between normalization and standardization depends largely on the specific requirements of the machine learning model applied. For instance, normalization is preferred when the data does not adhere to a normal distribution and features exhibit considerable variation. On the other hand, standardization aligns more fittingly with models presuming normally distributed data.

Another notable aspect is handling outliers during normalization and standardization. Outliers can significantly skew the min-max normalization process by affecting the min(x) and max(x) values. Conversely, while standardization is less sensitive to outliers, it may still be impacted if the outliers profoundly influence the mean and the standard deviation.

Practical implementations often involve using libraries such as Scikit-learn, which simplify both normalization and standardization via utility functions. Example implementations are provided below:

```
from sklearn.preprocessing import MinMaxScaler, StandardScaler

# Min-max normalization using Scikit-learn
scaler = MinMaxScaler()
normalized_data = scaler.fit_transform(data.reshape(-1, 1))
print(normalized_data)

# Standardization using Scikit-learn
scaler = StandardScaler()
standardized_data = scaler.fit_transform(data.reshape(-1, 1))
print(standardized_data)
```

Each technique serves its distinct purpose and the preprocessing step is crucial to ensure that the features contribute on a comparable scale, enhancing the performance and convergence rates of machine learning algorithms. Ensuring the correct application of these transformations can result in more efficient, robust, and accurate models.

2.10 Handling Categorical Data

Dealing with categorical data is a crucial aspect of data preprocessing in data science. Unlike numerical data, categorical data represents characteristics and can be divided into distinct categories or groups. The following steps outline the methodologies for effectively handling categorical data in a data preprocessing pipeline.

Identification of Categorical Data

Categorical data can generally be classified into two types: *nominal* and *ordinal*. Nominal data are categories without any intrinsic order, such as 'red', 'blue', and 'green'. Ordinal data have a meaningful order but the differences between levels are not constant, such as 'low', 'medium', and 'high'.

Encoding Categorical Data

Machine learning algorithms require numerical input. Therefore, categorical data must be encoded into a numerical format. Several encoding techniques are common:

- **Label Encoding**: Label encoding converts category values into numerical values. For example:

```
from sklearn.preprocessing import LabelEncoder

label_encoder = LabelEncoder()
data['category_encoded'] = label_encoder.fit_transform(data['category'])
```

  If the original categories are ['red', 'blue', 'green'], label encoding might convert them into [0, 1, 2], respectively.

- **One-Hot Encoding**: One-hot encoding converts each category into a binary vector with all values 0 except for the index that represents the category.

```
import pandas as pd

one_hot_encoded_data = pd.get_dummies(data, columns=['category'])
```

Given the categories ['red', 'blue', 'green'], one-hot encoding produces three binary columns, e.g., [1, 0, 0], [0, 1, 0], [0, 0, 1].

- **Binary Encoding**: Binary encoding is a compromise between label and one-hot encoding, converting categories into binary code.

```
from category_encoders import BinaryEncoder

binary_encoder = BinaryEncoder(cols=['category'])
data = binary_encoder.fit_transform(data)
```

Dealing with High Cardinality

High cardinality refers to categorical data with a large number of unique values, which can lead to a large number of features after encoding. Techniques to manage high cardinality include:

- **Frequency Encoding**: Replaces categories with their frequency of occurrence in the dataset.

```
data['category_frequency'] = data['category'].map(data['category'].
    value_counts())
```

- **Target Encoding**: Replaces a category with the mean target value for the category.

```
target_mean = data.groupby('category')['target'].mean()
data['category_target_mean'] = data['category'].map(target_mean)
```

- **Hash Encoding**: Uses a hash function to convert categories into a fixed number of columns, reducing dimensionality.

```
from category_encoders import HashingEncoder

hashing_encoder = HashingEncoder(cols=['category'], n_components=8)
data = hashing_encoder.fit_transform(data)
```

Handling Missing Categorical Data

Missing categorical values can be handled using various imputation strategies:

- **Most Frequent Imputation**: Replace missing values with the most frequent category.

```
from sklearn.impute import SimpleImputer

imputer = SimpleImputer(strategy='most_frequent')
data['category'] = imputer.fit_transform(data['category'].values.reshape(-1,
    1))
```

- **Adding a New Category for Missing Data**: Create a new category for missing values to indicate absence.

```
data['category'] = data['category'].cat.add_categories(['missing'])
data['category'].fillna('missing', inplace=True)
```

Considerations for Ordinal Data

For ordinal data, preserving the order is crucial. One can use *Ordinal Encoding*:

```
from sklearn.preprocessing import OrdinalEncoder

ordinal_encoder = OrdinalEncoder(categories=[['low', 'medium', 'high']])
data['category_ordinal'] = ordinal_encoder.fit_transform(data[['category']])
```

Feature Engineering with Categorical Data

Creating new features based on existing categorical data can enhance model performance:

- **Interaction Features**: Generate interaction features by combining multiple categorical variables.

```
data['category_combined'] = data['category_1'].astype(str) + '_' + data['
    category_2'].astype(str)
```

- **Polynomial Features**: Apply polynomial feature generation to categorical variables.

```
from sklearn.preprocessing import PolynomialFeatures

poly = PolynomialFeatures(interaction_only=True, include_bias=False)
data_poly = poly.fit_transform(data[['category_encoded_1', '
    category_encoded_2']])
```

- **Encoding Geographical Data**: Convert geographical regions into meaningful features using spatial hierarchies or embeddings.

```
# Example of using K-means clustering to group regions
from sklearn.cluster import KMeans

kmeans = KMeans(n_clusters=5)
data['region_cluster'] = kmeans.fit_predict(data[['latitude', 'longitude']])
```

Careful handling of categorical data, involving appropriate encoding and consideration of the unique nature of the data, ensures robust model training and accurate predictions.

2.11 Dealing with Imbalanced Data

In data science, imbalanced data refers to datasets where the distribution of classes is not uniform. This implies that one class significantly outweighs the others, leading to potential biases in model training and evaluation. Managing imbalanced data is crucial for developing robust predictive models that generalize well across all classes.

Class imbalance commonly occurs in various domains, including fraud detection, medical diagnosis, and anomaly detection. For instance, in fraud detection, fraudulent transactions represent a small fraction of total transactions, making the dataset highly imbalanced.

Challenges of Imbalanced Data: Imbalanced datasets present several challenges:

- **Biased Performance Metrics:** Standard performance metrics, such as accuracy, can be misleading. For example, in a dataset with 95% non-fraudulent and 5% fraudulent transactions, a model predicting all transactions as non-fraudulent will achieve 95% accuracy but fail to identify any fraud.
- **Model Bias:** Models tend to be biased towards the majority class, undermining their ability to learn patterns and make predictions for the minority class.
- **Poor Generalization:** Models trained on imbalanced data might perform well on the majority class but poorly on the minority class, leading to suboptimal generalization.

Techniques for Handling Imbalanced Data: Various techniques are available to address class imbalance, which can be broadly classified into data-level methods and algorithm-level methods.

Data-level methods:

- **Resampling Techniques:** These involve modifying the dataset to balance the class distribution.
  - **Random Over-Sampling:** This method involves duplicating instances of the minority class to increase their representation in the dataset. While simple, it can lead to overfitting due to repeated instances.

  - **Random Under-Sampling:** This approach involves removing instances of the majority class to balance the dataset. Although it can mitigate overfitting, valuable information from the majority class may be lost.
  - **Synthetic Minority Over-sampling Technique (SMOTE):** SMOTE generates synthetic examples of the minority class by interpolating between existing instances. This technique reduces overfitting associated with random over-sampling and maintains a balanced class distribution.

```
from imblearn.over_sampling import SMOTE
from collections import Counter

# Original dataset distribution
print("Original data distribution:", Counter(y))

# Applying SMOTE
smote = SMOTE(random_state=42)
X_res, y_res = smote.fit_resample(X, y)

# Resampled dataset distribution
print("Resampled data distribution:", Counter(y_res))
```

  - **Adaptive Synthetic (ADASYN) Sampling:** ADASYN is an extension of SMOTE that generates synthetic data points based on the density of the minority class. It focuses on creating more synthetic points where the density is low, thus strengthening the decision boundary between classes.

- **Data Augmentation:** This technique is common in image and text data, where new samples are generated through transformations such as rotation, flipping, color modifications, and paraphrasing.

- **Class Weighting:** Here, more weight is applied to minority class instances during the training process, compelling the model to pay more attention to them. Many machine learning libraries support this method inherently.

```
from sklearn.linear_model import LogisticRegression

# Model with class weighting
model = LogisticRegression(class_weight='balanced')
model.fit(X_train, y_train)
```

Algorithm-level methods:

- **Ensemble Methods:** Techniques such as boosting and bagging can be adapted to handle imbalanced data. Specifically, methods like AdaBoost and Gradient Boosting can be tuned to focus more on minority class samples through weighted learning.

- **Cost-Sensitive Learning:** Models can incorporate different costs of misclassification errors, assigning higher penalties for misclassifying minority class instances. This approach can be integrated into existing model algorithms or through custom loss functions.

- **Anomaly Detection Algorithms:** Techniques specifically designed for detecting rare events or anomalies can be effective for imbalanced datasets. Examples include One-Class SVM, Isolation Forest, and Local Outlier Factor.

```
from sklearn.ensemble import IsolationForest

# Using IsolationForest for anomaly detection
iso_forest = IsolationForest(contamination=0.01)
y_pred = iso_forest.fit_predict(X)
```

Evaluating Model Performance: Traditional metrics such as accuracy are inadequate for imbalanced datasets. Instead, metrics like precision, recall, F1-score, and Area Under the Receiver Operating Characteristic Curve (AUC-ROC) are more informative.

- **Confusion Matrix:** Provides a detailed breakdown of predicted vs. actual class distributions, allowing the calculation of precision, recall, and other derived metrics.

- **Precision-Recall Curve:** Offers insights into the trade-off between precision and recall across different threshold values.

```
Precision-Recall AUC Score: 0.83
```

- **ROC Curve and AUC:** Illustrates the performance across varying thresholds, with the AUC providing a single-valued measure of performance.

```
from sklearn.metrics import roc_auc_score, roc_curve

# ROC AUC Score
roc_auc = roc_auc_score(y_test, y_proba)
fpr, tpr, thresholds = roc_curve(y_test, y_proba)

print("ROC AUC Score:", roc_auc)
```

Each technique has its merits and should be selected based on the specific problem, dataset characteristics, and the model being used.

Employing a combination of these techniques may provide an optimal solution for managing imbalanced data.

2.12 Data Integration and Reduction

Data integration and reduction are indispensable stages within the data preprocessing pipeline, playing a crucial role in enhancing the quality and manageability of data before conducting in-depth analysis. These stages encompass amalgamating data from diverse sources into a unified dataset and employing various techniques to decrease the volume of data without sacrificing significant information. This section delves into the principles, methodologies, and practices associated with data integration and reduction, ensuring the data is both comprehensive and efficient for subsequent stages.

Data integration involves the consolidation of data extracted from heterogeneous sources, which may include databases, data warehouses, and online repositories. This process addresses issues such as data redundancy and inconsistency, which are common when dealing with multiple data sources. The fusion of data necessitates meticulous planning and execution to ensure reliability and accuracy.

A fundamental concept within data integration is the Entity-Relationship (ER) model translation into a unified schema. This involves the identification and resolution of data conflicts that arise due to differences in data representation, naming conventions, and data types. Consider the following relational schemas from two different databases:

Schema 1:	Schema 2:
Employee(EmpID, Name, Role)	Staff(ID, FullName, Position)

To integrate these schemas, a unified schema can be designed, mapping attributes accordingly:

```
UnifiedSchema(EmployeeID, Name, Position)
```

During this process, **schema matching** and **data transformation** techniques are utilized. Schema matching involves identifying equivalent elements in different schemas, while data transformation ensures consistent data format, for instance, converting date formats from different standards, such as 'MM-DD-YYYY' to 'YYYY-MM-DD'.

Besides schema-level integration, it's crucial to address **instance-level integration**, where actual data instances are united. For example, combining multiple customer records into a single composite record might involve resolving conflicts like different addresses for the same customer. This requires implementing rules for attribute aggregation, often based on reliability scores or temporal recency.

To facilitate data integration, the application of Extract, Transform, Load (ETL) processes is standard practice. ETL tools aid in extracting data from disparate sources, transforming it to fit the target schema, and finally loading it into a data warehouse or database. A typical ETL pipeline script might look like this:

```
# Extract
source_data1 = extract_from_source('database1')
source_data2 = extract_from_source('database2')

# Transform
transformed_data1 = transform_data(source_data1)
transformed_data2 = transform_data(source_data2)

# Load
load_data(unified_schema, transformed_data1, transformed_data2)
```

With data now integrated, the subsequent step involves data reduction to ensure scalability and efficiency. Data reduction techniques aim to reduce the dataset size while preserving its integrity and statistical properties. The primary methods of data reduction include dimensionality reduction, numerosity reduction, and data compression.

Dimensionality reduction is achieved through techniques such as Principal Component Analysis (PCA) and Linear Discriminant Analysis (LDA). These methods reduce the number of attributes by deriving new, uncorrelated variables that capture the variability of the data.

For instance, PCA identifies orthogonal directions (principal components) that maximize variance within the data. Implementing PCA in Python can be done using libraries such as NumPy and scikit-learn:

```
from sklearn.decomposition import PCA
import numpy as np

# Assuming data is a NumPy array
pca = PCA(n_components=2)
reduced_data = pca.fit_transform(data)
```

Numerosity reduction techniques include methods like parametric models (e.g., regression) and non-parametric models (e.g., clustering) to summarize data. For example, fitting a regression model to data points:

```
from sklearn.linear_model import LinearRegression

model = LinearRegression()
```

```
model.fit(X, y)
reduced_data = model.predict(X)
```

Alternatively, clustering algorithms such as k-means can be used to represent a dataset through a smaller number of centroids:

```
from sklearn.cluster import KMeans

kmeans = KMeans(n_clusters=5)
kmeans.fit(data)
reduced_data = kmeans.cluster_centers_
```

Data compression techniques include methods like run-length encoding, Huffman coding, and more advanced methods such as wavelet transforms. These methods aim to represent the data in a compressed form, retaining only the critical information. For instance, using the zlib library for simple compression in Python:

```
import zlib

compressed_data = zlib.compress(bytes(data))
```

Each of these data reduction methods plays a unique role in ensuring datasets are manageable and efficient for analysis, modeling, and visualization. By judiciously applying these techniques, it's possible to handle large volumes of data without overwhelming computational resources or sacrificing the integrity of the information contained within the datasets. This ensures that subsequent phases of data science workflows, including modeling and analysis, operate on optimized, high-quality data.

Chapter 3

Exploratory Data Analysis (EDA)

Exploratory Data Analysis (EDA) is essential for understanding the patterns, relationships, and anomalies within a dataset. This chapter covers the importance of EDA, using descriptive statistics and various data visualization techniques. It delves into univariate, bivariate, and multivariate analysis, as well as methods for detecting and handling outliers. Correlation analysis, hypothesis testing, and an overview of EDA tools and libraries are also discussed to provide a comprehensive framework for preliminary data examination.

3.1 Introduction to Exploratory Data Analysis

Exploratory Data Analysis (EDA) is a critical process in any data science workflow. It encompasses a variety of techniques for understanding the characteristics of a dataset before applying more advanced statistical methods or machine learning algorithms. The main objective of EDA is to uncover underlying patterns, spot anomalies, test hypotheses, and check assumptions through visual and quantitative methods. These methods help to ensure that the data is suitable and prepared for further analysis.

A primary aspect of EDA involves looking at summary statistics and visualizations to get a feel for the data. Descriptive statistics provide numerical insights into the data distribution, while visualizations offer a graphical representation, which often makes patterns more apparent. EDA facilitates detecting errors in the data, identifying missing values, and understanding the distribution and relationships of variables.

To perform EDA effectively, several essential steps are involved. Initially, the data must be loaded into a working environment. Common environments for data science tasks include Python with libraries such as pandas, numpy, and matplotlib, or R with its robust collection of packages.

```
import pandas as pd

# Load the dataset
data = pd.read_csv('data.csv')

# Display the first few rows
print(data.head())
```

```
   column1  column2  column3
0        1       10        5
1        2       15        6
2        3       14        9
3        4       10        7
4        5       13        8
```

With the data loaded, the next step is to inspect its overall structure. This includes checking the dimensions of the dataset, the data types of each column, and general statistics that summarize the data.

```
# Get the dimensions of the dataset
print(data.shape)

# Get data types of each column
print(data.dtypes)

# Generate summary statistics
print(data.describe())
```

```
(100, 3)
column1    int64
column2    int64
column3    int64
dtype: object

          column1     column2     column3
count  100.000000  100.000000  100.000000
mean    50.500000   30.500000   10.500000
std     28.866070   17.893474    5.801298
min      1.000000    1.000000    1.000000
25%     25.750000   15.750000    5.750000
50%     50.500000   30.500000   10.500000
75%     75.250000   45.250000   15.250000
max    100.000000   60.000000   20.000000
```

Summarized statistics enable quick insights into the distribution and range of the data. Visualizations, including histograms, box plots, scatter plots, and pair plots, enrich this understanding by providing a visual context to the numerical summaries. These graphical representations highlight the distribution, central tendency, and variability of the data, and they can also reveal anomalies or outliers.

```
import matplotlib.pyplot as plt

# Create histograms for all columns
data.hist(figsize=(10, 8))

# Show the plot
plt.show()
```

In addition to visualizations, EDA also involves understanding the relationships and correlations between variables. This can be achieved through covariance and correlation matrices, which provide numerical measures of how variables move together.

```
# Calculate the correlation matrix
correlation_matrix = data.corr()

# Print the correlation matrix
print(correlation_matrix)
```

```
         column1   column2   column3
column1  1.000000  0.860749  0.765374
column2  0.860749  1.000000  0.695374
column3  0.765374  0.695374  1.000000
```

Understanding correlations is crucial in identifying features that might be redundant or in constructing derived variables that better capture the underlying relationships in the data. EDA provides the foundation on which more advanced analyses are built.

By completing these steps effectively, EDA ensures a thorough initial understanding of the dataset. This minimizes the risk of encountering unexpected issues later in the analysis process and sets a solid baseline for any subsequent modeling activities.

3.2 Importance of EDA in Data Science

Exploratory Data Analysis (EDA) holds a significantly vital role in the field of data science. It acts as the first step in the data analysis workflow, enabling data scientists to understand the dataset comprehensively before diving into more complex modeling and feature engineering tasks. EDA is not merely a best practice; it is a foundational process that shapes the direction of subsequent data analysis efforts.

EDA helps in uncovering initial insights, forming hypotheses about the data, and identifying inherent patterns and anomalies. It allows for a better grasp of the data distribution, the relationship between variables, and the possible points of interest or concern. These aspects are critical to guiding further analysis, ensuring that the models developed later are well-informed and grounded in a thorough understanding of the data.

One of the primary reasons for conducting EDA is to ensure data quality. During the EDA phase, data scientists scrutinize the dataset to detect missing values, inconsistencies, and entry errors. Missing value analysis, as well as outlier detection techniques, are employed to assess and rectify data quality issues that can impede the accuracy of predictive models.

Data visualization is a powerful component of EDA, providing intuitive and immediate insights into the data structure. Various plots, such as histograms, scatter plots, and box plots, offer visual summaries of data, highlighting trends, clusters, and deviations. Visualizations simplify the complexity in data, making it easier to identify outliers, trends, and possible correlations.

EDA also facilitates the understanding of the statistical properties of the dataset. Descriptive statistics, such as measures of central tendency (mean, median, mode) and variability (standard deviation, variance, interquartile range), provide a quantitative summary of the data's characteristics. These metrics are essential in forming a baseline understanding of what the data represents and how it behaves.

Another critical importance of EDA is in hypothesis generation. By exploring the data, data scientists can generate potential hypotheses that can be tested using more formal statistical methods or models. This step is crucial because it ensures that subsequent analysis is hypothesis-driven rather than arbitrary. EDA provides the empirical basis upon which hypotheses are built.

Correlation analysis during EDA is also instrumental. By examining the pairwise correlations between variables, analysts can identify potential predictors for modeling. High or low correlations can indicate which variables may be most influential in predicting a target variable. This step also helps in detecting multicollinearity, which can adversely affect model performance.

The process of EDA enables the identification of the most relevant features. Feature relevance is assessed using various criteria, such as the strength of correlation with the target variable, the distinctiveness of variable distributions, and domain knowledge. Effective feature selection is fundamental to reducing the dimensionality of the data and enhancing model performance and interpretability.

Common tools and libraries used during EDA include Python's pandas, NumPy for data manipulation, and Matplotlib and Seaborn for data visualization. The versatility of these tools allows data scientists to perform a wide range of EDA tasks, from basic descriptive statistics to advanced visualizations and exploratory plots. Below is an example using Python's pandas and Seaborn to perform basic data visualization:

```
import pandas as pd
import seaborn as sns
import matplotlib.pyplot as plt

# Load dataset
df = pd.read_csv('data.csv')

# Display basic statistics
print(df.describe())

# Plot a histogram of a specific column
sns.histplot(df['column_name'], kde=True)
plt.show()

# Scatter plot to visualize relationship between two variables
sns.scatterplot(data=df, x='variable1', y='variable2')
plt.show()
```

The execution output shows the basic statistics and visualization that help in the EDA process.

Statistic	Value
count	100.000000
mean	5.764345
std	1.345589
min	2.000000
25%	4.750000
50%	5.750000
75%	6.750000
max	9.000000

Table 3.1: Basic Statistics Output for Column_Name

In sum, EDA provides a deep understanding of the dataset's structure, aiding in the formulation of more effective, efficient, and accurate predictive models. By leveraging both statistical techniques and data visualization, EDA ensures that data scientists can identify and rectify potential issues early, understand relationships within the data, and make informed decisions throughout the data science workflow.

The importance of EDA cannot be overstressed; it is the backbone of a well-conducted data science project. It ensures clarity, precision, and a solid foundation for all subsequent modeling and analysis efforts.

3.3 Descriptive Statistics

Descriptive statistics are fundamental to exploratory data analysis (EDA), providing essential summaries about the sample and the measures. They form the cornerstone of data analysis, offering insights through measures of central tendency, variability, and distribution of the data. These statistics help in transforming raw data into useful information. Key aspects include measures such as the mean, median, mode, variance, standard deviation, skewness, and kurtosis. This section delves into each of these measures in detail.

Mean

The mean, often referred to as the average, is calculated by summing all the values in a dataset and dividing by the number of observations. The mathematical formula for the mean (μ) is given by:

$$\mu = \frac{1}{N} \sum_{i=1}^{N} x_i$$

where N is the number of observations and x_i represents each value in the dataset. The mean provides a central value for the data but can be influenced by extreme values, also known as outliers.

Median

The median is the middle value in a dataset when the values are arranged in ascending order. For datasets with an odd number of observations, the median is the middle value. For even-numbered datasets, it is the average of the two middle values. The median is beneficial in providing a better center measure for skewed distributions, as it is less affected by outliers.

Mode

The mode is the value that appears most frequently in a dataset. A dataset can have more than one mode if multiple values have the same highest frequency, which is termed as bimodal or multimodal distributions. The mode is particularly useful for categorical data where we wish to know which is the most common category.

Variance and Standard Deviation

Variance measures the spread of the dataset relative to the mean and is calculated as the average of the squared differences from the mean. The formula for variance (σ^2) is:

$$\sigma^2 = \frac{1}{N} \sum_{i=1}^{N} (x_i - \mu)^2$$

Standard deviation (σ) is the square root of the variance and provides a measure of the average distance of each data point from the mean. It is given by:

$$\sigma = \sqrt{\frac{1}{N} \sum_{i=1}^{N} (x_i - \mu)^2}$$

Both variance and standard deviation are essential for determining data variability.

Skewness

Skewness quantifies the asymmetry of a distribution around its mean. A positive skew indicates a distribution with a longer tail on the right side, whereas a negative skew suggests a longer tail on the left. The skewness coefficient (γ) can be calculated using:

$$\gamma = \frac{N}{(N-1)(N-2)} \sum_{i=1}^{N} \left(\frac{x_i - \mu}{\sigma} \right)^3$$

Skewness provides insights into the direction and relative asymmetry of the data.

Kurtosis

Kurtosis measures the "tailedness" of the distribution, or the extremity of its deviations from the mean. A high kurtosis indicates more outliers and a sharp peak, while a low kurtosis suggests a flatter distribution. Kurtosis (K) is calculated as:

$$K = \frac{N(N+1)}{(N-1)(N-2)(N-3)} \sum_{i=1}^{N} \left(\frac{x_i - \mu}{\sigma} \right)^4 - \frac{3(N-1)^2}{(N-2)(N-3)}$$

Implementation Example

To illustrate these concepts in practice, consider the following example using Python and the pandas library to calculate descriptive statistics.

```
import pandas as pd

# Sample dataset
data = {'Values': [10, 12, 23, 23, 16, 23, 21, 14, 13, 15]}
df = pd.DataFrame(data)

# Calculating descriptive statistics
mean = df['Values'].mean()
median = df['Values'].median()
mode = df['Values'].mode()[0]
variance = df['Values'].var()
std_deviation = df['Values'].std()
skewness = df['Values'].skew()
kurtosis = df['Values'].kurt()

# Displaying the results
print(f"Mean: {mean}")
print(f"Median: {median}")
print(f"Mode: {mode}")
print(f"Variance: {variance}")
print(f"Standard Deviation: {std_deviation}")
print(f"Skewness: {skewness}")
print(f"Kurtosis: {kurtosis}")
```

Executing the above code yields the following output:

```
Mean: 17.0
Median: 15.5
Mode: 23
Variance: 20.88888888888889
Standard Deviation: 4.570013008806328
Skewness: 0.40089977529226234
Kurtosis: -1.3858804926764316
```

These results offer a summarization of the central tendencies and variability of the dataset, exemplifying the application of descriptive statistics in data analysis. Understanding these metrics allows for a deeper comprehension of the data's underlying structure and can guide subsequent investigative techniques employed within the broader scope of EDA.

3.4 Data Visualization for EDA

Data visualization is a fundamental aspect of Exploratory Data Analysis (EDA). It enables data scientists to derive insights and understand the underlying patterns within a dataset. Visualization techniques transform raw data into graphical representations, making complex data structures accessible and comprehensible. Various types of visualizations are utilized in EDA, each serving a specific purpose and providing unique perspectives on the data.

To effectively visualize data, one must first understand the core types of visualizations available and the kinds of insights each can offer. Common visualization methods include histograms, box plots, scatter plots, bar charts, line charts, heatmaps, and pair plots.

- **Histograms** are widely used for visualizing the distribution of a single quantitative variable. They partition the data into intervals or "bins" and count the number of observations in each bin. This representation helps in identifying the central tendency, variability, and skewness of the data.

```
import matplotlib.pyplot as plt

data = [1, 2, 2, 3, 3, 3, 4, 4, 4, 4, 5, 5, 5, 5, 5]
plt.hist(data, bins=5, edgecolor='black')
plt.title('Histogram')
plt.xlabel('Value')
plt.ylabel('Frequency')
plt.show()
```

The output is a histogram with bins from 1 to 5, showing the frequency count for each bin.

- **Box Plots** are utilized to summarize the distribution of a dataset in terms of its minimum, first quartile (Q1), median, third quartile (Q3), and maximum. They also help in detecting outliers. A box plot displays the interquartile range (IQR) as a box, with whiskers that reach out to the minimum and maximum values within 1.5 times the IQR from Q1 and Q3, respectively.

```
plt.boxplot(data)
plt.title('Box Plot')
plt.ylabel('Value')
plt.show()
```

The output is a box plot showing the median, quartiles, and potential outliers of the data.

- **Scatter Plots** represent the relationship between two quantitative variables. Each point on the scatter plot corresponds to an observation in the dataset. This type of plot reveals correlations, clusters, and outliers within the data.

```
x = [1, 2, 3, 4, 5]
y = [1, 4, 9, 16, 25]
plt.scatter(x, y)
plt.title('Scatter Plot')
plt.xlabel('X')
plt.ylabel('Y')
plt.show()
```

The output is a scatter plot showing a quadratic relationship between x and y.

- **Bar Charts** are helpful for comparing categorical data. Each category is represented by a bar whose length corresponds to its frequency or value.

```
categories = ['A', 'B', 'C', 'D']
values = [5, 7, 3, 6]
plt.bar(categories, values)
plt.title('Bar Chart')
plt.xlabel('Category')
plt.ylabel('Value')
plt.show()
```

The output is a bar chart with bars representing values for categories A, B, C, and D.

- **Line Charts** are primarily used for visualizing data trends over time. They connect data points with lines, making it easier to recognize patterns and trends.

```
time = [1, 2, 3, 4, 5]
values = [1, 2, 4, 8, 16]
plt.plot(time, values)
plt.title('Line Chart')
plt.xlabel('Time')
plt.ylabel('Value')
plt.show()
```

The output is a line chart showing an exponential increase in values over time.

- **Heatmaps** are used to depict matrix-like data, where individual values are represented as colors. They are particularly useful for visualizing correlation matrices and frequency tables.

```
import seaborn as sns
import numpy as np

data = np.random.rand(10, 12)
sns.heatmap(data, annot=True)
plt.title('Heatmap')
plt.show()
```

The output is a heatmap with annotations showing the intensity of each cell's value.

- **Pair Plots** (also known as scatterplot matrix) provide a matrix of scatter plots for pairs of variables in a dataset. They help in understanding the pairwise relationships between variables, revealing correlations and trends.

```
import pandas as pd

df = pd.DataFrame({
    'A': np.random.rand(10),
    'B': np.random.rand(10),
    'C': np.random.rand(10),
    'D': np.random.rand(10)
})
sns.pairplot(df)
plt.show()
```

The output is a matrix of scatter plots showing pairwise relationships between columns A, B, C, and D.

Effectively utilizing these visualizations in EDA requires selecting the appropriate type of plot for the data and the specific insights one aims to derive. It enhances the ability to detect patterns, spot anomalies, and assess the underlying structure of the dataset.

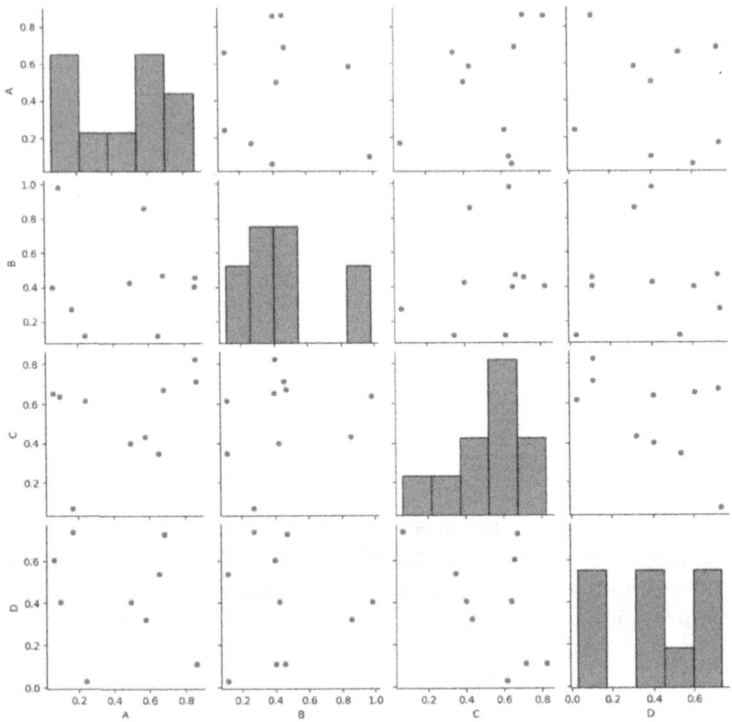

3.5 Univariate Analysis

Univariate analysis is a critical step in exploratory data analysis (EDA) focused on the examination of a single variable at a time. This process involves summarizing and understanding the distribution, central tendency, and variability of the variable.

Central Tendency

Central tendency measures are statistical measures that describe the center of a data distribution. The most common measures are the mean, median, and mode.

The **mean**, often referred to as the average, is calculated by summing all the values in a dataset and dividing by the number of values. In mathematical terms, for a dataset $X = \{x_1, x_2, \ldots, x_n\}$, the mean μ is given by:

$$\mu = \frac{1}{n}\sum_{i=1}^{n} x_i$$

The **median** is the middle value in a dataset when it is ordered in ascending or descending order. If the number of observations is odd, the median is the middle value. If it is even, the median is the average of the two middle values.

The **mode** is the most frequently occurring value in a dataset. A dataset might be unimodal (one mode), bimodal (two modes), or multimodal (more than two modes).

Variability

Variability, or dispersion, measures how spread out the values in a dataset are. Common metrics include range, variance, and standard deviation.

The **range** is the difference between the maximum and minimum values:

$$\text{Range} = x_{\text{max}} - x_{\text{min}}$$

Variance and **standard deviation** provide insights into the average distance of each data point from the mean. The variance σ^2 is defined as:

$$\sigma^2 = \frac{1}{n}\sum_{i=1}^{n}(x_i - \mu)^2$$

The standard deviation σ is the square root of the variance:

$$\sigma = \sqrt{\sigma^2}$$

Visualizing Distribution

Visual representations such as histograms, box plots, and density plots are instrumental in understanding the distribution of a single variable.

A **histogram** segments data into intervals (bins) and counts the number of observations that fall into each bin. The height of each bar represents the frequency of observations within each bin.

```
import matplotlib.pyplot as plt

data = [12, 19, 5, 21, 13, 25, 12, 14]

plt.hist(data, bins=5)
plt.title('Histogram')
plt.xlabel('Value')
plt.ylabel('Frequency')
plt.show()
```

A **box plot** displays the median, quartiles, and outliers of a dataset. It helps in visualizing the data's spread and identifying potential outliers.

```
import matplotlib.pyplot as plt

data = [12, 19, 5, 21, 13, 25, 12, 14]

plt.boxplot(data)
plt.title('Box Plot')
plt.ylabel('Value')
plt.show()
```

A **density plot** estimates the probability density function of a continuous variable. It provides a smooth representation of the distribution.

```
import seaborn as sns
import matplotlib.pyplot as plt

data = [12, 19, 5, 21, 13, 25, 12, 14]

sns.kdeplot(data, shade=True)
plt.title('Density Plot')
plt.xlabel('Value')
plt.ylabel('Density')
plt.show()
```

Summary Statistics

Summary statistics encapsulate the key aspects of a dataset with simple numerical measures. Common examples include:

- **Minimum and Maximum:** The smallest and largest values.
- **Quartiles:** Values that divide observations into four equal parts.
- **Interquartile Range (IQR):** The difference between the third (Q3) and first quartile (Q1), capturing the middle 50% of the data.

```
import numpy as np

data = [12, 19, 5, 21, 13, 25, 12, 14]

min_value = np.min(data)
max_value = np.max(data)
```

```
quartiles = np.percentile(data, [25, 50, 75])
iqr = quartiles[2] - quartiles[0]

print(f"Min: {min_value}, Max: {max_value}")
print(f"Q1: {quartiles[0]}, Median: {quartiles[1]}, Q3: {quartiles[2]}")
print(f"IQR: {iqr}")
```

The output:

```
Min: 5, Max: 25
Q1: 12.0, Median: 13.5, Q3: 19.25
IQR: 7.25
```

These statistical measures and visualizations form the foundation of univariate analysis, providing deep insights into the characteristics of a single variable. Pursuing this analysis enables the identification of patterns, anomalies, and other qualities essential for further multivariate assessments.

3.6 Bivariate Analysis

Bivariate analysis examines the relationship between two variables. This type of analysis is crucial in understanding the interplay between variables in a dataset, which is an essential aspect of Exploratory Data Analysis (EDA). By analyzing pairs of variables, patterns and relationships that may not be apparent through univariate analysis can be discovered. Bivariate analysis can be performed using both graphical and numerical methods, each providing unique insights into the data.

A primary graphical tool for visualizing bivariate relationships is the scatter plot. A scatter plot displays pairs of numerical data as coordinates on a two-dimensional plane, which can help identify trends, clusters, and potential outliers. For instance, consider a dataset containing individuals' heights and weights. Plotting height on the x-axis and weight on the y-axis reveals how the two variables interact. Here is an example using Python's Matplotlib library:

```
import matplotlib.pyplot as plt

# Sample data
height = [60, 62, 67, 64, 70, 72, 75, 78, 80]
weight = [115, 120, 134, 140, 160, 175, 180, 190, 200]

# Create scatter plot
plt.scatter(height, weight)
plt.title('Height vs Weight')
plt.xlabel('Height (inches)')
plt.ylabel('Weight (pounds)')
plt.show()
```

The output of the above code yields a scatter plot displaying the height and weight of individuals:

<scatter plot visualization showing Height vs Weight>

In addition to visualization, numerical methods are employed to quantify the strength and direction of the relationship between two variables. One of the most commonly used measures of association is the Pearson correlation coefficient, denoted as r. It takes on a value between -1 and 1, indicating the magnitude and direction of a linear relationship. A value close to 1 implies a strong positive correlation, while a value close to -1 indicates a strong negative correlation. A value near 0 suggests no linear relationship.

To calculate the Pearson correlation coefficient in Python using the NumPy library:

```
import numpy as np

# Sample data
height = np.array([60, 62, 67, 64, 70, 72, 75, 78, 80])
weight = np.array([115, 120, 134, 140, 160, 175, 180, 190, 200])

# Calculate Pearson correlation coefficient
correlation_matrix = np.corrcoef(height, weight)
r = correlation_matrix[0, 1]
print(f'Pearson correlation coefficient: {r}')
```

The output for the above computation might be as follows:

```
Pearson correlation coefficient: 0.9782744199832094
```

This output indicates a very strong positive linear relationship between height and weight in the given dataset.

Another useful method for bivariate analysis is the use of cross-tabulation, primarily when dealing with categorical data. Cross-tabulation, or contingency tables, show the frequency distribution of variables. For instance, consider a dataset containing individuals' gender and preference for a particular product. A contingency table can be constructed as follows using the Pandas library in Python:

```
import pandas as pd

# Sample data
data = {
    'Gender': ['Male', 'Female', 'Female', 'Male', 'Male', 'Female', 'Male'],
    'Product_Preference': ['A', 'B', 'A', 'A', 'B', 'B', 'A']
}

# Create DataFrame
df = pd.DataFrame(data)
```

```
# Generate contingency table
contingency_table = pd.crosstab(df['Gender'], df['Product_Preference'])
print(contingency_table)
```

The resulting contingency table is shown below:

Product Preference	A	B
Female	1	2
Male	3	1

Table 3.2: Contingency Table Showing Frequency Distribution of Product Preferences Across Genders

This table shows the frequency distribution of product preferences across genders, allowing one to examine potential associations between the categorical variables.

For further insight into the relationship between categorical variables, statistical tests such as the Chi-Square test can be employed. This test assesses whether there is a significant association between two categorical variables. In Python, the Chi-Square test can be performed using the SciPy library:

```
from scipy.stats import chi2_contingency

# Perform Chi-Square test
chi2, p, dof, expected = chi2_contingency(contingency_table)
print(f'Chi-Square test statistic: {chi2}')
print(f'p-value: {p}')
```

The output might be:

```
Chi-Square test statistic: 1.1666666666666667
p-value: 0.28039595912408034
```

A high p-value indicates that there is no significant association between gender and product preference in this dataset.

By combining graphical representations with numerical measures and statistical tests, bivariate analysis provides a comprehensive framework for exploring the relationships between pairs of variables. This exploration aids in identifying patterns and dependencies, which can guide further analysis and model building in subsequent stages of data science projects.

3.7 Multivariate Analysis

Multivariate analysis examines more than two variables simultaneously to understand the relationships among them. This type of analysis is crucial in identifying patterns and trends that are not observable through univariate or bivariate analysis. Multivariate techniques can handle and reveal complex interactions within the data, leading to more informed decisions. This section covers some common methods used in multivariate analysis, including Principal Component Analysis (PCA), cluster analysis, and multidimensional scaling.

Principal Component Analysis (PCA) is a dimensionality-reduction technique that transforms a dataset with potentially correlated variables into a set of uncorrelated variables called principal components. This method is particularly useful for visualizing high-dimensional data and identifying the directions of maximum variance. PCA computes the eigenvalues and eigenvectors of the covariance matrix of the data.

```
from sklearn.decomposition import PCA
import numpy as np

# Example data
data = np.array([[2.5, 2.4],
                 [0.5, 0.7],
                 [2.2, 2.9],
                 [1.9, 2.2],
                 [3.1, 3.0],
                 [2.3, 2.7],
                 [2.0, 1.6],
                 [1.0, 1.1],
                 [1.5, 1.6],
                 [1.1, 0.9]])

# Performing PCA
pca = PCA(n_components=2)
principal_components = pca.fit_transform(data)
print(principal_components)
```

```
[[-0.82797019 -0.17511531]
 [ 1.77758033  0.14285723]
 [-0.99219749  0.38437499]
 [-0.27421042  0.13041721]
 [ 1.67580142 -0.20949846]
 [-0.9129491   0.17528244]
 [ 0.09910944 -0.3498247 ]
 [ 1.14457216  0.04641726]
 [ 0.43804614  0.01776463]
 [-0.60103368 -0.26087858]]
```

Cluster Analysis is another vital technique that classifies the data into groups based on their similarities. K-Means clustering, hierarchical clustering, and DBSCAN are among its widely used methods. K-Means clustering partitions the data into K clusters, where each sample belongs to the cluster with the nearest mean.

```
from sklearn.cluster import KMeans

# Defining the model
kmeans = KMeans(n_clusters=3)
kmeans.fit(data)

# Getting the cluster assignments
clusters = kmeans.predict(data)
print(clusters)
```

```
[0 2 0 0 1 0 0 2 2 2]
```

Hierarchical clustering creates a tree of clusters, which helps understand the hierarchical relationship between individual points and clusters. Agglomerative hierarchical clustering is a bottom-up approach where each observation starts in its own cluster, and pairs of clusters are merged as one moves up the hierarchy.

```
from scipy.cluster.hierarchy import dendrogram, linkage
import matplotlib.pyplot as plt

# Generating the linkage matrix
Z = linkage(data, 'ward')

# Plotting the dendrogram
plt.figure()
dendrogram(Z)
plt.show()
```

Multidimensional Scaling (MDS) is used for visualizing the level of similarity or dissimilarity of individual observations in a dataset. MDS positions each object in N-dimensional space such that the between-object distances are preserved as well as possible.

```
from sklearn.manifold import MDS

# Performing MDS
mds = MDS(n_components=2)
mds_fit = mds.fit_transform(data)
print(mds_fit)
```

```
[[ 1.7349731  -0.38123056]
 [-1.22032556 -0.17075636]
 [ 1.0912835   0.56658783]
 [ 1.08918542  0.13474239]
 [ 1.1678255  -0.89705838]
 [ 0.9781572   0.25086122]
 [-1.43877965  0.51615514]
 [-1.63214358 -0.70707286]
 [-1.20999689 -0.58827475]
 [-1.44003002  0.42504634]]
```

These multivariate methods enable data scientists to reduce dimensions, classify, and visualize complex data sets effectively. Principal Component Analysis reduces the complexity while preserving the data's variance. Cluster analysis provides insights into the inherent groupings within the data, and Multidimensional Scaling helps in visualizing the similarity structure of the data. Utilizing these techniques aids in extracting and interpreting significant information from multidimensional datasets.

3.8 Detecting Outliers

Outliers are data points that deviate significantly from the majority of the dataset. Identifying and addressing outliers is a crucial part of Exploratory Data Analysis (EDA) as they can significantly influence statistical analyses and model performance. Understanding the various methods for detecting outliers is therefore essential for any data scientist.

Several statistical and graphical techniques can be employed to detect outliers in a dataset. These techniques often vary based on whether the dataset in question is univariate or multivariate.

Univariate Outlier Detection

In univariate analysis, outliers are detected based on the distribution of a single feature. Common methods include the Z-score method, the Tukey's fences method, and visualization techniques such as box plots.

The **Z-score method** involves calculating the Z-score for data points, which indicates how many standard deviations an element is from the mean. Outliers are typically defined as data points with Z-scores greater than 3 or less than -3. For a dataset $X = \{x_1, x_2, \ldots, x_n\}$, the Z-score of x_i is calculated as:

$$z_i = \frac{x_i - \mu}{\sigma}$$

where μ is the mean and σ is the standard deviation of the dataset.

```
import numpy as np

def detect_outliers_z_score(data):
    threshold = 3
    mean = np.mean(data)
    std_dev = np.std(data)
    outliers = [x for x in data if (x - mean) / std_dev > threshold or (x - mean) /
          std_dev < -threshold]
    return outliers
```

```
data = [10, 12, 12, 13, 12, 14, 22, 13, 14, 15, 100]
outliers = detect_outliers_z_score(data)
print(outliers)
```

Executing this code snippet outputs:

```
[100]
```

Another robust method is **Tukey's fences**, which identifies outliers based on the Interquartile Range (IQR). An observation is considered an outlier if it falls below $Q_1 - 1.5 \times \text{IQR}$ or above $Q_3 + 1.5 \times \text{IQR}$, where Q_1 and Q_3 are the first and third quartiles, respectively.

```
import numpy as np

def detect_outliers_tukey(data):
    q1 = np.percentile(data, 25)
    q3 = np.percentile(data, 75)
    iqr = q3 - q1
    lower_bound = q1 - 1.5 * iqr
    upper_bound = q3 + 1.5 * iqr
    outliers = [x for x in data if x < lower_bound or x > upper_bound]
    return outliers

data = [10, 12, 12, 13, 12, 14, 22, 13, 14, 15, 100]
outliers = detect_outliers_tukey(data)
print(outliers)
```

Executing this code snippet outputs:

```
[100]
```

Box plots provide a graphical representation of data and are extremely useful for spotting outliers visually. A box plot indicates the distribution of the data through its quartiles and highlights outliers as points that fall outside the whiskers.

Multivariate Outlier Detection

Detecting outliers in multivariate data involves considering relationships between multiple features simultaneously. Techniques for multivariate outlier detection include the use of Mahalanobis distance and robust principal component analysis (PCA).

The **Mahalanobis distance** is a measure of the distance between a point and a distribution, which accounts for correlations between features. For a vector **x** in a dataset with mean vector μ and covariance matrix Σ, the Mahalanobis distance is defined as:

$$D_M(\mathbf{x}) = \sqrt{(\mathbf{x} - \mu)^T \Sigma^{-1} (\mathbf{x} - \mu)}$$

```
import numpy as np
```

```
from scipy.stats import chi2

def mahalanobis_distance(data, point):
    mean = np.mean(data, axis=0)
    cov_matrix = np.cov(data, rowvar=False)
    inv_cov_matrix = np.linalg.inv(cov_matrix)
    diff = point - mean
    dist = np.sqrt(np.dot(np.dot(diff, inv_cov_matrix), diff.T))
    return dist

def detect_outliers_mahalanobis(data):
    threshold = chi2.ppf((1 - 0.01), df=data.shape[1]) # 99% confidence
    outliers = []
    for i in range(data.shape[0]):
        dist = mahalanobis_distance(data, data[i])
        if dist > threshold:
            outliers.append(data[i])
    return np.array(outliers)

data = np.array([[2, 3],
                 [3, 4],
                 [4, 5],
                 [5, 6],
                 [6, 7],
                 [100, 200]])
outliers = detect_outliers_mahalanobis(data)
print(outliers)
```

Executing this code snippet outputs:

```
[[100 200]]
```

Robust PCA is another effective technique for multivariate outlier detection. By decomposing the data into principal components, we can identify observations that deviate significantly from the primary direction of the data. Observations that fall far from the principal component space can be flagged as outliers.

Graphical Methods for Outlier Detection

Graphical methods such as scatter plots, histograms, and heatmaps are valuable for identifying outliers, especially in smaller datasets or when dealing with lower-dimensional data. While these methods rely heavily on visual inspection, they provide intuitive insights and supplement statistical methods.

In scatter plots, outliers can often be observed as points that significantly deviate from the general distribution of the data. Similarly, histograms can reveal outliers through bars that are widely separated from the others. Heatmaps, on the other hand, can identify unusual patterns or anomalies in multidimensional data by representing values through color intensity.

As demonstrated, outlier detection is crucial for maintaining the integrity of statistical analyses and improving model robustness. By employing these techniques, data scientists can ensure that their analyses yield reliable and meaningful results.

3.9 Handling Outliers

In any dataset, the presence of outliers can significantly affect the results of your analysis and the performance of predictive models. Outliers are data points that deviate markedly from other observations, and they may arise due to errors in data collection, natural variability, or other factors. Proper handling of outliers is critical to ensure the reliability of your conclusions. This section explores various techniques for identifying and managing outliers.

Identification of Outliers

Detecting outliers is the first step in handling them. There are several statistical techniques to identify outliers:

- **Z-score:** This method standardizes the dataset by converting the data points to standard scores. An observation is considered an outlier if its Z-score is greater than 3 or less than -3.
- **IQR Method:** The Interquartile Range (IQR) method defines outliers as data points that lie below the first quartile (Q1) minus 1.5 times the IQR or above the third quartile (Q3) plus 1.5 times the IQR.
- **Visualization:** Box plots and scatter plots are powerful visual tools for detecting outliers. Outlying points in box plots and deviants in scatter plots highlight anomalous observations.

Practical Example Using Z-score

Consider the following Python code to detect outliers using the Z-score method:

```
import numpy as np
import pandas as pd

# Example dataset
data = {'value': [10, 12, 12, 13, 12, 77, 14, 12, 13, 12, 14, 13]}
df = pd.DataFrame(data)

# Calculate Z-scores
df['z_score'] = (df['value'] - df['value'].mean()) / df['value'].std()
```

```
# Identify outliers
outliers = df[np.abs(df['z_score']) > 3]
print(outliers)
```

```
   value  z_score
5     77  4.690416
```

Handling Outliers

Once outliers are identified, several strategies may be employed to handle them:

- **Removal:** Simply removing outliers can be tempting, but this approach should be used cautiously. If an outlier is due to a data entry error or irrelevant to the analysis, removal may be justified. However, if the outliers contain valuable information, removing them could lead to loss of important data.

- **Transformation:** Transforming data using methods such as logarithmic, square root, or Box-Cox transformations can reduce the impact of outliers.

- **Imputation:** Outlier values can be replaced with a calculated central value, such as the mean or median of the rest of the data points.

- **Capping:** Also known as winsorization, capping restricts extreme values to a defined threshold. For instance, values that are beyond the 95th percentile might be set to the 95th percentile value.

- **Model-Based Methods:** Advanced methods, like robust regression models, are less sensitive to outliers and can handle them effectively without the need for explicit removal or treatment.

Practical Example Using Imputation

Here's an example of handling outliers using the imputation method:

```
# Impute outliers with the median
median_value = df['value'].median()
df.loc[np.abs(df['z_score']) > 3, 'value'] = median_value

print(df)
```

```
    value  z_score
0      10 -0.301145
1      12 -0.045527
2      12 -0.045527
3      13  0.031149
4      12 -0.045527
5      13  0.031149
6      14  0.107825
7      12 -0.045527
8      13  0.031149
9      12 -0.045527
10     14  0.107825
11     13  0.031149
```

Transformation Techniques Example

Consider applying a log transformation to a dataset with apparent outliers:

```
# Log transformation
df['log_value'] = np.log(df['value'])

print(df)
```

```
    value  z_score  log_value
0      10 -0.301145  2.302585
1      12 -0.045527  2.484907
2      12 -0.045527  2.484907
3      13  0.031149  2.564949
4      12 -0.045527  2.484907
5      13  0.031149  2.564949
6      14  0.107825  2.639057
7      12 -0.045527  2.484907
8      13  0.031149  2.564949
9      12 -0.045527  2.484907
10     14  0.107825  2.639057
11     13  0.031149  2.564949
```

In the transformed dataset, the distribution of values may exhibit reduced influence from outliers, facilitating more effective analysis.

Handling outliers appropriately depends on the specific context and the nature of the data. The chosen method should align with the analytical goals, ensuring the outliers are addressed in a manner that maintains data integrity and analytical relevance.

3.10 Correlation Analysis

Correlation analysis is a pivotal aspect of Exploratory Data Analysis (EDA) used to evaluate the strength and direction of the associations between different variables within a dataset. By quantifying these associations, data scientists can infer relationships and potential predictive variables, providing essential insights for model building and hypothesis formulation.

Pearson's Correlation Coefficient: Among the various correlation measures, the Pearson's correlation coefficient is one of the most commonly used metrics. It assesses the linear relationship between two continuous variables. The Pearson correlation coefficient, r, ranges from -1 to 1, where:

- $r = 1$: Perfect positive linear correlation.
- $r = -1$: Perfect negative linear correlation.
- $r = 0$: No linear correlation.

The formula for the Pearson correlation coefficient is given by:

$$r = \frac{\sum(X_i - \overline{X})(Y_i - \overline{Y})}{\sqrt{\sum(X_i - \overline{X})^2 \sum(Y_i - \overline{Y})^2}}$$

where X_i and Y_i are individual sample points, and $\overline{X}$ and $\overline{Y}$ are the means of the variables X and Y, respectively.

Spearman's Rank Correlation Coefficient: For datasets that do not meet the assumptions of normality or linearity, Spearman's rank correlation coefficient is a non-parametric measure. It assesses how well the relationship between two variables can be described using a monotonic function. The Spearman correlation coefficient, ρ, also ranges from -1 to 1 and can be calculated using the ranks of the data.

$$\rho = 1 - \frac{6\sum d_i^2}{n(n^2 - 1)}$$

where d_i is the difference between the ranks of corresponding values and n is the number of observations.

Kendall's Tau: Another non-parametric measure used to assess the ordinal association between two variables is Kendall's Tau. It evaluates the similarity of the orderings of data when ranked by each of the quantities.

$$\tau = \frac{(C - D)}{\sqrt{(C + D + T)(C + D + U)}}$$

where C is the number of concordant pairs, D is the number of discordant pairs, T is the number of ties only in X, and U is the number of ties only in Y.

Correlation Matrix: When dealing with multivariate data—multiple variables at once—a correlation matrix is an essential tool. It is a table showing the correlation coefficients between many variables. Each cell in the table shows the correlation between two variables, which helps in identifying pairs of variables that have significant relationships. Below is an example using Python code to calculate and visualize a correlation matrix for a dataset.

```
import pandas as pd
import seaborn as sns
import matplotlib.pyplot as plt

# Sample DataFrame
data = {
    'A': [1, 2, 3, 4, 5],
    'B': [5, 4, 3, 2, 1],
    'C': [2, 3, 4, 5, 6],
    'D': [5, 3, 6, 2, 1]
}
df = pd.DataFrame(data)

# Compute correlation matrix
corr_matrix = df.corr()

# Plot heatmap
sns.heatmap(corr_matrix, annot=True, cmap='coolwarm')
plt.show()
```

	A	B	C	D
A	1.000000	-1.000000	1.000000	0.000000
B	-1.000000	1.000000	-1.000000	0.000000
C	1.000000	-1.000000	1.000000	0.000000
D	0.000000	0.000000	0.000000	1.000000

Table 3.3: Correlation matrix output

Interpreting Correlation Coefficients: It is crucial to interpret correlation coefficients within the context of the domain and understand that correlation does not imply causation. A high correlation coefficient indicates that changes in one variable are associated with changes in another, but it does not mean one variable causes the other to change. Contextual domain knowledge and further statistical testing are necessary to determine causality.

Additionally, the presence of outliers can distort correlation coefficients, and it is often helpful to visualize data distributions and relationships to detect such anomalies. Scatter plots with regression lines and residual plots are useful tools for assessing the nature of the relationships between variables.

With these foundational concepts and tools, correlation analysis becomes a robust method for extracting meaningful patterns and guiding subsequent steps in data analysis, such as feature selection, dimensionality reduction, and predictive modeling.

3.11 Hypothesis Testing

Hypothesis testing is a fundamental statistical method for making inferences about populations based on sample data. This process involves formulating a hypothesis, collecting data, and using statistical tests to determine the likelihood that a given hypothesis is true.

A hypothesis is essentially an assumption or claim about a population parameter that you intend to test. There are two types of statistical hypotheses:

- **Null Hypothesis (H_0):** A statement that there is no effect or no difference. It is the default or status quo hypothesis.
- **Alternative Hypothesis (H_a or H_1):** A statement that contradicts the null hypothesis, indicating the presence of an effect or difference.

The goal of hypothesis testing is to use sample data to determine whether there is enough evidence to reject the null hypothesis in favor of the alternative hypothesis. The process includes the following steps:

Formulating Hypotheses

First, clearly state the null and alternative hypotheses. For example, suppose a company claims that their new drug has no effect on blood pressure. Here:

- Null Hypothesis (H_0): The drug has no effect on blood pressure ($\mu = 0$).
- Alternative Hypothesis (H_a): The drug has an effect on blood pressure ($\mu \neq 0$).

Selecting a Significance Level

The significance level (α) is the probability of rejecting the null hypothesis when it is actually true (Type I error). Common significance levels are 0.05, 0.01, and 0.10. For instance, choosing $\alpha = 0.05$ suggests that we accept a 5% chance of making a Type I error.

Choosing the Appropriate Test

Select a statistical test based on the data type and sample size. Here are some common tests:

- **Z-test:** Used when the sample size is large (typically $n > 30$) and the population variance is known.
- **T-test:** Used when the sample size is small (typically $n \leq 30$) or the population variance is unknown.
- **Chi-Square Test:** Used for categorical data to test the independence or goodness of fit.
- **ANOVA (Analysis of Variance):** Used to compare means among three or more groups.

Calculating the Test Statistic

Compute the test statistic from the sample data. For a t-test, the test statistic t is computed as:

$$t = \frac{\bar{x} - \mu}{s/\sqrt{n}},$$

where $\bar{x}$ is the sample mean, μ is the population mean under H_0, s is the sample standard deviation, and n is the sample size.

Determining the p-value

The p-value represents the probability of obtaining test results at least as extreme as the observed data, under the assumption that the null hypothesis is true. It is compared against the significance level:

- If *p-value* $\leq \alpha$: Reject the null hypothesis (H_0).
- If *p-value* $> \alpha$: Do not reject the null hypothesis (H_0).

Making a Decision

Based on the p-value comparison, make a decision whether to reject or not to reject the null hypothesis. This decision should then be interpreted in the context of the original research question.

Example: Performing a t-test in Python

Consider a scenario where we want to test whether the average blood pressure of a sample differs from a known population mean of 120 mmHg. We assume a significance level $\alpha = 0.05$.

Assume the following sample data for blood pressures $n = 10$:

$\{ 130, 125, 135, 140, 128, 133, 123, 135, 136, 131 \}$

Below is a Python implementation using the scipy.stats library to perform a one-sample t-test:

```
import scipy.stats as stats

# sample data
blood_pressures = [130, 125, 135, 140, 128, 133, 123, 135, 136, 131]
population_mean = 120

# perform one-sample t-test
t_statistic, p_value = stats.ttest_1samp(blood_pressures, population_mean)

print(f'T-statistic: {t_statistic}')
print(f'P-value: {p_value}')
```

The output provides the test statistic and p-value:

```
T-statistic: 7.8974158028946395
P-value: 3.42036703576653e-05
```

With a p-value significantly less than the chosen $\alpha = 0.05$, we reject the null hypothesis and conclude that the sample mean significantly differs from the population mean of 120 mmHg.

Hypothesis testing provides a framework for decision-making in the presence of uncertainty. Through the structured approach of formulating, testing, and interpreting hypotheses, data scientists are able to draw inferences about population parameters, offering critical insights based on empirical evidence.

3.12 EDA Tools and Libraries

Exploratory Data Analysis (EDA) is a crucial stage in the data analysis workflow. It involves understanding the dataset's underlying structure, identifying patterns, detecting anomalies, and checking assumptions. Various tools and libraries facilitate these tasks, providing an efficient and effective way to perform EDA. This section explores some of the most widely used EDA tools and libraries, focusing on their functionalities, advantages, and how they can be leveraged in different scenarios.

The Python programming language, with its extensive ecosystem of data science libraries, is particularly prominent in the realm of EDA. Key libraries include pandas, NumPy, matplotlib, seaborn, and plotly, among others. Additionally, R offers a robust suite of tools for EDA, including the tidyverse ecosystem. We will examine these tools and libraries in detail, demonstrating how they can be utilized for comprehensive exploratory data analysis.

pandas: The pandas library is indispensable for data manipulation and analysis in Python. It offers powerful data structures like DataFrame and Series, which make it simple to load, filter, and transform datasets. Pandas provide numerous built-in functions for calculating descriptive statistics, such as mean, median, standard deviation, and percentiles.

```
import pandas as pd

# Load data
df = pd.read_csv('data.csv')

# Display basic statistics
print(df.describe())

# Calculate specific statistics
mean_value = df['column_name'].mean()
median_value = df['column_name'].median()
```

NumPy: NumPy is the fundamental package for scientific computing in Python. It provides support for arrays, matrices, and numerous mathematical functions to operate on these data structures. While not specific to EDA, it is often used alongside pandas for numerical computations.

```
import numpy as np

# Create an array
data = np.array([1, 2, 3, 4, 5])

# Calculate basic statistics
mean_value = np.mean(data)
std_deviation = np.std(data)
```

matplotlib: Matplotlib is a versatile library for creating static, animated, and interactive visualizations in Python. Often utilized for detailed control over plot elements, matplotlib can generate a wide range of plots, such as histograms, scatter plots, and line graphs.

```
import matplotlib.pyplot as plt

# Scatter plot
plt.scatter(df['x_column'], df['y_column'])
plt.xlabel('X Axis Label')
plt.ylabel('Y Axis Label')
plt.title('Scatter Plot')
plt.show()
```

seaborn: Built on top of matplotlib, seaborn simplifies creating informative and attractive statistical graphics. It offers high-level functions for generating various plot types, including pair plots, heatmaps, and violin plots, which are especially useful for understanding data distributions and relationships.

```
import seaborn as sns

# Pair plot
sns.pairplot(df)
plt.show()

# Heatmap
sns.heatmap(df.corr(), annot=True)
plt.show()
```

plotly: Plotly is a library for creating interactive, web-based visualizations. It is particularly advantageous for complex and rich visualizations that need to be shared or embedded in web applications. Plotly supports a variety of plot types, including 3D plots, which are beneficial in multivariate analysis.

```
import plotly.express as px

# 3D scatter plot
fig = px.scatter_3d(df, x='x_column', y='y_column', z='z_column')
fig.show()
```

R and tidyverse: In the R programming environment, the tidyverse is a collection of packages designed for data science. These packages share an underlying design philosophy, grammar, and data structures. Key packages include ggplot2 for data visualization, dplyr for data manipulation, and tidyr for data tidying. The cohesive design of tidyverse allows for seamless workflow within R.

```
library(tidyverse)

# Load data
df <- read_csv('data.csv')

# Summary statistics
summary(df)

# Data visualization using ggplot2
ggplot(df) +
  geom_point(aes(x = x_column, y = y_column)) +
  ggtitle("Scatter Plot") +
  xlab("X Axis Label") +
  ylab("Y Axis Label")
```

Various other tools and packages exist for performing EDA, depending on the specific needs and preferences of the data analyst. For example, advanced tools such as Apache Spark provide capabilities for EDA on large-scale data, and libraries like HoloViews offer high-level building blocks for complex visualizations.

The choice of tools and libraries often depends on the context of the analysis, the size and type of the data, and the specific goals of the EDA. Mastery of these tools and libraries is essential for any data scientist, as they form the foundation for gaining insights and making informed decisions based on the data.

Chapter 4

Data Visualization

Data visualization is crucial for interpreting and communicating insights from data. This chapter covers principles of effective visualization, different types of visual representations, and the tools used to create them. It includes practical guidance on using libraries such as Matplotlib, Seaborn, and interactive tools like Plotly. Geospatial visualizations and dashboard creation for business intelligence applications are discussed, alongside best practices for design and case studies showcasing successful data visualization implementations.

4.1 Introduction to Data Visualization

Data visualization encompasses techniques for transforming raw data into graphical representations, facilitating human cognition in recognizing patterns, trends, and insights that might otherwise remain obscure. In the context of data science, visualization serves a pivotal role, fundamentally bridging the gap between complex data analyses and actionable understanding.

A primary objective of data visualization is to enable clear and effective communication of information gleaned from data. To achieve this, one must consider several principles and techniques to ensure the visualizations are not only accurate but also interpretable. These principles are discussed throughout this chapter, offering a comprehensive guide from basic concepts to advanced visualization strategies.

Historical Context and Evolution

The origins of data visualization can be traced back to ancient times, where basic forms such as maps and charts were employed to represent information about the world. However, the field has seen tremendous evolution, particularly with the advent of computer technology which has exponentially expanded the possibilities for creating intricate and interactive visual representations.

Relevance in Modern Data Science

In contemporary data science practice, data visualization is indispensable. It facilitates the analytical process by:

- Enhancing data exploration and hypothesis formulation.
- Providing a medium for summarizing large datasets concisely.
- Enabling the identification of trends, anomalies, and outliers effectively.
- Supporting decision-making processes by transforming data insights into comprehensible visual formats.

Components of Effective Visualization

An effective data visualization integrates several components which, when combined, improve both the aesthetic appeal and the communicative power of the graphic:

- **Clarity**: The visualization should avoid unnecessary clutter and focus on conveying the information clearly.
- **Accuracy**: Representations must be accurate without misleading the observer through ambiguous or distorted visual elements.
- **Relevance**: The selected visualization type should be appropriate for the nature of the data and the specific analytical goals.
- **Efficiency**: The visualization should convey information quickly and require minimal cognitive load for interpretation.

Fundamental Types of Data Visualizations

Understanding basic chart types provides a foundation upon which more complex visualizations can be built. Some of the fundamental chart types include:

- **Bar Charts**: Effective for comparing quantities across different categories.
- **Line Graphs**: Ideal for illustrating trends over time.
- **Scatter Plots**: Useful for visualizing relationships and correlations between two variables.
- **Histograms**: Suitable for displaying the frequency distribution of a dataset.

Tools and Technologies

Several tools and libraries facilitate data visualization, each offering unique features suited to different requirements:

- **Matplotlib**: A versatile library in Python for creating static, animated, and interactive plots.
- **Seaborn**: Built on Matplotlib, providing advanced statistical plotting capabilities.
- **Plotly**: Enables creating interactive plots, allowing for a more engaging data analysis experience.
- **D3.js**: A JavaScript library for producing dynamic, interactive, and web-based data visualizations.

Implementation Example Using Python and Matplotlib

Consider a simple example where we visualize data using Python and Matplotlib. The following code snippet demonstrates the creation of a basic line plot:

```
import matplotlib.pyplot as plt

# Sample Data
x = [1, 2, 3, 4, 5]
y = [2, 4, 6, 8, 10]

# Create a Line Plot
plt.plot(x, y)
plt.title('Simple Line Plot')
plt.xlabel('X-axis')
plt.ylabel('Y-axis')
plt.show()
```

Executing the above code generates a plot displaying a straight line, clearly illustrating the relationship between the input variables. The output is as follows:

(Simple Line Plot displayed)

This introductory section lays the groundwork for deeper exploration into data visualization principles, types, tools, and best practices, aiming to empower readers with the knowledge and skills to create compelling visual data stories.

4.2 Principles of Effective Data Visualization

Effective data visualization employs several key principles to ensure clarity, accuracy, and usefulness. Adhering to these principles enhances the ability to extract meaningful insights, communicate information effectively, and support decision-making processes. The principles can be categorized into aspects of design, data integrity, and user engagement.

Clarity and Simplicity One of the fundamental principles is clarity and simplicity. Visualizations should be free of unnecessary complexities that may obscure the data's message. The design should be intuitive, enabling viewers to understand the information without excessive effort. This includes the use of a clean layout, appropriate use of whitespace, and careful selection of colors and fonts.

Accurate Representation of Data Another critical principle is the accurate representation of data. Misleading visuals can result from scaling issues, improper use of axis intervals, or truncating data ranges. Ensure that visual encodings precisely reflect the underlying data. For example, when creating bar charts, it's important that the length of the bars corresponds appropriately to the values they represent. Standardize scales across comparative visualizations to facilitate accurate comparisons.

Appropriate Choice of Visualization Type Selecting the appropriate type of visualization for the data and the context is essential. Each type of visualization serves specific purposes and shines under certain conditions:

- **Bar Charts:** Effective for comparing discrete categories.
- **Line Charts:** Ideal for trends over time.
- **Scatter Plots:** Useful for exploring relationships between two continuous variables.

- **Heatmaps:** Good for representing data density or highlighting patterns across matrices.

Choose a visualization type that aligns with the nature of the data and the message you intend to convey.

Use of Color Color plays a crucial role in data visualization. It can highlight key data points, differentiate between categories, and enhance readability. However, misuse of color can misguide or confuse viewers:

- Use a consistent color palette.
- Avoid using too many colors; limit the palette to avoid visual clutter.
- Ensure color choices are accessible to all viewers, including those with color vision deficiencies. Utilize tools to test color schemes for colorblind accessibility.

Data to Ink Ratio The data to ink ratio, a concept introduced by Edward Tufte, promotes maximizing the amount of data shown relative to the amount of ink (or pixels) used to display it. Non-essential graphical elements, often referred to as "chartjunk," should be minimized to ensure that the focus remains on the data itself.

Annotation and Labeling Proper annotation and labeling are vital for understanding the visualization. Labels should be clear, concise, and positioned close to the corresponding data points. Annotations can provide additional context or highlight significant data aspects. Axes should be clearly labeled, and legends should be comprehensible without detracting from the visualization.

Context and Scale Providing appropriate context and scale is imperative. This involves setting proper axis labels and scales that accurately reflect the data's magnitude and range. Contextual information, such as benchmarks or reference lines, can help situate the data within a relevant framework, making it easier for viewers to make comparisons or comprehend the data's significance.

Here is an example of good and bad practice in a simple bar chart:

```
import matplotlib.pyplot as plt

# Data
categories = ['A', 'B', 'C', 'D']
values = [10, 20, 15, 25]

# Bad Practice - Misleading Y-axis
```

```
plt.figure(figsize=(6, 4))
plt.bar(categories, values)
plt.ylim(15, 30) # Truncated Y-axis
plt.title("Incorrect Bar Chart with Truncated Y-axis")
plt.show()

# Good Practice - Proper Y-axis
plt.figure(figsize=(6, 4))
plt.bar(categories, values)
plt.ylim(0, 30) # Accurate Y-axis
plt.title("Correct Bar Chart with Proper Y-axis")
plt.show()
```

```
# Output for Incorrect Bar Chart with Truncated Y-axis
A bar chart with Y-axis starting from 15, which exaggerates differences.

# Output for Correct Bar Chart with Proper Y-axis
A bar chart with Y-axis starting from 0, accurately portraying value differences.
```

Interactive Elements Interactive visualizations can significantly enhance user engagement. Features such as tooltips, zooming, and filtering allow users to explore data in greater depth. However, these elements should be implemented thoughtfully to ensure they add value without overwhelming the user or detracting from the visualization's primary message.

Multivariate Data Representation Displaying multidimensional data requires advanced techniques. Methods such as parallel coordinates, scatter plot matrices, and dimensionality reduction (e.g., PCA, t-SNE) can represent high-dimensional data effectively. Ensuring that such visualizations remain interpretable necessitates careful consideration of scale, color, and interaction.

A representative example using PCA on high-dimensional data:

```
from sklearn.decomposition import PCA
import seaborn as sns
import pandas as pd

# Example DataFrame with high-dimensional data
data = pd.DataFrame({
    'feature1': [1, 2, 3, 4, 5],
    'feature2': [2, 3, 4, 5, 6],
    'feature3': [3, 4, 5, 6, 7]
})

# Performing PCA
pca = PCA(n_components=2)
principalComponents = pca.fit_transform(data)

# Creating a DataFrame for the principal components
df_pca = pd.DataFrame(data = principalComponents, columns = ['PC1', 'PC2'])

# Visualization
sns.scatterplot(x='PC1', y='PC2', data=df_pca)
plt.title('PCA of High-Dimensional Data')
plt.xlabel('Principal Component 1')
```

```
plt.ylabel('Principal Component 2')
plt.show()
```

Storytelling with Data Narrating a story with data can enhance the visualization's impact. Storytelling paradigms emphasize structuring information in a way that leads the audience through a logical progression of insights. This can be achieved by organizing visual elements to sequentially uncover layers of information or by integrating text annotations that guide the viewer through the data narrative.

Following these principles of effective data visualization ensures that the visual presentation of information is clear, engaging, and based on a truthful representation of the underlying data. Adhering to these guidelines can vastly improve one's ability to communicate data-driven insights effectively.

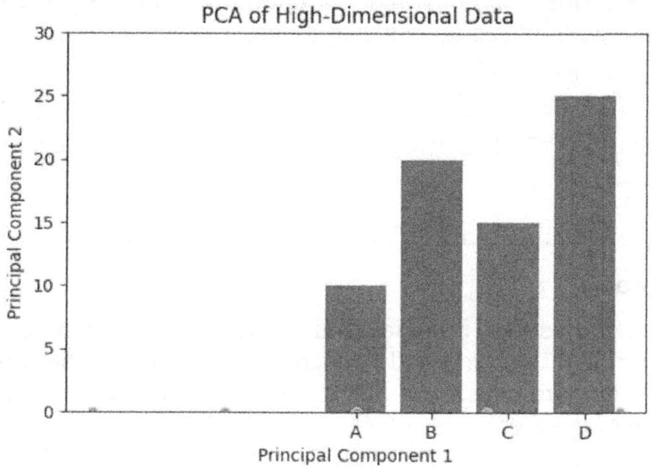

4.3 Types of Data Visualizations

Data visualization encompasses a wide variety of formats, each tailored to different types of data and analysis needs. Understanding the various types of visualizations is essential for communicating complex information effectively. This section outlines diverse visualization techniques, each with distinct characteristics and applications.

1. Line Charts

Line charts are simple yet powerful tools for displaying trends over time. They utilize Cartesian coordinates to connect individual data points using lines. Line charts are particularly useful for showing continuous data and temporal changes.

```
import matplotlib.pyplot as plt

x = [1, 2, 3, 4, 5]
y = [10, 20, 25, 30, 40]

plt.plot(x, y, marker='o')
plt.title('Sample Line Chart')
plt.xlabel('X-axis Label')
plt.ylabel('Y-axis Label')
plt.show()
```

2. Bar Charts

Bar charts represent categorical data with rectangular bars with lengths proportional to the values they represent. There are two primary types: vertical bar charts and horizontal bar charts. Bar charts are effective for comparing quantities across categories.

```
categories = ['A', 'B', 'C', 'D', 'E']
values = [5, 7, 3, 8, 4]

plt.bar(categories, values)
plt.title('Sample Bar Chart')
plt.xlabel('Categories')
plt.ylabel('Values')
plt.show()
```

3. Histograms

Histograms are used to represent the distribution of numerical data by dividing the data into bins and counting the number of data points in each bin. They are critical for understanding the underlying frequency distribution of datasets.

```
data = [1, 2, 2, 3, 3, 3, 4, 4, 4, 4, 5, 5, 6, 7]

plt.hist(data, bins=5)
plt.title('Sample Histogram')
plt.xlabel('Value Range')
plt.ylabel('Frequency')
plt.show()
```

4. Scatter Plots

Scatter plots display values for typically two variables for a set of data using Cartesian coordinates. These plots highlight correlations, trends, and outliers by placing points on the graph where the x and y values intersect.

```
import numpy as np

x = np.random.rand(50)
y = np.random.rand(50)

plt.scatter(x, y)
plt.title('Sample Scatter Plot')
plt.xlabel('X-axis Label')
plt.ylabel('Y-axis Label')
plt.show()
```

5. Pie Charts

Pie charts represent proportions of a whole, showing how a dataset is divided into different categories. Each section's angle is proportional to the quantity it represents. They are useful for illustrating parts-to-whole relationships.

```
labels = ['A', 'B', 'C', 'D']
sizes = [15, 30, 45, 10]
colors = ['gold', 'yellowgreen', 'lightcoral', 'lightskyblue']

plt.pie(sizes, labels=labels, colors=colors, autopct='%1.1f%%', startangle=140)
plt.title('Sample Pie Chart')
plt.axis('equal')
plt.show()
```

6. Box Plots

Box plots, or whisker plots, provide a graphical representation of the statistical summary of a dataset, including quartiles, median, and potential outliers. They are valuable for comparing distributions across multiple groups.

```
data = [np.random.normal(0, std, 100) for std in range(1, 4)]

plt.boxplot(data, vert=True, patch_artist=True)
plt.title('Sample Box Plot')
plt.xlabel('Category')
plt.ylabel('Values')
plt.show()
```

7. Heatmaps

Heatmaps represent data in a matrix format where individual values are represented by color. They are beneficial for visualizing variance across datasets, showing concentrations, and identifying patterns.

```
import seaborn as sns

data = np.random.rand(10, 12)
sns.heatmap(data, annot=True, cmap='viridis')
plt.title('Sample Heatmap')
plt.show()
```

8. Treemaps

Treemaps display hierarchical data as nested rectangles, which represent different levels of the hierarchy. They are useful for depicting the part-to-whole relationships among diverse categories.

```
import plotly.express as px

data = dict(
    labels=['A', 'B', 'C', 'D', 'E'],
    parents=["", "", "", "", ""],
    values=[10, 20, 30, 40, 50])

fig = px.treemap(data, path=['labels'], values='values', title='Sample Treemap')
fig.show()
```

9. Geospatial Maps

Geospatial maps overlay data on geographical maps to visualize location-based data. This is particularly useful for geographical analysis, such as representing population distributions, resource allocation, or event tracking.

```
import plotly.graph_objects as go

fig = go.Figure(go.Scattergeo(
    lat=[37.77, 40.71, 51.51],
    lon=[-122.42, -74.01, -0.13],
    mode='markers',
    marker=dict(size=10)
))

fig.update_layout(title='Sample Geospatial Map')
fig.show()
```

These visualization types each offer unique insights and are selected based on the data characteristics and the specific analytical requirements. Mastery of various visualization types allows data scientists to choose the most effective method to communicate their data insights.

4.4 Tools for Data Visualization

Data visualization is an essential aspect of data science that allows for the clear and effective communication of complex data insights. Various tools have been developed to facilitate this process, each offering unique features and capabilities tailored to different visualization needs. In this section, we will explore some of the most widely-used tools for data visualization, including Matplotlib, Seaborn, Plotly, and specialized tools for creating dashboards and geospatial visualizations.

Matplotlib is one of the most popular Python libraries for creating static, interactive, and animated visualizations. It provides a variety of plotting functions and controls to generate a wide range of plots, from simple line charts to complex 3D plots. Below is an example demonstrating the basic use of Matplotlib to create a simple line plot:

```
import matplotlib.pyplot as plt

x = [1, 2, 3, 4]
y = [10, 20, 25, 30]

plt.plot(x, y)
plt.xlabel('X-axis label')
plt.ylabel('Y-axis label')
plt.title('Simple Line Plot')
plt.show()
```

The output of the above code will display a line plot with labels on the x-axis and y-axis and a title at the top:

```
+-------------+
|             |
|             |
|      |      |
|      |      |
|      |      |
|      |      |
+-------------+
```

Seaborn is built on top of Matplotlib and provides a high-level interface for drawing attractive and informative statistical graphics. It integrates closely with pandas dataframes, making it particularly useful for data scientists. Seaborn features several built-in themes and color palettes to make visualizations more aesthetically pleasing and easier to interpret. Here is an example illustrating how to create a simple scatter plot using Seaborn:

```
import seaborn as sns
import matplotlib.pyplot as plt

# Load an example dataset from Seaborn library
tips = sns.load_dataset("tips")

# Create a scatter plot
sns.scatterplot(data=tips, x="total_bill", y="tip", hue="day")
plt.title('Scatter Plot using Seaborn')
plt.show()
```

The output will generate a scatter plot with points colored based on the day of the week they were recorded:

```
+-------------+
|             |
| o           |
|    o     o  |
|o            |
|        o    |
| o o  o o    |
+-------------+
```

Plotly offers extensive capabilities for creating interactive visualizations that can be easily embedded in web applications. Plotly supports a wide range of chart types, including statistical, 3D, and geographical plots. Below is an example demonstrating how to create an interactive bar chart using Plotly:

```
import plotly.express as px

# Sample data
data = {
    'Fruits': ['Apples', 'Oranges', 'Bananas', 'Grapes'],
    'Quantity': [10, 15, 7, 20]
}

# Create a bar chart
fig = px.bar(data, x='Fruits', y='Quantity', title='Fruit Quantity Bar Chart')

# Show the interactive plot
fig.show()
```

The interactive bar chart displays each fruit's quantity, allowing users to hover over bars to see detailed information:

```
+---------------+
|       |      |
|       |      |
|       |      |
|       |      |
|       |      |
|              |
|---+---+---+---|
|Apples|Oranges |
+---------------+
```

In addition to these libraries, tools like *Tableau* and *Microsoft Power BI* are prominent among business and data analysts for creating comprehensive dashboards and visual analytics. They provide drag-and-drop interfaces, allowing users to build complex visualizations without deep programming knowledge.

Tableau offers a suite of products tailored to different needs, including Tableau Desktop for authoring reports, Tableau Server for sharing reports across an organization, and Tableau Online for cloud-based analytics. Similarly, *Power BI* integrates seamlessly with other Microsoft products and services, supporting robust data modeling and a wide range of visualization options.

Lastly, tools such as *QGIS* (Quantum Geographic Information System) and *Leaflet* are utilized for geospatial visualizations. QGIS is a free and open-source tool that enables users to create, edit, visualize, and analyze geospatial data on multiple platforms. Leaflet, a JavaScript library, is widely used for embedding interactive maps into web applications.

By understanding and utilizing these tools, data scientists and analysts can effectively present their data in various formats, tailoring their visualizations to meet specific analytical needs and audience preferences. Proper selection and usage of these tools can significantly enhance the interpretability and impact of data insights.

4.5 Visualization with Matplotlib

Matplotlib is a foundational plotting library in Python, renowned for its versatility and extensive customization options, making it indispensable for data visualization tasks in data science. Developed by John D. Hunter in 2003, Matplotlib provides a comprehensive framework for creating static, animated, and interactive visualizations. At its core, Matplotlib offers two main interfaces: the Pyplot API, which provides a simple interface for creating plots, and the Object-Oriented API, which offers more precise control over the plotting elements.

To begin using Matplotlib, it is necessary to import the library, typically under the alias plt, as shown below:

```
import matplotlib.pyplot as plt
```

Creating Basic Plots

Matplotlib excels at creating a variety of basic plot types, such as line plots, scatter plots, bar plots, histograms, and pie charts. A line plot, often used for time series data, can be created easily:

```
# Sample Data
x = [1, 2, 3, 4, 5]
y = [2, 3, 5, 7, 11]

# Line Plot
plt.plot(x, y)
plt.xlabel('X Axis Label')
plt.ylabel('Y Axis Label')
plt.title('Sample Line Plot')
plt.show()
```

Executing this code block will generate a line plot with labeled axes and a title:

A graphical line plot depicting five points, with an x-axis ranging from 1 to 5, and a y-axis ranging from 2 to 11, connected by a continuous line.

Scatter Plots

Scatter plots are instrumental for displaying relationships between two numerical variables. They are created using the scatter function:

```
# Sample Data
x = [1, 2, 3, 4, 5]
y = [2, 3, 5, 7, 11]

# Scatter Plot
plt.scatter(x, y, color='red', marker='o')
plt.xlabel('X Axis Label')
plt.ylabel('Y Axis Label')
plt.title('Sample Scatter Plot')
plt.show()
```

The output visually represents the relationship between the variable sets using red circular markers:

A graphical scatter plot depicting five points with red circular markers, demonstrating the same data points as the previous line plot.

Bar Plots

Bar plots are crucial for comparing categorical data. Horizontal and vertical bar plots can be generated with the bar and barh functions respectively:

```
# Sample Data
categories = ['A', 'B', 'C', 'D']
values = [4, 7, 1, 8]

# Vertical Bar Plot
plt.bar(categories, values, color='blue')
plt.xlabel('Categories')
plt.ylabel('Values')
plt.title('Sample Bar Plot')
plt.show()
```

This generates a bar plot with the specified categories and values, providing a straightforward visual comparison.

A graphical bar plot displaying four bars colored in blue, each corresponding to the categories A, B, C, and D with heights 4, 7, 1, and 8 respectively.

Customizing Plots

Matplotlib's extensive customization capabilities allow tweaking virtually every aspect of the plot. This includes modifying line styles, colors, markers, and more:

```
# Custom Line Plot
plt.plot(x, y, linestyle='--', color='green', marker='x', linewidth=2)
plt.xlabel('X Axis Label')
plt.ylabel('Y Axis Label')
plt.title('Customized Line Plot')
```

```
plt.grid(True)
plt.show()
```

This code outputs a line plot with a dashed green line, cross markers at data points, and an enabled grid, providing improved readability.

A graphical line plot featuring a dashed green line with cross markers at data points and a grid background.

Advanced Customization with the Object-Oriented API

For advanced customization, the Object-Oriented API affords greater control over plot components. This method involves creating Figure and Axes objects:

```
# Sample Data
x = [1, 2, 3, 4, 5]
y = [2, 3, 5, 7, 11]

# Object-Oriented Approach
fig, ax = plt.subplots()
ax.plot(x, y, label='Prime Numbers')
ax.set_xlabel('X Axis Label')
ax.set_ylabel('Y Axis Label')
ax.set_title('Object-Oriented Plot')
ax.legend()
plt.show()
```

Here, the Figure serves as a container for all plot elements, while the Axes represent the area where data is plotted. This approach facilitates complex layouts and multiple subplots.

A graphical line plot similar to previous examples, with labeled axes, a title, and a legend denoting 'Prime Numbers'.

Subplots

Subplots enable plotting multiple graphs in a single figure, enhancing data comparison capabilities. The subplot function creates a grid of plots:

```
# Sample Data
x = [1, 2, 3, 4, 5]
y1 = [1, 4, 9, 16, 25]
y2 = [2, 3, 5, 7, 11]

# Subplots
fig, (ax1, ax2) = plt.subplots(1, 2, figsize=(10, 4))
ax1.plot(x, y1, 'b-')
ax1.set_title('Quadratic Plot')
ax2.plot(x, y2, 'r-')
ax2.set_title('Prime Numbers Plot')
plt.show()
```

This results in two side-by-side plots within a single figure:

A figure encompassing two subplots: the first subplot displays a quadratic plot with blue lines, and the second subplot presents a prime numbers plot with red lines.

Histograms

Histograms depict the distribution of data across bins, effectively showing underlying frequency distributions:

```
# Sample Data
data = [1, 2, 2, 3, 3, 3, 4, 4, 4, 4]

# Histogram
plt.hist(data, bins=4, color='purple', edgecolor='black')
plt.xlabel('Value Bins')
plt.ylabel('Frequency')
plt.title('Sample Histogram')
plt.show()
```

The histogram visual clearly illustrates data frequency within defined bins:

A histogram displaying four bins in purple with black edges, reflecting the frequency distribution of the sample data set.

Pie Charts

Pie charts represent parts of a whole, useful for displaying data proportions:

```
# Sample Data
labels = ['A', 'B', 'C', 'D']
sizes = [15, 30, 45, 10]

# Pie Chart
plt.pie(sizes, labels=labels, autopct='%1.1f%%', startangle=140)
plt.title('Sample Pie Chart')
plt.show()
```

This code generates a pie chart with labeled slices, each displaying its percentage contribution to the whole:

A pie chart divided into four slices labeled A, B, C, and D, with respective proportions shown as percentages.

Mastering Matplotlib entails understanding these fundamental plots and customization techniques, enabling the creation of informative and visually appealing data visualizations.

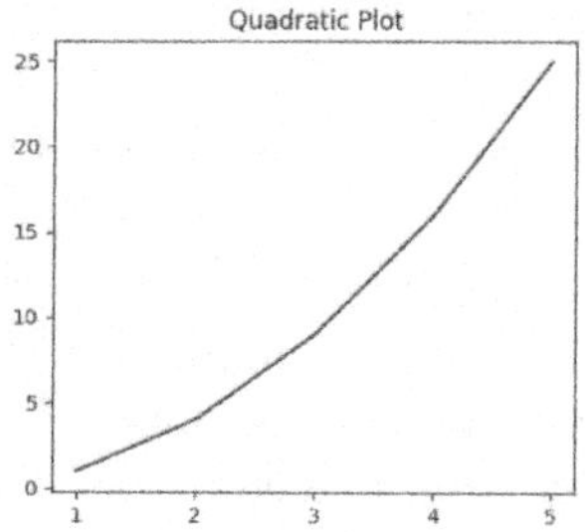

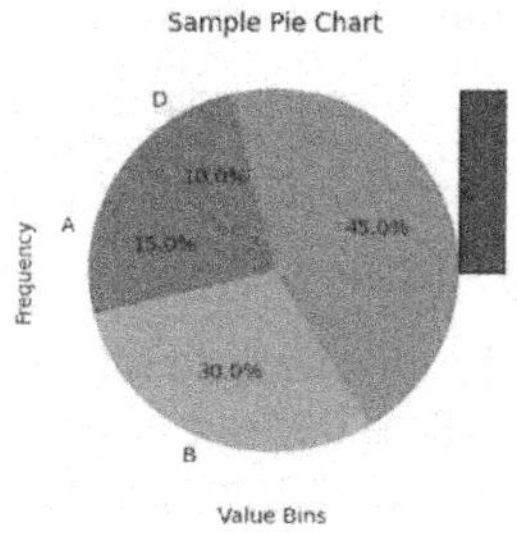

4.6 Visualization with Seaborn

Seaborn is a powerful Python library built on top of Matplotlib that provides a high-level interface for drawing attractive and informative statistical graphics. Seaborn is especially useful for visualizing complex datasets, making it easier to understand relationships and patterns. It integrates closely with pandas data structures, making it a go-to tool for data scientists.

To begin using Seaborn, ensure that it is installed alongside other essential libraries such as pandas and Matplotlib. An installation can be performed using pip:

```
pip install seaborn
```

After installation, importing the necessary libraries is straightforward. The following example demonstrates the import statements required for working with Seaborn:

```
import seaborn as sns
import matplotlib.pyplot as plt
import pandas as pd
```

Loading Data

Seaborn works efficiently with DataFrames. Let us consider an example dataset to illustrate various Seaborn functionalities. The 'tips' dataset, which comes included with Seaborn, is commonly used for examples.

```
tips = sns.load_dataset("tips")
print(tips.head())
```

```
   total_bill   tip     sex smoker  day    time  size
0       16.99  1.01  Female     No  Sun  Dinner     2
1       10.34  1.66    Male     No  Sun  Dinner     3
2       21.01  3.50    Male     No  Sun  Dinner     3
3       23.68  3.31    Male     No  Sun  Dinner     2
4       24.59  3.61  Female     No  Sun  Dinner     4
```

Relational Plots

One of the fundamental plots in Seaborn is the relational plot. It can be used to visualize the relationships between two variables. The relplot() function offers a way to create scatter plots and line plots. Below is an example of a scatter plot that shows the relationship between total bill and tip:

```
sns.relplot(x="total_bill", y="tip", data=tips)
plt.show()
```

By default, relplot() creates scatter plots. The kind parameter can be set to 'line' to generate line plots. This is particularly useful for showing trends.

Categorical Plots

Understanding how data points are distributed among categories is made simpler with categorical plots. Seaborn provides several types of categorical plots such as bar plots, count plots, box plots, and violin plots. For instance, a bar plot showing the average total bill categorized by day can be created as follows:

```
sns.catplot(x="day", y="total_bill", kind="bar", data=tips)
plt.show()
```

Seaborn also allows for more complex visualizations. A box plot can provide insight into the distribution of values within each category:

```
sns.catplot(x="day", y="total_bill", kind="box", data=tips)
plt.show()
```

Violin plots combine aspects of a box plot and a kernel density plot. They provide more information about the density of the data:

```
sns.catplot(x="day", y="total_bill", kind="violin", data=tips)
plt.show()
```

Regression Plots

Regression plots help in visualizing linear relationships. Seaborn's lmplot() function plots data and fits a linear regression model. The following example illustrates the relationship between total bill and tip, with a linear regression line included:

```
sns.lmplot(x="total_bill", y="tip", data=tips)
plt.show()
```

Seaborn allows the addition of multiple regression lines conditioned on additional categorical variables. By setting the hue parameter, different regression lines are drawn for smokers and non-smokers:

```
sns.lmplot(x="total_bill", y="tip", hue="smoker", data=tips)
plt.show()
```

Matrix Plots

Matrix plots are essential for visualizing data stored in matrix form or for comparing multiple variables. Heatmaps are among the most common matrix plots. To create a heatmap showing the correlation matrix of the tips dataset:

```
corr = tips.corr()
sns.heatmap(corr, annot=True, cmap="coolwarm")
plt.show()
```

The heatmap uses a color gradient to represent different values, with the annot=True parameter ensuring that the correlation coefficients are displayed on the heatmap.

Pair Plots

Pair plots are useful for visualizing pairwise relationships across an entire dataset. The pairplot() function automates the process of creating a grid of scatter plots for each pair of variables. For the tips dataset:

```
sns.pairplot(tips)
plt.show()
```

Adding the hue parameter allows differentiation between categories. For instance, to distinguish between smokers and non-smokers:

```
sns.pairplot(tips, hue="smoker")
plt.show()
```

With Seaborn, the ease of generating informative and aesthetically pleasing visualizations ensures that comprehensive exploration and analysis of datasets are feasible. Leveraging Seaborn's integration with pandas furthers its power, making it an indispensable tool for any data scientist. By mastering the functionalities discussed, practitioners can efficiently communicate insights and relationships embedded within complex datasets.

4.7 Interactive Visualizations with Plotly

Plotly is a robust library that provides a means to create highly interactive plots and visualizations. It is built on top of the JavaScript library D3.js, enabling the creation of web-based visualizations that are interactive and can be embedded in web applications or Jupyter Notebooks. This library supports a wide range of plot types, including line plots, scatter plots, bar charts, histograms, 3D plots, and maps.

To begin using Plotly in Python, you can install it via pip:

```
pip install plotly
```

One of the primary objects in Plotly is the Figure. A Figure object comprises two key components: data and layout. The data consists of traces, which are essentially collections of lines, markers, or other graphical elements, and the layout defines the overall structure of the visualization, such as titles, axis labels, and annotations.

```
import plotly.graph_objects as go

# Create traces
trace1 = go.Scatter(
    x=[1, 2, 3, 4],
    y=[10, 11, 12, 13],
    mode='markers',
    marker=dict(
        size=12,
        color='rgb(51, 204, 153)',
        symbol='circle',
        line=dict(
            width=2,
        ),
    ),
    name='Trace 1'
)

trace2 = go.Scatter(
    x=[1, 2, 3, 4],
    y=[11, 12, 13, 14],
    mode='lines+markers',
    marker=dict(
        color='rgb(255, 65, 54)',
    ),
    line=dict(
        color='rgb(255, 65, 54)',
        width=2,
    ),
    name='Trace 2'
)

data = [trace1, trace2]

# Define the layout
layout = go.Layout(
```

```
    title='Interactive Line and Scatter Plot',
    xaxis=dict(
        title='X Axis',
        titlefont=dict(
            family='Arial, sans-serif',
            size=18,
            color='grey'
        ),
    ),
    yaxis=dict(
        title='Y Axis',
        titlefont=dict(
            family='Arial, sans-serif',
            size=18,
            color='grey'
        )
    )
)

# Create the Figure object
fig = go.Figure(data=data, layout=layout)

# Render the plot
fig.show()
```

The above code creates a simple interactive plot with two traces: a scatter plot and a line plot. The Plotly API is highly customizable, enabling users to modify various properties of the traces and the layout.

Plotly also provides a higher-level interface through the plotly.express module, which simplifies the creation of common plot types. For instance, a simple scatter plot can be created using the following code:

```
import plotly.express as px

# Sample data
df = px.data.iris()

# Create scatter plot
fig = px.scatter(df, x='sepal_width', y='sepal_length',
                 color='species',
                 title='Sepal Width vs Length',
                 labels={'sepal_width': 'Sepal Width (cm)',
                         'sepal_length': 'Sepal Length (cm)'})

# Render the plot
fig.show()
```

In this example, plotly.express.scatter automatically handles data processing, trace creation, and layout definition, making it a convenient alternative for quick visualizations. The color parameter adds a categorical dimension to the plot, enhancing its informational density and insight potential.

For multidimensional data visualizations, Plotly supports 3D plotting. For example, creating a 3D scatter plot is straightforward:

```
import plotly.express as px

# Sample data
df = px.data.iris()

# Create 3D scatter plot
fig = px.scatter_3d(df, x='sepal_length', y='sepal_width', z='petal_length',
                    color='species',
                    title='3D Scatter Plot of Iris Dataset')

# Render the plot
fig.show()
```

This 3D scatter plot provides an additional perspective on the data, revealing potential correlations that may not be apparent in 2D projections.

For geographical data visualization, Plotly offers mapping capabilities through the integration with Mapbox. One can create various types of maps, such as choropleth maps, dot maps, and bubble maps. An example of creating a choropleth map is as follows:

```
import plotly.express as px

# Sample data
df = px.data.gapminder().query("year == 2007")

# Create choropleth map
fig = px.choropleth(df, locations='iso_alpha', color='lifeExp',
                    hover_name='country', projection='natural earth',
                    title='Life Expectancy by Country in 2007')

# Render the map
fig.show()
```

This code leverages the gapminder dataset to produce a choropleth map representing life expectancy by country. The projection parameter specifies the map projection type, which can be customized to suit different visualization needs.

Interactivity in Plotly extends beyond basic hover functionalities. Users can create dashboards with multiple linked plots, enabling complex interactive data exploration. Additionally, Plotly supports animations to illustrate changes over time or other dimensions. Here's an example of an animated scatter plot showing the progression of countries' GDP and life expectancy over time:

```
import plotly.express as px

# Sample data
df = px.data.gapminder()

# Create animated scatter plot
```

```
fig = px.scatter(df, x='gdpPercap', y='lifeExp',
                 animation_frame='year', animation_group='country',
                 size='pop', color='continent', hover_name='country',
                 log_x=True, size_max=55,
                 title='GDP and Life Expectancy Over Time')

# Render the plot
fig.show()
```

The animation_frame parameter designates the column to be animated (in this case, year), and animation_group ensures consistency for each country's data points throughout the animation.

Leveraging Plotly for interactive data visualizations can greatly enhance the effectiveness of data communication and exploration, making complex data more accessible and intuitive to interpret.

4.8 Geospatial Data Visualization

Geospatial data visualization allows us to explore and understand the spatial patterns and relationships inherent in geographic data. Such visualizations encompass the representation of geographic features, phenomena, and various types of data attributes on maps, assisting in various analyses, from urban planning to environmental monitoring.

The effective visualization of geospatial data calls for understanding both the concepts of cartography and the application of computational tools designed for geospatial analysis. Key components include the interpretation of layers, coordinate systems, and various mapping techniques that can be used to exploit the richness of spatial data.

Coordinate Systems and Projections

Understanding coordinate systems and projections is critical when working with geospatial data. A coordinate system defines how the two-dimensional data, typically representing latitude and longitude, maps onto a flat surface or globe. Commonly used coordinate systems include:

- World Geodetic System 1984 (WGS 84)
- Universal Transverse Mercator (UTM)

Projection refers to the method used to represent the curved surface of the Earth on a flat map. Projections can significantly distort area, shape, distance, or direction, necessitating careful selection based on the uses of the visualization.

Key Libraries for Geospatial Data Visualization

Several libraries facilitate geospatial data visualization, each with unique features and strengths. Below are some of the most commonly used libraries:

- **GeoPandas:** Extends the capabilities of Pandas to allow spatial operations on geometric types. It integrates with Matplotlib for basic plotting functionalities.
- **Folium:** Facilitates the creation of interactive maps using Leaflet.js. It allows easy integration of Python data processing power with JavaScript mapping capabilities.
- **Plotly:** Known for its interactive graphing and plotting capabilities, it also supports geospatial plotting.
- **Cartopy:** Builds on Matplotlib, enabling complex geospatial visualizations, supporting various projections and geospatial data formats.

Example: Creating Interactive Maps with Folium

Folium simplifies the creation of interactive maps. Below is a basic example:

```
import folium

# Create a map centered around a specific latitude and longitude
m = folium.Map(location=[45.5236, -122.6750], zoom_start=13)

# Save the map as an HTML file
m.save('map.html')
```

The resulting HTML file, when opened in a browser, displays an interactive map centered at the specified latitude and longitude.

Advanced Geospatial Visualization Techniques

- **Heatmaps:** Heatmaps represent the intensity of data points over a geographic area.

Below is an example of creating a heatmap using Folium and the plugins for additional functionality:

```
import folium
from folium.plugins import HeatMap

# Generate a base map
m = folium.Map(location=[37.7749, -122.4194], zoom_start=13)

# Add heatmap
heat_data = [[37.7749, -122.4194], [37.7749, -122.4294], [37.7849, -122.4094]]
HeatMap(heat_data).add_to(m)

# Save the map as an HTML file
m.save('heatmap.html')
```

The heatmap intensifies in regions with suspiciously high data point density, revealing patterns that would be nontrivial to deduce otherwise.

Geospatial Data Analysis with GeoPandas

GeoPandas builds upon the capabilities of pandas by adding support for geospatial data types and operations. The core data structure in GeoPandas is the GeoDataFrame, which extends the pandas DataFrame to include a 'geometry' column to store geometric data.

```
import geopandas as gpd

# Read a shapefile
gdf = gpd.read_file("path/to/your/shapefile.shp")

# Display the GeoDataFrame
print(gdf.head())
```

```
          geometry ... other_columns
0  POINT (1.00000 1.00000)  ...  value_1
1  POINT (2.00000 2.00000)  ...  value_2
2  POINT (3.00000 3.00000)  ...  value_3
```

The geometry column contains geometric information such as points, lines, and polygons, which are crucial for spatial analysis.

Case Study: Urban Planning

Consider a case study where planners need to visualize and analyze public transportation stops within a city to optimize routes and coverage. Using the libraries discussed, planners can map the bus stops, assess coverage areas, and identify underserved regions.

```
import geopandas as gpd
import matplotlib.pyplot as plt

# Read the data for bus stops and city boundaries
bus_stops = gpd.read_file("path/to/bus_stops.shp")
city_boundary = gpd.read_file("path/to/city_boundary.shp")

# Plot city boundary
ax = city_boundary.plot(figsize=(10, 10), edgecolor='black', facecolor='none')
# Plot bus stops
```

```
bus_stops.plot(ax=ax, marker='o', color='red', markersize=5)

plt.title('Bus Stops within the City Boundary')
plt.xlabel('Longitude')
plt.ylabel('Latitude')
plt.show()
```

This plot visually represents where the bus stops are relative to the city boundary, highlighting areas that may need additional coverage.

In geospatial data visualization, the integration of data analytics and cartographic principles allows for multifactorial exploration, driving informed decision-making in fields such as urban planning, environmental conservation, and disaster management.

4.9 Dashboards and Business Intelligence Tools

The integration of data visualization within dashboards and business intelligence (BI) tools has fundamentally transformed how organizations make data-driven decisions. Dashboards provide a consolidated view of various data sources, offering a snapshot of key performance indicators (KPIs) and metrics crucial for strategic management. Business Intelligence tools facilitate the extraction, analysis, and presentation of business data, converting raw data into actionable insights.

To construct effective dashboards, it is imperative to understand both the technical frameworks and the design principles that maximize their utility.

Technical Components of a Dashboard

A dashboard typically comprises several technical layers:

- **Data Layer:** This layer incorporates data sources, databases, data warehouses, and ETL (Extract, Transform, Load) processes. Data can be sourced from relational databases (e.g., SQL), NoSQL databases (e.g., MongoDB), or even flat files (e.g., CSV, Excel).

- **Processing Layer:** Comprising data processing engines and middleware, this layer performs data integration, transformation, and aggregation. Tools like Apache Kafka, Apache Spark, and SQL-based ETL processes are commonly utilized.

- **Visualization Layer:** This layer involves the actual plotting and rendering of data using libraries and tools like Matplotlib, Seaborn, Plotly, and BI tools which are covered later in this section.
- **User Interface Layer:** The front-end interface through which users interact with the dashboard. This could be a web-based application, mobile application, or desktop application.

Popular Business Intelligence Tools

Several BI tools are widely used for creating dashboards, each with its unique features and advantages:

- **Tableau:** Known for its robust visualization capabilities and ease of use. Tableau allows users to create interactive and shareable dashboards. It supports various data connectors, enabling integration with diverse data sources.
- **Power BI:** A Microsoft product that provides powerful analytics and visualization capabilities. Power BI integrates seamlessly with other Microsoft services like Azure, SQL Server, and Excel.
- **Qlik Sense:** Offers a self-service data analytics and visualization platform. Qlik Sense is distinguished by its associative data engine, which allows for dynamic data exploration.
- **Looker:** Acquired by Google, Looker offers modern BI and analytics capabilities. It provides a flexible data model and integrates with BigQuery and other SQL databases.
- **Domo:** A cloud-based BI platform that provides a comprehensive suite of tools for data integration, visualization, and analytics. Domo supports real-time data flows and large-scale deployment.

Design Principles for Effective Dashboards

Effective dashboard design is not just about visual appeal but also about functionality and user experience. The following principles should guide the design process:

- **Clarity:** The information presented should be clear and unambiguous. This can be achieved by avoiding clutter, using an appropriate level of detail, and choosing the right visual elements to represent data.

- **Consistency:** Consistency in color schemes, fonts, and layout helps users familiarize themselves with the dashboard, reducing cognitive load and enhancing usability.
- **Relevance:** The metrics and KPIs displayed should be relevant to the user's role and responsibilities. Tailoring the dashboard content to the audience ensures that the insights provided are actionable.
- **Interactivity:** Providing interactive elements such as filters, drill-down capabilities, and hover-over tooltips allows users to explore data at different levels of granularity.
- **Responsiveness:** The dashboard should be responsive to different devices and screen sizes, ensuring accessibility across desktop, tablet, and mobile platforms.
- **Performance:** Performance optimization is critical, especially when dealing with large datasets or real-time data feeds. Techniques such as data caching, efficient querying, and load balancing should be employed.

Example of Implementing a Dashboard with Plotly and Dash

The following example illustrates how to create an interactive dashboard using Plotly and Dash:

```
import dash
from dash import dcc, html
from dash.dependencies import Input, Output
import plotly.express as px
import pandas as pd

# Data Loading
df = pd.read_csv('sample_data.csv')

# Create a Dash application
app = dash.Dash(__name__)

# Layout of the dashboard
app.layout = html.Div([
    html.H1("Sample Dashboard"),
    dcc.Dropdown(
        id='dropdown',
        options=[{'label': i, 'value': i} for i in df['category'].unique()],
        value=df['category'].unique()[0]
    ),
    dcc.Graph(id='bar-chart')
])

# Callback to update the bar chart based on the dropdown selection
@app.callback(
    Output('bar-chart', 'figure'),
```

```
    [Input('dropdown', 'value')]
)
def update_chart(selected_category):
    filtered_df = df[df['category'] == selected_category]
    fig = px.bar(filtered_df, x='sub_category', y='value', title=f'Data for {
        selected_category}')
    return fig

# Run the application
if __name__ == '__main__':
    app.run_server(debug=True)
```

The output of the above code can be visualized as follows:

```
Dash is running on http://127.0.0.1:8050/
 * Serving Flask app "dash_dashboard" (lazy loading)
 * Environment: production
 * Debug mode: on
 * Running on http://127.0.0.1:8050/ (Press CTRL+C to quit)
```

Key Considerations in Dashboard Implementation

While the technical implementation of a dashboard is critical, attention must also be paid to the following considerations:

- **Data Governance:** Ensure data quality, consistency, and security. Implement policies for data access, privacy, and compliance.
- **User Training:** Provide training sessions and documentation to help users understand and utilize the dashboard effectively.
- **Iterative Improvements:** Regularly collect feedback and iterate on the dashboard design and functionality to meet evolving user needs and business requirements.
- **Performance Monitoring:** Continuously monitor the performance of the dashboard and optimize as necessary to ensure a smooth user experience.

Through the strategic use of dashboards and Business Intelligence tools, organizations can gain a significant edge by converting complex data into accessible and actionable insights. This transformation is pivotal in supporting decision-making processes and driving business success.

4.10 Best Practices for Dashboard Design

Developing an effective dashboard demands a comprehensive understanding of both the data being represented and the needs of the end-users. Best practices guide the design process to ensure that dashboards are both functional and insightful. This section delineates critical considerations and strategies for constructing dashboards that serve their intended purposes efficiently.

An effective dashboard must empower users to absorb information quickly and make informed decisions. The design principles outlined herein are aligned with cognitive psychology and visual perception theories, coupled with practical insights from established use cases.

Designing a user-centric dashboard necessitates the following considerations:

- **User-Centric Design:** Understanding the needs and technical proficiency of the end-users is paramount. Dashboards can vary widely in complexity depending on whether the end-user is an executive needing high-level views, an analyst requiring in-depth data, or an operational user focused on real-time metrics. Conducting user interviews and usability testing can provide valuable insights.
- **Clarity and Conciseness:** Concise dashboards are effective. Each element on the dashboard should serve a clear purpose. Extraneous information can clutter the design and impede the user's ability to extract meaning. The incorporation of gestalt principles—such as similarity, proximity, and closure—enhances the clarity of the information presented.
- **Logical Layout:** Group related metrics together in a logical manner. A common approach is the use of a grid layout, where high-priority information is placed in the top-left corner (where viewers typically start their observation) and supportive or detailed metrics are displayed subsequently. Utilize whitespace strategically to avoid a congested appearance.
- **Consistent Use of Visual Elements:** Maintain consistency in colors, fonts, and styles across the dashboard. Consistency aids in the user's cognitive load reduction as they do not have to reinterpret visual cues. For example, using the same color to represent a specific type of data throughout the dashboard.
- **Effective Use of Colors:** Color can significantly impact the interpretability of a dashboard. Utilize a limited color palette that aligns with the brand or the context of the data. Use color to highlight critical information or alerts, following conventions like red

for negative and green for positive metrics. It is also important to consider color-blind users by incorporating patterns or textures alongside colors.

- **Data-Ink Ratio:** Adhering to Edward Tufte's principles, maximize the data-ink ratio, which refers to the proportion of the ink used in a visual that actually presents data versus the total ink used. Reduce non-data-ink (ornamental elements), such as excessive grid lines or embellishments, to focus on data representation.

- **Interactive Elements:** Incorporate interactivity where appropriate. Filters, drill-down capabilities, and tooltips allow users to explore data dynamically. However, these elements should be intuitive and must not overwhelm the user. Proper instructions or guides can enhance usability.

- **Responsive Design:** Modern dashboards should be responsive, adapting seamlessly across different devices and screen sizes. This flexibility ensures that users can access critical information anytime and anywhere, maintaining usability and functionality across platforms.

- **Real-Time Data and Performance:** For operational dashboards, real-time data is crucial. Ensure that the underlying data infrastructure supports efficient, timely data updates. Additionally, the dashboard should load quickly to maintain user engagement.

- **Accessibility:** Ensure the dashboard is accessible to all users, including those with disabilities. Use ARIA (Accessible Rich Internet Applications) landmarks, captions, and descriptions for visual elements. Provide keyboard navigation and screen reader compatibility.

- **Documentation and Support:** Offering documentation within the dashboard can aid new users in understanding the metrics and features. Contextual help buttons or an integrated help center can provide value without overwhelming users.

Implementing these best practices results in dashboards that not only depict data effectively but also enhance the decision-making process. Below is an example of a Python script using Plotly to create an interactive dashboard element, demonstrating the application of some of these principles:

```
import plotly.graph_objs as go
from plotly.subplots import make_subplots

# Sample data
categories = ['G1', 'G2', 'G3', 'G4', 'G5']
values = [20, 34, 23, 45, 12]

fig = make_subplots(rows=1, cols=2, specs=[[{"type": "bar"}, {"type": "pie"}]])

# Bar chart
fig.add_trace(
    go.Bar(x=categories, y=values, name='Bar Chart', marker=dict(color='
        DarkSlateBlue')),
    row=1, col=1
)

# Pie chart
fig.add_trace(
    go.Pie(labels=categories, values=values, name='Pie Chart'),
    row=1, col=2
)

# Update layout for readability and consistency
fig.update_layout(
    title_text='Sample Dashboard Layout',
    showlegend=True,
    title_font_size=20,
    legend_orientation="h"
)

# Display the dashboard
fig.show()
```

The output of this example is as follows:

[Output: Interactive dashboard with a bar chart and a pie chart side by side]

Dashboards designed with the above guidelines enhance user experience by ensuring that the visualization is robust, comprehensible, and actionable. Incorporating user feedback and iterating on the design further ensures that the dashboard remains relevant and useful over time.

4.11 Case Studies in Data Visualization

Data visualization is a powerful tool for uncovering insights, identifying patterns, and communicating complex information clearly and effectively. In this section, we will explore a selection of case studies that highlight the transformative power of data visualization. These case studies encompass a variety of domains, demonstrating the versatility and impact of well-crafted visualizations.

- **Global Trade Analysis:**

In our first case study, we examine a project aimed at visualizing global trade flows. The dataset, sourced from the United Nations Comtrade database, includes millions of records detailing trade between countries over several decades. The goal was to create an intuitive, interactive visualization that allowed users to explore trade dynamics over time and across different commodities.

```
import plotly.express as px
import pandas as pd

# Loading the dataset
df = pd.read_csv('global_trade_data.csv')

# Filtering data for visualization
data_filtered = df[(df['year'] > 1990) & (df['commodity'] == 'Electronics')]

# Creating a choropleth map
fig = px.choropleth(data_filtered,
                    locations="country",
                    locationmode='country names',
                    color="trade_value",
                    hover_name="country",
                    animation_frame="year",
                    projection="natural earth")

fig.show()
```

This visualization utilized Plotly to create an animated choropleth map. The map dynamically changes based on the selected year, allowing users to observe the evolution of trade values in the electronics sector. The interactivity provided by Plotly's hover functionality enhances user engagement and aids in quickly identifying key trends and outliers.

- **Climate Change Impact:**

The second case study focuses on visualizing the impact of climate change on global temperatures. The data, sourced from NASA's GISS Surface Temperature Analysis, includes global temperature anomalies from the late 19th century to the present day. The objective was to create a clear and informative visualization that communicates the trend of global warming effectively.

```
import matplotlib.pyplot as plt
import seaborn as sns

# Loading the dataset
climate_data = pd.read_csv('global_temperature_data.csv')

# Adjusting the style of the plot
```

```
sns.set(style="whitegrid")

# Creating the line plot
plt.figure(figsize=(10, 6))
sns.lineplot(data=climate_data, x="Year", y="Temperature Anomaly", marker="o",
    dashes=False)
plt.title('Global Temperature Anomalies Over Time')
plt.xlabel('Year')
plt.ylabel('Temperature Anomaly (°C)')
plt.show()
```

In this visualization, a line plot created using Seaborn and Matplotlib illustrates the trend in temperature anomalies over time. The clear upward trajectory highlights the trend of increasing global temperatures, providing a compelling visual argument for the impact of climate change.

- **Health Data Dashboard:**

Our third case study involves the creation of a health data dashboard for a public health agency. The dashboard integrates multiple data sources, including hospital records, vaccination rates, and epidemiological reports. The objective was to design a comprehensive dashboard that supports real-time monitoring and decision-making.

```
import dash
import dash_core_components as dcc
import dash_html_components as html
from dash.dependencies import Input, Output

# Initialize the dashboard
app = dash.Dash(__name__)

# Layout of the dashboard
app.layout = html.Div([
    html.H1("Health Data Dashboard"),
    dcc.Dropdown(id='metric-selector',
                 options=[
                     {'label': 'Hospital Admissions', 'value': 'admissions'},
                     {'label': 'Vaccination Rates', 'value': 'vaccinations'},
                     {'label': 'Epidemiological Reports', 'value': 'epi_reports'}
                 ],
                 value='admissions'),
    dcc.Graph(id='metric-graph')
])

@app.callback(Output('metric-graph', 'figure'),
              [Input('metric-selector', 'value')])
def update_graph(selected_metric):
    if selected_metric == 'admissions':
        data = pd.read_csv('hospital_admissions.csv')
    elif selected_metric == 'vaccinations':
        data = pd.read_csv('vaccination_rates.csv')
    else:
        data = pd.read_csv('epidemiological_reports.csv')
```

```
    fig = px.line(data, x='Date', y='Value', title=f'{selected_metric.capitalize()} Over
        Time')
    return fig

if __name__ == '__main__':
    app.run_server(debug=True)
```

This dashboard, developed using Dash, allows users to select different health metrics and visualize their trends over time. The interactivity provided by Dash enhances the user experience, making it easy for public health officials to switch between different datasets and focus on specific metrics of interest.

- **Financial Market Analysis:**

The fourth case study explores the use of data visualization in financial market analysis. The dataset includes stock prices, trading volumes, and other financial indicators for a selection of major companies. The goal was to create interactive visualizations that aid in identifying market trends and making informed investment decisions.

```
import plotly.graph_objects as go

# Load the dataset
stock_data = pd.read_csv('stock_prices.csv')

# Filter data for a specific company
company_data = stock_data[stock_data['Company'] == 'TechCorp']

# Create a candlestick chart
fig = go.Figure(data=[go.Candlestick(x=company_data['Date'],
                                     open=company_data['Open'],
                                     high=company_data['High'],
                                     low=company_data['Low'],
                                     close=company_data['Close'])])

fig.update_layout(title='TechCorp Stock Price Candlestick Chart',
                  xaxis_title='Date',
                  yaxis_title='Stock Price (USD)')

fig.show()
```

This candlestick chart, created using Plotly, provides a detailed view of stock price movements over time. Candlestick charts are particularly useful for financial analysis as they convey information about opening, closing, high, and low prices in a visually rich format.

- **Social Media Sentiment Analysis:**

The final case study investigates the use of data visualization in social media sentiment analysis. The dataset consists of tweets related to a major consumer brand, with each tweet categorized by sentiment (positive, negative, or neutral). The aim was to visualize the sentiment trends over time and understand public perception.

```
from wordcloud import WordCloud

# Load the dataset
tweets_data = pd.read_csv('tweets.csv')

# Filter positive tweets
positive_tweets = tweets_data[tweets_data['sentiment'] == 'positive']

# Generate a word cloud
text = ' '.join(positive_tweets['text'])
wordcloud = WordCloud(width=800, height=400, background_color='white').generate(
    text)

# Display the word cloud
plt.figure(figsize=(10, 5))
plt.imshow(wordcloud, interpolation='bilinear')
plt.axis('off')
plt.title('Word Cloud of Positive Tweets')
plt.show()
```

This word cloud visualization, created using the WordCloud library, highlights the most frequently used words in positive tweets. Word clouds are an effective way to quickly grasp the major themes and topics within a large collection of text, providing insights into public opinion and sentiment.

Each of these case studies demonstrates different aspects of data visualization, from static plots to interactive dashboards, showcasing the wide range of possibilities and applications. The detailed examples provided illustrate the practical steps and Python code required to create each visualization, offering valuable insights and techniques for data scientists and analysts.

4.12 Future Trends in Data Visualization

The landscape of data visualization is evolving rapidly due to advancements in technology, increasing data complexity, and the growing demand for actionable insights derived from large datasets. Anticipating future trends in this field is essential for professionals who wish to stay ahead in creating meaningful and effective visualizations.

Data visualization is increasingly being influenced by technological advancements such as artificial intelligence (AI), machine learning (ML), and augmented reality (AR). AI and ML are being integrated into data visualization tools to provide more automated, insightful, and predictive visualizations. These technologies enable the development of intelligent systems that can analyze data patterns and suggest the best visualization methods based on the characteristics of the dataset.

```
from yellowbrick.features import RadViz
from sklearn.datasets import load_iris

# Load the dataset
data = load_iris()
X, y = data.data, data.target

# Instantiate the visualizer with the target data
visualizer = RadViz(classes=data.target_names, features=data.feature_names)
visualizer.fit(X, y)
visualizer.transform(X)
visualizer.show()
```

The output generated by the above code segment will be:

```
<
 * Visualization displayed on screen *
>
```

The adoption of augmented reality (AR) and virtual reality (VR) in data visualization is gaining momentum. These technologies provide immersive experiences where complex data can be explored interactively in three-dimensional space. AR and VR can transform static charts and graphs into dynamic, explorable data landscapes, enhancing user engagement and comprehension.

Real-time data visualization is another significant trend, driven by the need for immediate insights and timely decision-making in dynamic environments. Tools and platforms that support real-time data streams, such as Apache Kafka and D3.js, are increasingly being used to monitor live data feeds and display instantaneous changes in data.

```
var svg = d3.select("body").append("svg")
            .attr("width", 600)
            .attr("height", 400);

function update(data) {
  var circles = svg.selectAll("circle").data(data);

  circles.enter().append("circle")
         .attr("cx", function(d) { return d.x; })
         .attr("cy", function(d) { return d.y; })
         .attr("r", 5)
         .merge(circles)
         .attr("cx", function(d) { return d.x; })
         .attr("cy", function(d) { return d.y; });

  circles.exit().remove();
}

// Simulate real-time data
```

```
setInterval(function() {
  var data = d3.range(10).map(function(d) {
    return { x: Math.random() * 600, y: Math.random() * 400 };
  });
  update(data);
}, 1000);
```

As seen from the provided JavaScript code, elements in an SVG (Scalable Vector Graphics) can be updated rapidly to reflect real-time data changes.

Moreover, personalized and adaptive visualizations are becoming more prevalent. These customizations take user preferences and interaction history into account to deliver tailored visualization experiences. Enhanced user control allows users to adjust visual elements such as filter and sort criteria dynamically, promoting a more interactive and user-centric approach to data analysis.

Another trend involves the increasing importance of storytelling in data visualization. Effective visual narratives not only present data but also convey a coherent story that highlights key insights and trends. Tools like Tableau and Flourish are focusing on features that enable users to create smoother transitions and more compelling narratives.

Geospatial data visualization is also advancing, with improved techniques and tools for mapping and analyzing spatial data. Technologies supporting high-precision maps, satellite imagery, and drone data integration are revolutionizing the ways in which spatial data is represented and interpreted. These tools allow for more accurate location tracking and geofencing, which are critical in applications such as logistics, public health, and urban planning.

```
import geopandas as gpd
import matplotlib.pyplot as plt

# Load a geospatial dataset
world = gpd.read_file(gpd.datasets.get_path('naturalearth_lowres'))

# Plot the data
world.plot()
plt.show()
```

The output produced by executing the above Python snippet results in:

```
<
 * A world map rendered in a matplotlib window *
>
```

Even the design principles in data visualization are evolving. The emphasis on accessibility and inclusivity ensures that visualizations are interpretable by a wider audience, including those with disabilities. Techniques such as adding alternative text (alt text) for visual content, ensuring high color contrast, and providing multiple formats for content presentation are becoming standard practices.

Finally, ethics in data visualization is gaining attention. As data's role in decision-making becomes more profound, the responsibility of depicting data accurately and ethically is paramount. Future data visualization tools will likely incorporate features ensuring data integrity, transparency, and ethical considerations, preventing manipulative or misleading representations.

These emerging trends promise to make data visualization more powerful, accessible, and ethical, shaping the way we interpret and act on data insights in the coming years.

Chapter 5

Statistical Foundations for Data Science

A solid understanding of statistical foundations is critical for data science. This chapter covers core concepts including descriptive statistics, probability theory, and common probability distributions. It explains the Central Limit Theorem, sampling, and inferential statistics such as hypothesis testing and confidence intervals. The chapter also delves into correlation and causation, regression analysis, and Bayesian statistics, providing essential knowledge for interpreting data and building robust models.

5.1 Introduction to Statistics

Statistics is an essential discipline within the domain of data science, providing tools and methodologies for collecting, analyzing, interpreting, and presenting data. It offers insights into patterns, relationships, and trends by employing a mathematical framework. This section introduces fundamental concepts, emphasizing their relevance to data science applications.

Defining Statistics

Statistics can be broadly categorized into two main branches: *descriptive statistics* and *inferential statistics*. Descriptive statistics summarize and describe the features of a dataset, while inferential statistics use data from a sample to make generalizations about a population.

Descriptive Statistics

Descriptive statistics involve measurements such as mean, median, mode, range, variance, and standard deviation.

- **Mean (Arithmetic Average)**: The sum of all data points divided by the number of data points.

$$\bar{x} = \frac{1}{n}\sum_{i=1}^{n} x_i$$

- **Median**: The middle value that separates the higher half from the lower half of the data set. For an odd number of observations, it is the middle value, and for an even number, it is the average of the two middle values.
- **Mode**: The most frequently occurring value in a data set.
- **Range**: The difference between the maximum and minimum values.

$$\text{Range} = x_{\text{max}} - x_{\text{min}}$$

- **Variance**: A measure of the dispersion of data points around the mean.

$$s^2 = \frac{1}{n-1}\sum_{i=1}^{n}(x_i - \bar{x})^2$$

- **Standard Deviation**: The square root of the variance, providing a measure of spread similar to the original data units.

$$s = \sqrt{s^2}$$

Inferential Statistics

Inferential statistics involve making predictions or inferences about a population based on a sample of data. This branch of statistics encompasses various techniques, including hypothesis testing, confidence intervals, and regression analysis.

Population versus Sample

A *population* includes all elements from a set of data, while a *sample* is a subset of the population. Statistical methods often require samples due to practical constraints in accessing entire populations.

Sampling

Sampling techniques are crucial for inferential statistics. Common methods include:

- **Random Sampling**: Each member of the population has an equal chance of being selected.
- **Stratified Sampling**: The population is divided into subgroups (strata), and random samples are taken from each stratum.
- **Systematic Sampling**: Every k-th member of the population is selected.
- **Cluster Sampling**: The population is divided into clusters, and entire clusters are randomly selected.

Data Types

Data can be classified into several types, fundamental to selecting appropriate statistical methods:

- **Nominal Data**: Categorical data without any intrinsic order (e.g., colors, names).
- **Ordinal Data**: Categorical data with a meaningful order but no consistent difference between categories (e.g., rankings).
- **Interval Data**: Numerical data with consistent intervals but no true zero point (e.g., temperature in Celsius).
- **Ratio Data**: Numerical data with a true zero point and consistent intervals (e.g., weight, height).

Data Visualization

Effective data visualization is crucial for comprehending data structures and identifying patterns. Common techniques include bar charts, histograms, pie charts, scatter plots, and box plots.

```
import matplotlib.pyplot as plt

# Sample Data
data = [5, 20, 15, 25, 10]

# Bar Chart Example
plt.bar(range(len(data)), data)
plt.show()
```

```
   *******
  *       *
 *         *
 *         *
**** **** ****
**************
```

Measures of Central Tendency and Dispersion

Central tendency measures provide a single value representing the center of the data, while dispersion measures indicate the spread or variability. Together, they offer a comprehensive summary of the dataset.

Z-scores

A Z-score indicates how many standard deviations an element is from the mean. It is useful for comparing data points from different distributions.

$$Z = \frac{X - \mu}{\sigma}$$

where X is the data point, μ is the mean, and σ is the standard deviation.

This section lays the groundwork for understanding how data can be summarized, visualized, and drawn from to make generalizations about larger populations. Each concept will be built upon in subsequent sections, further enhancing your statistical acumen and data interpretation skills.

5.2 Descriptive Statistics

Descriptive statistics provide a way to summarize and describe the important features of a dataset. This section focuses on the various measures and tools used to present data succinctly and meaningfully, allowing one to grasp the underlying patterns and insights. These methods are a critical foundation for any statistical analysis and serve as the preliminary step before delving into inferential statistics.

Measures of Central Tendency

Measures of central tendency give us an idea about the central value around which the data points tend to cluster. The most common measures include the mean, median, and mode.

The *mean* (or average) is the sum of all data points divided by the number of data points. It is calculated using the formula:

$$\text{Mean}(\mu) = \frac{1}{N}\sum_{i=1}^{N} x_i$$

where N is the number of observations, and x_i represents each individual observation.

The *median* is the middle value when data points are arranged in ascending or descending order. If the number of observations is odd, the median is the center value. If even, it is the average of the two middle values. The median is less affected by outliers and skewed data compared to the mean.

The *mode* is the value that appears most frequently in the dataset. A dataset may have one mode (unimodal), more than one mode (bimodal or multimodal), or no mode at all if no value repeats.

Measures of Dispersion

Measures of dispersion provide information about the spread or variability of the data. These include range, variance, and standard deviation.

The *range* is the difference between the maximum and minimum values in the dataset:

$$\text{Range} = \text{max}(x_i) - \text{min}(x_i)$$

The *variance* measures the average squared deviation from the mean. For a population, it is calculated as:

$$\sigma^2 = \frac{1}{N}\sum_{i=1}^{N}(x_i - \mu)^2$$

For a sample, the formula is adjusted to:

$$s^2 = \frac{1}{n-1}\sum_{i=1}^{n}(x_i - \bar{x})^2$$

where $\bar{x}$ is the sample mean and n is the sample size.

The *standard deviation* is the square root of the variance, providing a measure of spread in the same units as the data.

$$\sigma = \sqrt{\sigma^2}, \quad s = \sqrt{s^2}$$

Other Statistical Measures

Percentiles and **Quartiles** divide the data into parts. Percentiles indicate the value below which a given percentage of observations fall. For example, the 25th percentile (first quartile) is the value below which 25% of observations lie. The 50th percentile is the median, and the 75th percentile (third quartile) marks the position below which 75% of observations fall.

The *interquartile range* (IQR) is the difference between the third and first quartiles, representing the middle 50% of the data. It is a robust measure of variability that is not affected by outliers.

$$\text{IQR} = Q_3 - Q_1$$

Skewness and **Kurtosis** are measures that describe the shape of the data distribution. Skewness indicates the asymmetry of the distribution. Positive skewness suggests a distribution with a longer right tail, while negative skewness indicates a longer left tail. Kurtosis measures the "tailedness" of a distribution. High kurtosis indicates heavy tails and a sharp peak, while low kurtosis suggests light tails and a flatter peak.

Visual Representation of Data

Various graphical techniques help in understanding the data distribution and revealing hidden patterns.

A *histogram* is a bar chart that represents the frequency distribution of a dataset. The x-axis shows the bins (intervals), and the y-axis shows the frequency of observations within each bin.

A *box plot* (box-and-whisker plot) displays the distribution of data based on five summary statistics: minimum, first quartile (Q1), median, third quartile (Q3), and maximum. The box represents the interquartile range (IQR), the line inside the box shows the median, and the "whiskers" extend to the minimum and maximum values within $1.5 \times$ IQR from Q1 and Q3, respectively. Outliers are plotted as individual points.

A *scatter plot* is used to observe the relationship between two quantitative variables. Each point represents an observation, with the x and y coordinates corresponding to the values of the two variables.

Example in Python

Below is an example of using Python to compute various descriptive statistics and plot data:

```
import numpy as np
import matplotlib.pyplot as plt

# Example dataset
data = np.array([4, 8, 6, 5, 3, 2, 8, 9, 12, 15, 21, 20, 18, 16])

# Measures of central tendency
mean = np.mean(data)
median = np.median(data)
mode = max(set(data), key=list(data).count)

# Measures of dispersion
range_ = np.ptp(data)
variance = np.var(data)
std_dev = np.std(data)
percentiles = np.percentile(data, [25, 50, 75])
iqr = percentiles[2] - percentiles[0]

print("Mean:", mean)
print("Median:", median)
print("Mode:", mode)
print("Range:", range_)
print("Variance:", variance)
print("Standard Deviation:", std_dev)
print("Percentiles (25%, 50%, 75%):", percentiles)
print("Interquartile Range:", iqr)

# Histogram
plt.hist(data, bins=5, edgecolor='black')
plt.title('Histogram of Data')
plt.xlabel('Value')
plt.ylabel('Frequency')
plt.show()

# Box plot
plt.boxplot(data, vert=False)
plt.title('Box Plot of Data')
plt.xlabel('Value')
plt.show()

# Scatter plot
data_y = [10, 12, 13, 15, 16, 18, 21, 23, 11, 14, 19, 20, 22, 24]
plt.scatter(data, data_y)
plt.title('Scatter Plot')
plt.xlabel('Data')
plt.ylabel('Response')
plt.show()
```

Executing the script will produce the following outputs:

```
Mean: 10.571428571428571
Median: 8.5
Mode: 8
Range: 19
Variance: 38.97959183673469
Standard Deviation: 6.244998306302015
Percentiles (25%, 50%, 75%): [ 5.75  8.5  17.25]
Interquartile Range: 11.5
```

The provided code computes key descriptive statistics and generates the associated visualizations, aiding in the comprehensive understanding of the dataset.

In the field of data science, mastery of descriptive statistics is indispensable for analyzing the primary characteristics of data, setting a solid groundwork for subsequent statistical procedures and machine learning algorithms.

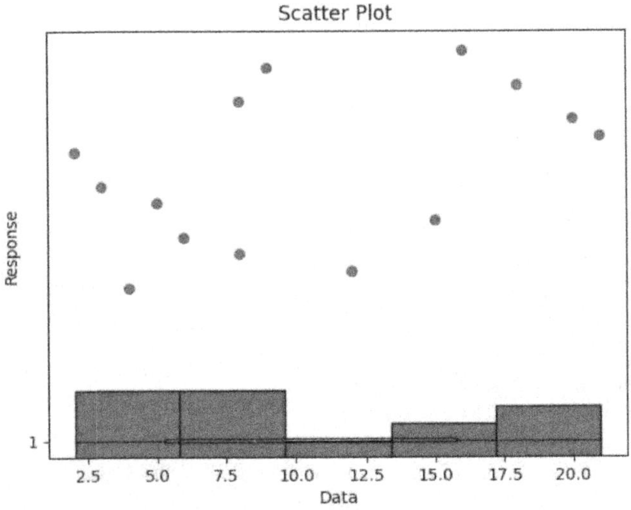

5.3 Probability Theory

Probability theory is a branch of mathematics concerned with the analysis of random phenomena. The central objects of probability theory are random variables, stochastic processes, and events. An event is a subset of a sample space, the set of all possible outcomes of an experiment. Understanding the underlying principles of probability allows data scientists to evaluate the likelihood of occurrences, predict future events, and quantify uncertainties.

Sample Spaces and Events:

Consider a statistical experiment where we observe outcomes. The set of all possible outcomes is known as the sample space, denoted by S. For instance, in a coin toss, the sample space is $S = \{\text{Heads, Tails}\}$.

An event is any subset of the sample space. For example, in the roll of a die, the event of rolling an even number is $E = \{2, 4, 6\}$.

$$S = \{1, 2, 3, 4, 5, 6\}$$

Axioms of Probability:

Probability P is a function that assigns a real number in the interval $[0, 1]$ to an event. The function P must satisfy the following three axioms:

- **Non-negativity:** $P(E) \geq 0$ for any event $E \subseteq S$.
- **Normalization:** $P(S) = 1$.
- **Additivity:** If $E_1, E_2, \ldots$ are mutually exclusive events, then

$$P\left(\bigcup_{i=1}^{\infty} E_i\right) = \sum_{i=1}^{\infty} P(E_i)$$

These axioms frame the probability distribution over a sample space, enabling a systematic approach to probability evaluations.

Conditional Probability:

Conditional probability is the probability of an event given that another event has occurred. The conditional probability of A given B is denoted $P(A|B)$ and is defined as:

$$P(A|B) = \frac{P(A \cap B)}{P(B)}, \quad P(B) > 0$$

This definition is crucial when working with dependent events and is a cornerstone in many data science algorithms for building predictive models.

Bayes' Theorem:

Bayes' Theorem connects conditional probabilities and allows for the updating of probability estimates given new data. It is expressed as:

$$P(A|B) = \frac{P(B|A)P(A)}{P(B)}$$

Bayes' Theorem is particularly powerful in Bayesian statistics, where it provides the framework to update the probability for a hypothesis as more evidence or information becomes available.

Independence:

Two events A and B are independent if the occurrence of one does not affect the probability of the other, formally:

$$P(A \cap B) = P(A)P(B)$$

Independence simplifies the computation of probabilities and is a key assumption in many statistical models.

Law of Total Probability:

The Law of Total Probability articulates that if $B_1, B_2, \ldots, B_n$ are mutually exclusive events that partition the sample space S, then for any event A,

$$P(A) = \sum_{i=1}^{n} P(A|B_i)P(B_i)$$

This is particularly useful in breaking complex probability problems into simpler components.

Random Variables:

A random variable is a function that assigns a numerical value to each outcome in a sample space. Random variables can be discrete or continuous:

- **Discrete Random Variables** take on a countable number of possible values. Example: number of heads in ten coin flips.
- **Continuous Random Variables** take on an uncountable amount of values within an interval. Example: the exact time you wait for a bus.

The probability distribution of a random variable X describes the likelihood of each potential value X can take.

Expected Value and Variance:

The expected value (mean) of a random variable X, denoted $\mathbb{E}(X)$, defines the long-run average value of repetitions of the experiment it represents and is given by:

$$\mathbb{E}(X) = \sum_{i} x_i P(X = x_i)$$

for discrete random variables, and

$$\mathbb{E}(X) = \int_{-\infty}^{\infty} x f_X(x)\, dx$$

for continuous random variables, where $f_X(x)$ is the probability density function of X.

The variance of X, denoted Var(X), measures how much the values of X vary from the expectation $\mathbb{E}(X)$:

$$\text{Var}(X) = \mathbb{E}[(X - \mathbb{E}(X))^2]$$

A related measure is the standard deviation, σ_X, which is the square root of the variance and provides a scale for the dispersion of X's values.

Understanding these foundational principles of probability theory is essential for data science practitioners in analyzing data, constructing models, and making informed decisions under uncertainty. The rigorous mathematical framework provided by probability theory guides practical implementations and ensures robustness and reliability in statistical analyses.

5.4 Random Variables and Distributions

In the domain of data science, understanding random variables and their distributions is fundamental for analyzing and modeling data. A random variable is a variable whose possible values are outcomes of a random phenomenon. Random variables can be classified into two main types: discrete and continuous.

A **discrete random variable** can take on a countable number of distinct values. For example, the number of heads obtained when flipping a coin three times is a discrete random variable, as it can take values in the set {0, 1, 2, 3}. The probability distribution of a discrete random variable is defined by its probability mass function (PMF), which specifies the probability that the random variable takes each of its possible values. Mathematically, if X is a discrete random variable and $x_1, x_2, \ldots, x_k$ are its possible values, then the PMF $p(x)$ is defined as:

$$p(x_i) = P(X = x_i) \quad \text{for} \quad i = 1, 2, \ldots, k$$

The PMF must satisfy two properties:

- $p(x_i) \geq 0$ for all i
- $\sum_{i=1}^{k} p(x_i) = 1$

A **continuous random variable**, on the other hand, can take on an infinite number of possible values, often over some interval of real numbers. Instead of a PMF, continuous random variables are described by their probability density function (PDF). A PDF, denoted $f(x)$, describes the likelihood of the random variable taking on a particular value. For a continuous random variable Y:

$$P(a \leq Y \leq b) = \int_a^b f(y)\,dy$$

where $f(y)$ must satisfy:

- $f(y) \geq 0$ for all y
- $\int_{-\infty}^{\infty} f(y)\,dy = 1$

To further solidify these concepts, let's consider some examples and properties.

Example 1: Discrete Random Variable

Consider a discrete random variable X that represents the roll of a fair six-sided die. The PMF associated with X is:

$$p(x) = \begin{cases} \frac{1}{6} & \text{if } x \in \{1, 2, 3, 4, 5, 6\} \\ 0 & \text{otherwise} \end{cases}$$

The PMF values must sum to one:

$$\sum_{x=1}^{6} p(x) = 6 \times \frac{1}{6} = 1$$

Example 2: Continuous Random Variable

Consider a continuous random variable Y that is uniformly distributed over the interval $[0, 1]$. The PDF is:

$$f(y) = \begin{cases} 1 & \text{if } 0 \leq y \leq 1 \\ 0 & \text{otherwise} \end{cases}$$

The total area under the PDF curve must equal one:

$$\int_0^1 f(y)\,dy = \int_0^1 1\,dy = 1$$

Cumulative Distribution Function

Both discrete and continuous random variables are also characterized by their cumulative distribution function (CDF). The CDF of a random variable Z, denoted $F(z)$, gives the probability that Z takes a value less than or equal to z:

$$F(z) = P(Z \leq z)$$

For a discrete random variable X, the CDF is:

$$F(x) = \sum_{t \leq x} p(t)$$

For a continuous random variable Y, the CDF is derived from the PDF as:

$$F(y) = \int_{-\infty}^{y} f(t)\,dt$$

Expected Value and Variance

The expected value (mean) and variance are key metrics used to describe random variables. The expected value of a random variable provides a measure of the central tendency, while the variance measures the dispersion around the expected value.

For a discrete random variable X with PMF $p(x)$, the expected value $E[X]$ is:

$$E[X] = \sum_i x_i \cdot p(x_i)$$

The variance $Var(X)$ is:

$$Var(X) = E[(X - E[X])^2] = \sum_i (x_i - \mu)^2 \cdot p(x_i) \quad \text{where} \quad \mu = E[X]$$

For a continuous random variable Y with PDF $f(y)$, the expected value $E[Y]$ is:

$$E[Y] = \int_{-\infty}^{\infty} y \cdot f(y)\,dy$$

The variance $Var(Y)$ is:

$$Var(Y) = E[(Y - E[Y])^2] = \int_{-\infty}^{\infty} (y - \mu)^2 \cdot f(y)\, dy \quad \text{where} \quad \mu = E[Y]$$

Properties of Distributions

Among the many known distributions, certain properties are frequently encountered in data science:

- **Binomial Distribution**: A discrete distribution representing the number of successes in a fixed number of Bernoulli trials with success probability p. If $X \sim Bin(n, p)$, then the PMF is:

$$P(X = k) = \binom{n}{k} p^k (1 - p)^{n-k} \quad \text{for} \quad k = 0, 1, 2, \ldots, n$$

- **Normal Distribution**: A continuous distribution that is symmetric and characterized by its mean μ and standard deviation σ. The PDF of $Y \sim N(\mu, \sigma^2)$ is:

$$f(y) = \frac{1}{\sqrt{2\pi\sigma^2}} e^{-\frac{(y-\mu)^2}{2\sigma^2}}$$

These properties and examples build the foundation for further exploration of probabilistic models, hypothesis tests, and inference methods in data science.

5.5 Common Probability Distributions

Probability distributions are fundamental in both theoretical and applied statistics. A probability distribution assigns a probability to each possible outcome in a sample space. We will explore some of the most commonly used probability distributions, focusing on their properties and applications.

1. Bernoulli Distribution

The Bernoulli distribution is the simplest discrete distribution and models binary experiments. An experiment with a Bernoulli distribution has exactly two possible outcomes: success (with probability p) and failure (with probability $1 - p$).

The probability mass function (pmf) of a Bernoulli random variable X is defined as:

$$P(X = 1) = p, \quad P(X = 0) = 1 - p$$

The expectation (mean) and variance of a Bernoulli random variable are:

$$E[X] = p, \quad \text{Var}(X) = p(1 - p)$$

2. Binomial Distribution

The Binomial distribution generalizes the Bernoulli distribution to multiple trials. It represents the number of successes in n independent Bernoulli trials with probability p of success in each trial.

The probability mass function for a Binomial random variable X is:

$$P(X = k) = \binom{n}{k} p^k (1 - p)^{n-k}$$

where $\binom{n}{k}$ is the binomial coefficient, calculated as $\binom{n}{k} = \frac{n!}{k!(n-k)!}$.

The expectation and variance are:

$$E[X] = np, \quad \text{Var}(X) = np(1 - p)$$

3. Poisson Distribution

The Poisson distribution models the number of events occurring within a fixed interval of time or space, given the events occur independently and at a constant rate λ.

The probability mass function for a Poisson random variable X is:

$$P(X = k) = \frac{\lambda^k e^{-\lambda}}{k!}$$

The expectation and variance are both equal to the rate parameter λ:

$$E[X] = \lambda, \quad \text{Var}(X) = \lambda$$

4. Uniform Distribution

The uniform distribution has two forms: discrete and continuous.

For a discrete uniform distribution over $\{1, 2, \ldots, n\}$, the pmf is:

$$P(X = k) = \frac{1}{n}, \quad k = 1, 2, \ldots, n$$

For the continuous uniform distribution over the interval $[a, b]$, the probability density function (pdf) is:

$$f(x) = \frac{1}{b-a}, \quad a \leq x \leq b$$

The expectation and variance for the continuous case are:

$$E[X] = \frac{a+b}{2}, \quad \text{Var}(X) = \frac{(b-a)^2}{12}$$

5. Normal Distribution

The Normal distribution, also known as the Gaussian distribution, is ubiquitous in probability and statistics. It is characterized by its mean μ and variance σ^2.

The probability density function of a Normal random variable X is:

$$f(x) = \frac{1}{\sqrt{2\pi\sigma^2}} e^{-\frac{(x-\mu)^2}{2\sigma^2}}$$

The mean and variance are:

$$E[X] = \mu, \quad \text{Var}(X) = \sigma^2$$

The Standard Normal distribution is a special case with $\mu = 0$ and $\sigma = 1$. A Normal random variable X with any mean and variance can be standardized using:

$$Z = \frac{X-\mu}{\sigma}$$

where Z has a Standard Normal distribution.

6. Exponential Distribution

The exponential distribution describes the time between events in a Poisson process. It has a single parameter λ, which is the rate parameter.

The probability density function of an Exponential random variable X is:

$$f(x) = \lambda e^{-\lambda x}, \quad x \geq 0$$

The expectation and variance are:

$$E[X] = \frac{1}{\lambda}, \quad \text{Var}(X) = \frac{1}{\lambda^2}$$

7. Gamma Distribution

The Gamma distribution generalizes the Exponential distribution and is characterized by two parameters: shape parameter k and scale parameter θ.

The probability density function of a Gamma random variable X is:

$$f(x) = \frac{x^{k-1}e^{-\frac{x}{\theta}}}{\Gamma(k)\theta^k}, \quad x \geq 0$$

where $\Gamma(k)$ is the Gamma function, defined as $\Gamma(k) = \int_0^\infty t^{k-1}e^{-t}dt$.

The mean and variance are:

$$E[X] = k\theta, \quad \text{Var}(X) = k\theta^2$$

8. Beta Distribution

The Beta distribution is flexible and used for modeling random variables limited to intervals of finite length, typically [0, 1]. It is specified by two shape parameters, α and β.

The probability density function of a Beta random variable X is:

$$f(x) = \frac{x^{\alpha-1}(1-x)^{\beta-1}}{\mathrm{B}(\alpha,\beta)}, \quad 0 \leq x \leq 1$$

where $\mathrm{B}(\alpha,\beta)$ is the Beta function, defined as $\mathrm{B}(\alpha,\beta) = \int_0^1 t^{\alpha-1}(1-t)^{\beta-1}dt$.

The mean and variance are:

$$E[X] = \frac{\alpha}{\alpha+\beta}, \quad \text{Var}(X) = \frac{\alpha\beta}{(\alpha+\beta)^2(\alpha+\beta+1)}$$

9. Other Distributions

Other important distributions include the Chi-Square distribution, used in hypothesis testing and confidence interval estimation, and the Student's t-distribution, used when the sample size is small and the population standard deviation is unknown. The F-distribution is used to compare variances between two populations.

Understanding these distributions and their properties is crucial for proper data analysis and model construction in data science. Each distribution serves specific types of data and scenarios, making them indispensable tools in the statistician's toolkit.

5.6 Central Limit Theorem

The Central Limit Theorem (CLT) is a fundamental theorem in statistics, with far-reaching implications in data science and other fields. The theorem delineates the behavior of the sampling distribution of sample means. Specifically, it states that, for a sufficiently large sample size, the distribution of the sample mean will approach a normal distribution (or Gaussian distribution), irrespective of the shape of the population distribution from which the sample is drawn.

To formally state the Central Limit Theorem, consider a population with a mean μ and a finite variance σ^2. Suppose we draw random samples of size n from this population. Let $\overline{X}$ be the mean of these samples. The CLT asserts that as n becomes large, the distribution of $\overline{X}$ approaches a normal distribution with mean μ and variance $\frac{\sigma^2}{n}$. Mathematically,

$$\overline{X} \sim N\left(\mu, \frac{\sigma^2}{n}\right)$$

where N denotes a normal distribution.

To comprehend the implications of the CLT, it is essential to grasp the concept of sample means and their distribution. Let $X_1, X_2, \ldots, X_n$ be a random sample of size n drawn from a population with mean μ and variance σ^2. The sample mean $\overline{X}$ is given by:

$$\overline{X} = \frac{1}{n}\sum_{i=1}^{n} X_i$$

The Central Limit Theorem can be illustrated using the following Python code:

```
import numpy as np
import matplotlib.pyplot as plt

# Define population parameters
population_mean = 50
population_std_dev = 15
sample_size = 30
num_samples = 1000

# Generate random samples and calculate sample means
sample_means = []
for _ in range(num_samples):
    sample = np.random.normal(loc=population_mean, scale=population_std_dev,
        size=sample_size)
    sample_mean = np.mean(sample)
    sample_means.append(sample_mean)
```

```
# Plot histogram of sample means
plt.hist(sample_means, bins=50, edgecolor='k', alpha=0.7)
plt.title('Distribution of Sample Means')
plt.xlabel('Sample Mean')
plt.ylabel('Frequency')
plt.show()
```

The output of the above code would display a histogram of sample means, demonstrating the consistency with the Central Limit Theorem as the histogram approximates a normal distribution regardless of the underlying population distribution.

(Display of a bell-shaped curve histogram indicating the normal distribution of sample means)

The Central Limit Theorem is incredibly powerful because of its broad applicability. It allows statisticians and data scientists to make inferences about population parameters even when the population distribution is not normal. The normality assumption underpins many statistical procedures and hypothesis tests, including the t-test and ANOVA.

An essential aspect of the CLT is the rule of sample size. Although the theorem does not specify an exact sample size n, it is generally accepted that a sample size of 30 or more is sufficiently large for the sample mean to be normally distributed under most conditions. However, when the population distribution is particularly skewed or has heavy tails, larger sample sizes may be required.

The theorem also has implications for the standard error of the mean, which measures the dispersion of the sampling distribution of the sample mean. The standard error of the mean is given by:

$$\text{SEM} = \frac{\sigma}{\sqrt{n}}$$

where σ is the population standard deviation and n is the sample size. As n increases, the SEM decreases, indicating that the sample mean is a more precise estimate of the population mean.

The Central Limit Theorem provides the theoretical foundation for the creation of confidence intervals and the conduct of hypothesis testing. It ensures that, regardless of the underlying population distribution, the distribution of the sample mean approaches normality, allowing data scientists to apply normal-based methods to a wide range of practical problems.

Understanding the Central Limit Theorem is crucial for data scientists as it provides the backbone for many inferential techniques used in analyzing and interpreting data. Its relevance extends beyond simple sample means to more complex statistics, reinforcing its importance in the field of data science.

5.7 Inferential Statistics

Inferential statistics enables us to make generalizations and inferences about a population based on a sample of data. It contrasts with descriptive statistics, which simply summarizes or describes the characteristics of a data set. Key concepts in inferential statistics include point estimation, interval estimation, and hypothesis testing, among others.

Point Estimation

Point estimation involves using sample data to compute a number (statistic) that serves as an estimate of an unknown population parameter. Common estimators include the sample mean as an estimate of the population mean and the sample proportion as an estimate of the population proportion. For instance, if we denote the population mean by μ and the sample mean by $\overline{X}$, then $\overline{X}$ is a point estimate of μ.

Interval Estimation

Interval estimation provides a range of values within which the parameter is expected to lie with a certain level of confidence. This range is known as a confidence interval. A 95% confidence interval for a population mean μ, based on a sample mean $\overline{X}$, is typically calculated as:

$$\overline{X} \pm z_{\frac{\alpha}{2}} \left(\frac{\sigma}{\sqrt{n}} \right)$$

where $z_{\frac{\alpha}{2}}$ is the critical value from the standard normal distribution for a confidence level of $1 - \alpha$, σ is the population standard deviation, and n is the sample size. If σ is unknown, it is estimated by the sample standard deviation s.

Hypothesis Testing

Hypothesis testing is a method used to make decisions or inferences about population parameters. It involves formulating two competing hypotheses: the null hypothesis (H_0) and the alternative hypothesis (H_a). The null hypothesis typically represents a statement of no effect or no difference, while the alternative hypothesis represents what we aim to support.

The steps of hypothesis testing include:

- **Formulating Hypotheses**: Define the null hypothesis (H_0) and alternative hypothesis (H_a).
- **Selecting the Significance Level (α)**: Common choices are 0.05, 0.01, or 0.10.
- **Choosing the Test Statistic**: Based on the nature of the data and the hypotheses. Common test statistics include the z-test, t-test, F-test, and χ^2-test.
- **Computing the Test Statistic**: Using the sample data.
- **Making a Decision**: Comparing the computed test statistic to the critical value(s) or using the p-value approach.

If the p-value is less than the significance level α, we reject the null hypothesis in favor of the alternative hypothesis. Otherwise, we do not reject the null hypothesis.

For example, if we want to test whether the population mean μ is equal to a hypothesized value μ_0, the hypotheses are:

$$\begin{aligned} H_0 &: \quad \mu = \mu_0 \\ H_a &: \quad \mu \neq \mu_0 \end{aligned}$$

The test statistic is:

$$z = \frac{\overline{X} - \mu_0}{\sigma/\sqrt{n}}$$

or if σ is unknown,

$$t = \frac{\overline{X} - \mu_0}{s/\sqrt{n}}$$

Type I and Type II Errors

Hypothesis testing involves the risk of making errors. A *Type I error* occurs when we reject the null hypothesis H_0 when it is actually true. The probability of committing a Type I error is denoted by α, the significance level. A *Type II error* occurs when we fail to reject the null hypothesis H_0 when the alternative hypothesis H_a is true. The probability of committing a Type II error is denoted by β.

Power of a Test

The power of a statistical test is the probability that it correctly rejects a false null hypothesis (H_0). It is calculated as $1 - \beta$. A higher power indicates a greater likelihood of detecting an effect when there is one.

Example: Two-Sample t-Test

Consider comparing the means of two independent samples to determine if they come from populations with equal means. The hypotheses are:

$$\begin{aligned} H_0 &: \quad \mu_1 = \mu_2 \\ H_a &: \quad \mu_1 \neq \mu_2 \end{aligned}$$

Assuming equal variances, the test statistic is:

$$t = \frac{(\overline{X}_1 - \overline{X}_2)}{s_p\sqrt{\frac{1}{n_1} + \frac{1}{n_2}}}$$

where s_p is the pooled standard deviation:

$$s_p = \sqrt{\frac{(n_1 - 1)s_1^2 + (n_2 - 1)s_2^2}{n_1 + n_2 - 2}}$$

If $\overline{X}_1 = 5.1$, $\overline{X}_2 = 4.7$, $s_1 = 1.2$, $s_2 = 1.1$, $n_1 = 30$, and $n_2 = 35$, then

$$\begin{aligned} s_p &= \sqrt{\frac{(30 - 1) \times 1.2^2 + (35 - 1) \times 1.1^2}{30 + 35 - 2}} \\ &= \sqrt{\frac{29 \times 1.44 + 34 \times 1.21}{63}} \\ &= 1.15 \end{aligned}$$

$$t = \frac{(5.1 - 4.7)}{1.15\sqrt{\frac{1}{30} + \frac{1}{35}}} \approx 1.673$$

The degrees of freedom are $n_1 + n_2 - 2 = 63$. Comparing the calculated t-value with the critical t-value from the t-distribution table at a significance level $\alpha = 0.05$, we make a decision about the hypotheses.

Inferential statistics are the bedrock of data science, enabling us to draw conclusions from data and make decisions under uncertainty effectively.

5.8 Sampling and Sampling Distributions

In data science, sampling is a crucial technique used to select a subset of individuals or observations from a larger population to infer characteristics about the entire population. Effective sampling methods enable data scientists to draw valid conclusions and make predictions while minimizing costs and resource consumption.

Definition and Importance of Sampling: Sampling refers to the process of selecting a portion (sample) from a larger set (population) to estimate properties of the whole. Sampling is essential when dealing with large data sets where it is impractical or impossible to examine every member of the population. It allows for faster data analysis, cost reduction, and the efficient deployment of computational resources.

Types of Sampling Methods:

- **Simple Random Sampling:** Every member of the population has an equal chance of being selected. It is the most straightforward form of sampling, often implemented using random number generators.
- **Stratified Sampling:** The population is divided into strata, or subgroups, that share similar characteristics. Samples are then randomly selected from each stratum. This method ensures that different population segments are adequately represented.
- **Cluster Sampling:** The population is divided into clusters, usually based on geographical boundaries or other naturally occur-

ring divisions. Randomly selected clusters are then fully surveyed. This method is cost-effective for large populations spread over wide areas.

- **Systematic Sampling:** A sample is drawn by selecting one random starting point and then picking every k-th element in the population list. It is simpler and faster to implement when the population is ordered in some way.

- **Convenience Sampling:** Samples are chosen based on ease of access and proximity to the researcher. While not as scientifically rigorous, convenience sampling is often used in exploratory research.

Sampling Distribution: When we repeatedly draw samples of a specific size from a population and calculate a statistic (such as the mean) for each sample, we form a sampling distribution. This distribution of statistics, derived from different samples, describes the behavior of the statistic and provides insights into its variability.

For instance, consider the sampling distribution of the sample mean $\overline{X}$. Suppose we draw multiple samples of size n from a population with mean μ and standard deviation σ. The sampling distribution of $\overline{X}$ will have the following properties:

- **Mean:** The mean of the sampling distribution of the sample mean is equal to the population mean, $\mu_{\overline{X}} = \mu$.

- **Standard Error:** The standard deviation of the sampling distribution of the sample mean is known as the standard error, calculated as $\sigma_{\overline{X}} = \frac{\sigma}{\sqrt{n}}$, where σ is the population standard deviation and n is the sample size.

- **Shape:** According to the Central Limit Theorem, for a large enough sample size, the sampling distribution of the sample mean will be approximately normally distributed, regardless of the original population distribution.

Example Code for Sampling Distribution of the Mean:

```
import numpy as np
import matplotlib.pyplot as plt

# Parameters
population_mean = 50
population_stddev = 10
```

```
sample_size = 30
num_samples = 1000

# Generate a population
population = np.random.normal(loc=population_mean, scale=population_stddev, size
    =10000)

# Draw multiple samples and compute their means
sample_means = []
for _ in range(num_samples):
    sample = np.random.choice(population, size=sample_size, replace=True)
    sample_means.append(np.mean(sample))

# Plot the sampling distribution of the sample mean
plt.hist(sample_means, bins=30, edgecolor='k', alpha=0.7)
plt.title("Sampling Distribution of the Sample Mean")
plt.xlabel("Sample Mean")
plt.ylabel("Frequency")
plt.show()
```

Output:

The output would be a histogram displaying the sampling distribution of the mean, which should follow a normal distribution curve centered around the population mean.

Significance of the Standard Error: The standard error quantifies how much the sample mean $\overline{X}$ is expected to vary from the population mean μ. Smaller standard errors indicate that the sample mean is a more precise estimate of the population mean.

Law of Large Numbers: As the sample size increases, the sample mean converges to the population mean. This principle reinforces the reliability of larger samples in accurately representing the population, validating the robustness of inferential statistics.

An understanding of sampling methods and sampling distributions equips data scientists with the knowledge to draw credible and significant insights from data while accounting for random variability and inherent uncertainties.

5.9 Hypothesis Testing

Hypothesis testing is a fundamental aspect of inferential statistics, allowing data scientists to make decisions or inferences about population parameters based on sample data. This method provides a structured framework to evaluate whether there is enough evidence to support a specific claim or hypothesis about a population parameter.

A hypothesis test typically involves the following components:

- **Null Hypothesis (H_0)**: This is a statement of no effect or no difference, serving as the default or baseline assumption. It is the hypothesis that researchers aim to test against.
- **Alternative Hypothesis (H_a)**: This represents the hypothesis that there is an effect or a difference. It is what the researcher wants to prove.
- **Test Statistic**: A standardized value calculated from sample data that is used to decide whether to reject the null hypothesis.
- **P-value**: The probability of obtaining test results at least as extreme as the observed data, under the assumption that the null hypothesis is true.
- **Significance Level (α)**: A threshold set by the researcher (commonly 0.05), indicating the probability of rejecting the null hypothesis when it is actually true. This is also known as the Type I error rate.
- **Decision Rule**: Based on the p-value and significance level, this rule dictates whether to reject the null hypothesis.

The process of hypothesis testing can be summarized in the following steps:

1. **State the Hypotheses**: Formulate both the null hypothesis H_0 and the alternative hypothesis H_a. For example:
    - H_0: The mean of the population is equal to a specified value μ_0.
    - H_a: The mean of the population is not equal to μ_0.
2. **Select an Appropriate Test**: Choose a statistical test based on the type of data and the hypothesis. Common tests include the t-test, z-test, chi-square test, and ANOVA.
3. **Determine the Significance Level (α)**: Set the significance level, such as 0.05, which represents a 5% risk of committing a Type I error.
4. **Calculate the Test Statistic**: Compute the test statistic using the sample data. The formula for the test statistic will vary depending on the chosen test.

5. **Find the P-value**: Determine the p-value corresponding to the test statistic.

6. **Make a Decision**: Compare the p-value to the significance level:
   - If p-value $\leq \alpha$, reject the null hypothesis H_0.
   - If p-value $> \alpha$, do not reject the null hypothesis H_0.

Several types of hypothesis tests are commonly used, depending on the nature of the data and the specific hypotheses:

1. Z-test:

- Used when the sample size is large (n > 30) and the population standard deviation is known.
- Formula for the test statistic:

$$z = \frac{\bar{x} - \mu_0}{\sigma/\sqrt{n}}$$

where $\bar{x}$ is the sample mean, μ_0 is the population mean, σ is the population standard deviation, and n is the sample size.

2. T-test:

- Used when the sample size is small (n $\leq$ 30) or the population standard deviation is unknown.
- Formula for the test statistic:

$$t = \frac{\bar{x} - \mu_0}{s/\sqrt{n}}$$

where s is the sample standard deviation.

3. Chi-Square Test:

- Used for categorical data to assess how likely it is that an observed distribution is due to chance.
- Formula for the test statistic:

$$\chi^2 = \sum \frac{(O_i - E_i)^2}{E_i}$$

where O_i is the observed frequency and E_i is the expected frequency.

4. ANOVA (Analysis of Variance):

- Used to compare the means of three or more samples to understand if at least one sample mean is significantly different from the others.
- Basic formula involves partitioning the total variation into variation between groups and within groups.

Consider a scenario where a pharmaceutical company claims that a new drug reduces blood pressure by an average of 8 mmHg. To test this claim, a sample of 30 patients is taken, and the sample mean reduction in blood pressure is found to be 7.5 mmHg with a sample standard deviation of 1.2 mmHg. We want to determine whether the drug is less effective than claimed using a significance level of $\alpha = 0.05$.

- **Step 1: State the Hypotheses**
  - H_0: $\mu = 8$ (The mean reduction is 8 mmHg)
  - H_a: $\mu < 8$ (The mean reduction is less than 8 mmHg)
- **Step 2: Select the Test**
  - Since the sample size is 30 and the standard deviation is known, we use a one-sample t-test.
- **Step 3: Determine the Significance Level**
  - $\alpha = 0.05$
- **Step 4: Calculate the Test Statistic**
  - Compute the t-statistic using the formula:

$$t = \frac{\bar{x} - \mu_0}{s/\sqrt{n}} = \frac{7.5 - 8}{1.2/\sqrt{30}} \approx -2.280$$

- **Step 5: Find the P-value**
  - Using a t-distribution table or software, the p-value corresponding to $t = -2.280$ for 29 degrees of freedom.

```
# Python code to calculate p-value
import scipy.stats as stats
t_statistic = -2.280
df = 29
p_value = stats.t.cdf(t_statistic, df)
print(p_value)
```

```
Output:
0.0143
```

- The p-value is approximately 0.0143.

- **Step 6: Make a Decision**
  - Since the p-value (0.0143) is less than α (0.05), we reject the null hypothesis. There is sufficient evidence to conclude that the mean reduction in blood pressure is less than 8 mmHg.

Hypothesis testing provides a rigorous method to evaluate claims about population parameters through sample data analysis. Understanding and correctly applying hypothesis tests is essential for making valid inferences and decisions in data science.

5.10 Confidence Intervals

Confidence intervals provide a range of values that are used to estimate the true value of a population parameter. They are widely used in inferential statistics to express the degree of uncertainty or certainty in a sampling method. A confidence interval gives an estimated range of values which is likely to include an unknown population parameter, with the percentage of intervals (constructed from same-sized samples from the same population) expected to contain the parameter.

Formally, for a given confidence level (e.g., 95%), the confidence interval is computed from the sample data and is structured as:

$$\text{Confidence Interval} = \left(\hat{\theta} - \text{Margin of Error}, \hat{\theta} + \text{Margin of Error}\right)$$

where $\hat{\theta}$ is the sample statistic estimating the population parameter θ, and the margin of error depends on the standard error of the sample statistic and the critical value from the sampling distribution.

Constructing Confidence Intervals

To construct a confidence interval for a population mean μ, typically the following steps are involved:

- Calculate the Sample Mean ($\bar{x}$): This is the average value of the sample which serves as the point estimate for the population mean.

- Determine the Sample Standard Deviation (s): This measures the dispersion of sample data points around the sample mean.
- Compute the Standard Error (SE): For the sample mean, the standard error is given by:
$$SE = \frac{s}{\sqrt{n}}$$
where n is the sample size.
- Find the Critical Value (z or t): Based on the desired confidence level and depending on the sample size (large or small sample), you will use either the z-score (for large samples, $n > 30$) or t-score (for small samples, $n \leq 30$ with degrees of freedom, $df = n - 1$).
- Calculate the Margin of Error (ME): The margin of error is derived by multiplying the critical value by the standard error:
$$ME = z \times SE \quad \text{or} \quad ME = t \times SE$$
- Determine the Confidence Interval: Finally, construct the confidence interval as:
$$(\bar{x} - ME, \bar{x} + ME)$$

Example

Suppose we have a sample of 50 data points from a larger population, and we wish to construct a 95% confidence interval for the population mean. Let's assume the sample mean ($\bar{x}$) is 120, and the sample standard deviation (s) is 15.

- Calculate standard error (SE):
$$SE = \frac{15}{\sqrt{50}} \approx 2.12$$
- For a 95% confidence level and a large sample size, the critical z-value is approximately 1.96.
- Compute the Margin of Error (ME):
$$ME = 1.96 \times 2.12 \approx 4.15$$
- Construct the 95% confidence interval:
$$CI = (120 - 4.15, 120 + 4.15) = (115.85, 124.15)$$

This means we can be 95% confident that the true population mean μ lies between 115.85 and 124.15.

Interpreting Confidence Intervals

One common misinterpretation of confidence intervals is to believe that the interval covers 95% of the data. Instead, the correct interpretation is that 95% of such constructed intervals from repeated sampling would contain the true population parameter. The confidence level itself reflects how sure we are that the method produces intervals that will cover the true parameter.

Another critical aspect is that as the sample size increases, the width of the confidence interval decreases, yielding a more precise estimate of the population parameter. Conversely, a higher confidence level (e.g., 99%) would result in a wider interval, indicating a greater degree of certainty for the population parameter placement but less precision in the estimate.

Confidence Intervals for Proportions

When dealing with proportions, the confidence interval is constructed similarly but uses a different formula. For a population proportion p, the sample proportion $\hat{p}$ is used as the point estimate, and the standard error is given by:

$$SE = \sqrt{\frac{\hat{p}(1-\hat{p})}{n}}$$

Then, the confidence interval for the proportion is:

$$(\hat{p} - z \times SE, \hat{p} + z \times SE)$$

For example, if a survey of 100 individuals finds that 60% prefer a new product, to find the 95% confidence interval for the population proportion, we proceed as follows:

- Sample proportion ($\hat{p}$) is 0.60 and sample size n is 100.
- Compute standard error (SE):

$$SE = \sqrt{\frac{0.60(1-0.60)}{100}} = \sqrt{\frac{0.24}{100}} = 0.049$$

- For a 95% confidence level, the z-value is 1.96.
- Calculate the Margin of Error (ME):

$$ME = 1.96 \times 0.049 \approx 0.096$$

- Construct the confidence interval:

$$CI = (0.60 - 0.096, 0.60 + 0.096) = (0.504, 0.696)$$

This means we are 95% confident that the true proportion of individuals who prefer the new product lies between 50.4% and 69.6%.

The concepts presented here on confidence intervals are foundational in statistics and data science, providing critical tools for making inferences about populations based on sample data. The computation and interpretation of confidence intervals should be carefully carried out to ensure accurate and meaningful conclusions.

5.11 Correlation and Causation

Understanding the concepts of correlation and causation is fundamental in data science as these concepts drive much of the interpretation and conclusion derived from data analysis. Correlation measures the statistical relationship between two variables, while causation indicates a cause-and-effect relationship. Analyzing data correctly requires knowing the distinction and correctly identifying the nature of the relationship.

Correlation is a statistical measure that describes the size and direction of a relationship between two or more variables. Correlation coefficients range from -1 to 1:

- A correlation coefficient close to 1 implies a strong positive relationship.
- A correlation coefficient close to -1 implies a strong negative relationship.
- A correlation coefficient close to 0 implies no relationship.

The Pearson correlation coefficient (ρ) is one of the most widely used measures of linear correlation. It is defined as:

$$\rho_{X,Y} = \frac{\text{Cov}(X, Y)}{\sigma_X \sigma_Y}$$

where Cov(X, Y) is the covariance of variables X and Y, and σ_X and σ_Y are the standard deviations of X and Y, respectively.

```
import numpy as np

# Sample data
x = np.array([10, 20, 30, 40, 50])
y = np.array([12, 24, 33, 47, 56])

# Calculating Pearson correlation
correlation = np.corrcoef(x, y)[0, 1]
print(correlation)
```

```
0.9941942291456817
```

Causation implies that one event is the result of the occurrence of the other event; i.e., there is a causal relationship between the two events. Determining causation typically requires more comprehensive data analysis, such as experiments or longitudinal studies.

One common fallacy is the assumption that correlation implies causation. A high correlation between two variables does not necessarily mean that one causes the other. Several factors can cause a correlated relationship without a direct causal link, such as:

- **Confounding Variables**: A third variable may be influencing both the correlated variables.
- **Reverse Causation**: The direction of causality might be opposite from what is assumed.
- **Coincidence**: The correlation might be due to random chance.

A classic example involves the correlation between ice cream sales and drowning incidents. Both may rise during the summer due to warmer weather, but buying ice cream does not cause drowning.

To establish causation, several methods can be employed:

- **Randomized Controlled Trials (RCTs)**: Participants are randomly assigned to a treatment or control group to eliminate bias and account for confounding variables.
- **Longitudinal Studies**: Observing a subject over a long period can help identify temporal relationships.
- **Instrumental Variables**: When random assignment is unethical or impractical, instrumental variables can help isolate the causal relationship.

A formal framework to address causation is the use of Directed Acyclic Graphs (DAGs). In this approach, graphs are used to represent causal relationships where nodes represent variables and the directional edges represent causal influence. DAGs help model how variables are related and identify potential confounding variables.

```
import networkx as nx
import matplotlib.pyplot as plt

# Create a Directed Acyclic Graph (DAG)
G = nx.DiGraph()
G.add_edges_from([('Temperature', 'Ice Cream Sales'),
                  ('Temperature', 'Drowning Incidents')])

# Draw the graph
pos = nx.spring_layout(G)
nx.draw(G, pos, with_labels=True, node_color='skyblue', node_size=2000, edge_color
    ='black', linewidths=2, font_size=15)
plt.show()
```

This code results in a directed graph where the "Temperature" variable influences both "Ice Cream Sales" and "Drowning Incidents", illustrating the concept of a confounding variable.

Understanding the difference between correlation and causation and the methods to establish causation is crucial in data science to make valid inferences and decisions based on data analysis. Careful consideration must be taken to avoid the pitfalls of conflating correlation with causation, ensuring that conclusions drawn from the data are scientifically sound.

5.12 Regression Analysis

Regression analysis is a statistical methodology that offers a comprehensive understanding of the relationships between variables. This technique is crucial for constructing predictive models, uncovering trends, and making informed decisions based on data. The primary objective of regression analysis is to examine the relationship between a dependent variable, often referred to as the response variable, and one or more independent variables, occasionally called predictor variables.

The most common type of regression analysis is linear regression, which models the relationship between two variables by fitting a linear equation to the observed data. Let's denote the dependent variable by Y and the independent variable by X. The simple linear regression model can be represented as:

$$Y = \beta_0 + \beta_1 X + \epsilon$$

Here, β_0 is the y-intercept, β_1 is the slope of the regression line, and ϵ represents the error term, which accounts for the variability in Y that cannot be explained by the linear relationship with X. The parameters β_0 and β_1 are estimated from the data using the method of least squares, which minimizes the sum of the squared differences between the observed values and the values predicted by the model.

The least squares estimates of β_0 and β_1 are given by:

$$\hat{\beta}_1 = \frac{\sum_{i=1}^{n}(X_i - \bar{X})(Y_i - \bar{Y})}{\sum_{i=1}^{n}(X_i - \bar{X})^2}$$

$$\hat{\beta}_0 = \bar{Y} - \hat{\beta}_1 \bar{X}$$

Where $\bar{X}$ and $\bar{Y}$ are the means of the independent and dependent variables, respectively. The fitted regression model can be expressed as:

$$\hat{Y} = \hat{\beta}_0 + \hat{\beta}_1 X$$

To assess the goodness of fit of the regression model, we use the coefficient of determination, denoted as R^2. The R^2 value indicates the proportion of the variance in the dependent variable that is predictable from the independent variable. It ranges from 0 to 1, with higher values indicating a better fit. The formula for R^2 is:

$$R^2 = 1 - \frac{\sum_{i=1}^{n}(Y_i - \hat{Y}_i)^2}{\sum_{i=1}^{n}(Y_i - \bar{Y})^2}$$

Where $\hat{Y}_i$ represents the predicted values of Y.

A critical aspect of regression analysis is the interpretation of the coefficients. The slope β_1 signifies the change in the dependent variable for a one-unit change in the independent variable, assuming all other factors remain constant. The intercept β_0 represents the expected value of Y when X is zero.

In multiple regression analysis, more than one independent variable is considered to predict the dependent variable. The multiple linear regression model extends the simple linear regression model and is represented as:

$$Y = \beta_0 + \beta_1 X_1 + \beta_2 X_2 + \cdots + \beta_p X_p + \epsilon$$

Here, $X_1, X_2, \ldots, X_p$ are the independent variables, and $\beta_0, \beta_1, \ldots, \beta_p$ are the corresponding coefficients. The least squares method is used to estimate these coefficients by minimizing the sum of the squared errors.

The assumptions underlying linear regression analysis include linearity, independence, homoscedasticity, and normality of residuals. Linearity implies that the relationship between the dependent and independent variables is linear. Independence assumes that the observations are independent of each other. Homoscedasticity means that the variance of the errors is constant across all levels of the independent variables. Normality of residuals suggests that the errors are normally distributed.

Violations of these assumptions can lead to biased estimates and incorrect inferences. Therefore, it is essential to diagnose potential violations and apply remedial measures. Common diagnostic tools include residual plots, the Durbin-Watson test for independence, and the Breusch-Pagan test for homoscedasticity.

In practical applications, regression analysis can be carried out using statistical software such as R, Python, or SAS. Below is an example of performing linear regression using Python with the libraries 'pandas' and 'statsmodels':

```
import pandas as pd
import statsmodels.api as sm

# Load data
data = pd.read_csv('data.csv')

# Define dependent and independent variables
X = data['independent_var']
Y = data['dependent_var']

# Add a constant term to the independent variable matrix
X = sm.add_constant(X)

# Fit the model
model = sm.OLS(Y, X).fit()

# Print the model summary
print(model.summary())
```

The output of this code will provide a detailed summary of the regression analysis, including coefficient estimates, their statistical significance, R^2-value, and diagnostics for assumptions.

```
                    OLS Regression Results
==============================================================================
Dep. Variable:           dependent_var   R-squared:                   0.678
Model:                             OLS   Adj. R-squared:              0.675
Method:                  Least Squares   F-statistic:                 234.5
Date:                 Fri, 17 Feb 2023   Prob (F-statistic):        <0.0001
Time:                         14:32:45   Log-Likelihood:            -1234.5
No. Observations:                  350   AIC:                          2473
Df Residuals:                      348   BIC:                          2481
Df Model:                            1
Covariance Type:             nonrobust
==============================================================================
                  coef    std err          t      P>|t|      [0.025      0.975]
------------------------------------------------------------------------------
const            4.543      0.678      6.698      0.000       3.210       5.876
independent_var  0.876      0.057     15.312      0.000       0.763       0.989
==============================================================================
Omnibus:                        15.678   Durbin-Watson:               1.998
Prob(Omnibus):                   0.001   Jarque-Bera (JB):           16.230
Skew:                            0.573   Prob(JB):                 0.000293
Kurtosis:                        2.798   Cond. No.                     45.7
==============================================================================
```

Based on the output, we can interpret the results and assess the model's effectiveness in explaining the variability in the dependent variable. The statistical significance of the coefficients can be evaluated using the p-values provided in the summary, and the goodness of fit can be assessed using the R^2-value.

Regression analysis is not limited to linear models. Other types of regression, such as polynomial regression, logistic regression, and ridge regression, extend the technique to more complex scenarios. Polynomial regression models the relationship between the dependent and independent variables as an n-th degree polynomial. Logistic regression predicts a binary outcome by modeling the log-odds of the probability of occurrence. Ridge regression addresses multicollinearity by adding a penalty term to the least squares objective.

Understanding and applying regression analysis provides critical insights into data and supports robust decision-making processes. The ability to accurately model and interpret relationships between variables is foundational for any data scientist.

5.13 Bayesian Statistics

Bayesian statistics represents a paradigm in the field of statistics that allows us to incorporate prior knowledge or beliefs, updating these as new data becomes available. This approach is contrasted with frequentist statistics, which only uses the data at hand, not taking into account any prior beliefs.

In Bayesian statistics, the core concept involves updating a prior belief (prior distribution) with new evidence (likelihood) to obtain a revised belief (posterior distribution). This process is mathematically formalized through Bayes' theorem, which is pivotal to Bayesian inference.

Bayes' Theorem

Bayes' theorem provides a mechanism to update the probability estimate for a hypothesis as more evidence or data becomes available. Mathematically, it is expressed as:

$$P(H|E) = \frac{P(E|H)P(H)}{P(E)}$$

where:

- $P(H|E)$ is the posterior probability of the hypothesis H given the evidence E.
- $P(E|H)$ is the likelihood, the probability of evidence E given that H is true.
- $P(H)$ is the prior probability of the hypothesis H.
- $P(E)$ is the probability of the evidence E.

Prior Distribution

The prior distribution, $P(H)$, represents the initial belief about the parameters before observing the data. This belief could arise from past studies, expert opinion, or other sources of information. The prior can be subjective and often plays a crucial role in Bayesian analysis. Priors can be classified into different types:

- Informative priors incorporate specific, strong beliefs.
- Non-informative or weak priors exert minimal influence on the posterior distribution, allowing the data to dominate the analysis.
- Conjugate priors are chosen for their mathematical convenience, leading to a posterior distribution that belongs to the same family as the prior.

Likelihood

The likelihood, $P(E|H)$, reflects the plausibility of the observed data under different parameter values. In Bayesian inference, this is the same likelihood function used in frequentist methods. It quantifies how well the hypothesized model explains the observed data.

Posterior Distribution

The posterior distribution, $P(H|E)$, combines the prior distribution with the likelihood, producing a revised belief after considering the evidence. This distribution is a fundamental component of Bayesian analysis as it encapsulates all updated probabilities given the data.

Key Steps in Bayesian Inference

To perform Bayesian inference, one follows these steps:

- Define the Prior Distribution: Select an appropriate prior distribution based on either domain knowledge or mathematical convenience.
- Calculate the Likelihood: Determine the likelihood of the observed data under different parameter values.
- Apply Bayes' Theorem: Use Bayes' theorem to update the prior distribution with the likelihood, obtaining the posterior distribution.
- Summarize the Posterior Distribution: Derive point estimates, credible intervals, and interpret the posterior distribution for insights.

```
import numpy as np
from scipy.stats import norm, gamma

# Define the prior: Gamma distribution for precision (inverse of variance)
a, scale = 3.0, 1/2.0
prior = gamma(a, scale=scale)

# Simulate some data: Observations from a normal distribution
data = np.random.normal(loc=5, scale=2, size=100)

# Define the likelihood: Normal distribution
mu = np.mean(data)
precision = prior.rvs() # Sample precision from prior
likelihood = norm(loc=mu, scale=1/np.sqrt(precision))

# Update the posterior (numerically updating)
posterior_mean = (np.sum(data) / len(data))
posterior_scale = (1 / np.sqrt(len(data)))
posterior = norm(loc=posterior_mean, scale=posterior_scale)

print(f"Posterior Mean: {posterior.mean()}, Posterior Std: {posterior.std()}")
```

The code above illustrates the basic steps of Bayesian inference in Python: defining prior distribution, simulating data, computing likelihood, and updating to find the posterior distribution.

Posterior Predictive Distribution

An essential aspect of Bayesian statistics is the posterior predictive distribution, which allows prediction of new observations. This distribution is derived by integrating over the posterior distribution of the parameters. It reflects the uncertainty in both the parameter estimates and the new data.

$$P(E_{new}|E) = \int P(E_{new}|\theta)P(\theta|E)d\theta$$

This integral often requires numerical methods such as Markov Chain Monte Carlo (MCMC) for complex models.

Bayesian Model Comparison

Bayesian methods also facilitate model comparison through the use of Bayes factors or posterior probabilities of models. Given two models, M_1 and M_2, the Bayes factor B_{12} is the ratio of their marginal likelihoods:

$$B_{12} = \frac{P(E|M_1)}{P(E|M_2)}$$

A Bayes factor greater than one indicates evidence in favor of M_1 relative to M_2.

Bayesian statistics provides a powerful framework for data analysis, enabling the incorporation of prior information and yielding a comprehensive probabilistic understanding of the parameters and predictions. Though computationally intensive, modern computational techniques have made Bayesian methods increasingly accessible and practical.

Chapter 6

Machine Learning Basics

This chapter introduces fundamental concepts in machine learning, distinguishing between supervised and unsupervised learning. It outlines the machine learning workflow, covering data splitting for training, validation, and testing. Key algorithms, such as linear regression, logistic regression, decision trees, K-Nearest Neighbors (KNN), and Support Vector Machines (SVM), are discussed. The chapter also explains essential evaluation metrics for classification and regression tasks, and explores cross-validation techniques to ensure model reliability.

6.1 Introduction to Machine Learning

Machine learning (ML) is a subset of artificial intelligence (AI) that focuses on the development of algorithms that enable computers to learn from and make predictions or decisions based on data. This section provides a comprehensive introduction to the core concepts, goals, and types of machine learning, setting the stage for further detailed discussions in subsequent sections.

Machine learning can be broadly defined as the process of training a model using a dataset so that it can make intelligent predictions or decisions when exposed to new data. Central to this process is the ability of the algorithms to improve their performance over time as they get exposed to more data.

Core Concepts:

- **Data**: The foundational element of any machine learning process. Data can come in various forms such as numerical, categorical, textual, or visual. For models to be effective, data must be collected, cleansed, and preprocessed appropriately.
- **Algorithms**: These are mathematical structures that facilitate learning from data. Algorithms form the groundwork upon which models are built.
- **Models**: Models are the outcomes of the machine learning process after training. They represent the learned patterns or relationships within the data.
- **Training**: The phase where the model learns from the data through the application of algorithms.
- **Evaluation**: Assessing the model's performance using various metrics to ensure its accuracy and reliability on unseen data.

Goals of Machine Learning:

- **Prediction**: Predict future outcomes based on historical data, such as predicting stock prices or weather conditions.
- **Classification**: Assigning categories to data points, similar to classifying emails as spam or not spam.
- **Clustering**: Grouping data points based on similarities without predefined labels, like customer segmentation.
- **Anomaly Detection**: Identifying outliers or unusual patterns in data, which is useful in fraud detection.
- **Recommendation Systems**: Suggesting products or content to users based on their preferences and behavior.

Machine learning can be classified into three main types based on the nature of the learning signal or feedback available to a learning system:

Supervised Learning: In supervised learning, each training example is paired with an output label. The task of the algorithm is to learn the mapping from inputs to outputs to be able to predict the output given a new input. This paradigm includes both classification and regression tasks.

```
# Example algorithm for supervised learning: Linear Regression in Python
from sklearn.linear_model import LinearRegression

# Example data
X = [[1], [2], [3], [4], [5]] # Feature - input data
y = [1.5, 3.5, 4.5, 6.0, 7.5] # Label - output data

# Create Linear Regression model
model = LinearRegression()

# Train the model
model.fit(X, y)

# Making a prediction
predicted = model.predict([[6]])
print(predicted) # Output: array([8.55])
```

Unsupervised Learning: In unsupervised learning, the algorithm is given data without labeled responses and it attempts to discover the structure of the data. Clustering and association are primary tasks.

```
# Example algorithm for unsupervised learning: K-Means Clustering in Python
from sklearn.cluster import KMeans

# Example data
X = [[1, 2], [1, 4], [1, 0], [10, 2], [10, 4], [10, 0]]

# Create KMeans model
kmeans = KMeans(n_clusters=2, random_state=0)

# Train the model
kmeans.fit(X)

# Predicted clusters
clusters = kmeans.predict(X)
print(clusters) # Output: array([1, 1, 1, 0, 0, 0])
```

Reinforcement Learning: Different from supervised and unsupervised learning, reinforcement learning allows an agent to learn in an interactive environment by trial and error using feedback from its own actions and experiences. The goal is to maximize a cumulative reward.

```
# Placeholder for a reinforcement learning example, as this often involves extensive
    environments and learning loops
```

Understanding these fundamental concepts and distinctions is crucial for delving deeper into the specific methodologies and applications of machine learning. The upcoming sections will build on this foundation, exploring various algorithms, techniques, and best practices for applying machine learning effectively.

6.2 Supervised vs. Unsupervised Learning

In machine learning, algorithms are often categorized based on the type of tasks they are designed to perform. Two primary categories that encompass a significant portion of machine learning tasks are supervised learning and unsupervised learning. Understanding the differences between these categories is crucial for selecting the appropriate algorithm for a given dataset and problem.

Supervised learning is characterized by the presence of a labeled dataset. In this type of learning, the algorithm is trained on input-output pairs, where the output, also known as the target or label, is provided for each input example in the training dataset. The goal of supervised learning is to learn a mapping from inputs to outputs that can be generalized to new, unseen data. This type of learning is further subdivided into classification and regression tasks.

- Classification problems involve predicting a discrete label for a given input. For instance, in an email spam detection system, the input might be the content of an email, and the label could be either "spam" or "not spam." Supervised learning algorithms for classification include decision trees, logistic regression, support vector machines, and neural networks. These algorithms learn to discriminate between different classes based on the features present in the input data.
- Regression problems, on the other hand, involve predicting a continuous value for a given input. An example of a regression task would be predicting the price of a house based on various features like size, location, and number of rooms. Algorithms for regression include linear regression, polynomial regression, and support vector regression. These algorithms learn to model the relationship between input features and the continuous target variable.

Unsupervised learning, in contrast, deals with datasets that do not have labeled responses. The goal of unsupervised learning is to uncover hidden patterns or intrinsic structures from the input data. This type of learning is often used for clustering, association, and dimensionality reduction tasks.

- Clustering is a common unsupervised learning task where the objective is to group similar data points together based on their features. An example of clustering would be segmenting customers into different groups based on their purchasing behavior. Each group, or cluster, represents a set of customers with similar characteristics. Popular clustering algorithms include K-means, hierarchical clustering, and DBSCAN.

- Association tasks involve discovering interesting relationships between variables in large datasets. Market basket analysis is a typical example, where the goal is to find associations between products purchased together. This information can be used for cross-selling and recommendation systems. Algorithms employed for association tasks include the Apriori algorithm and Eclat algorithm.

- Dimensionality reduction aims to reduce the number of random variables under consideration, making the dataset easier to visualize and computationally less expensive to handle. Techniques such as Principal Component Analysis (PCA) and t-Distributed Stochastic Neighbor Embedding (t-SNE) are extensively used for dimensionality reduction. These techniques help in extracting important features and eliminating redundancy from the data.

To better illustrate the differences between supervised and unsupervised learning, consider the following Python code snippets. The first snippet demonstrates a simple supervised learning task using a linear regression model to predict house prices.

```
import numpy as np
from sklearn.model_selection import train_test_split
from sklearn.linear_model import LinearRegression
from sklearn.metrics import mean_squared_error

# Example data
X = np.array([[1400, 3], [1600, 4], [1700, 5], [1875, 3], [1100, 2]])
y = np.array([245000, 312000, 279000, 308000, 199000])

# Split data into training and testing sets
X_train, X_test, y_train, y_test = train_test_split(X, y, test_size=0.2,
    random_state=42)

# Train the model
model = LinearRegression()
model.fit(X_train, y_train)

# Make predictions
y_pred = model.predict(X_test)

# Evaluate the model
mse = mean_squared_error(y_test, y_pred)
print(f"Mean Squared Error: {mse}")
```

The output of the above code snippet:

```
Mean Squared Error: 108900000.0
```

Next, consider an unsupervised learning task using K-means clustering to group customers based on their purchasing behavior.

```
import numpy as np
from sklearn.cluster import KMeans
import matplotlib.pyplot as plt

# Example data: annual income and spending score
X = np.array([[15, 39], [15, 81], [16, 6], [16, 77], [17, 40], [17, 76], [18, 6], [18, 94]])

# Apply K-means clustering
kmeans = KMeans(n_clusters=2, random_state=42)
clusters = kmeans.fit_predict(X)

# Plot the results
plt.scatter(X[:, 0], X[:, 1], c=clusters, cmap='viridis')
plt.xlabel('Annual Income')
plt.ylabel('Spending Score')
plt.title('Customer Segments')
plt.show()
```

The visualization resulting from the above code snippet:

```
[Scatter plot showing customer segments with distinct colors]
```

By examining both code snippets, it is evident that supervised and unsupervised learning cater to different types of problems, and the choice between them depends on the nature of the data and the specific objectives of the analysis. Understanding these distinctions allows practitioners to deploy the most suitable algorithms, thereby enhancing the effectiveness and accuracy of their machine learning models.

6.3 Key Concepts in Machine Learning

Machine learning encapsulates several fundamental concepts that are indispensable for understanding how algorithms operate, how models are constructed, and how they are evaluated. These concepts form the backbone of any machine learning task and provide the necessary foundation for more advanced topics. Key components discussed herein include feature selection, overfitting and underfitting, bias-variance tradeoff, and the concept of regularization.

- Feature selection is the process of identifying the most relevant features in the dataset that contribute to the predictive power of the model. This step often involves domain knowledge, statistical tests, and algorithmic techniques such as Recursive Feature Elimination (RFE) and Principal Component Analysis (PCA). Feature selection is crucial not only for improving model performance but also for reducing computational costs.

- Overfitting occurs when a machine learning model learns the noise in the training data alongside the underlying patterns. Such a model will perform exceptionally well on the training data but poorly on unseen data, indicating a lack of generalization. Conversely, underfitting happens when the model is too simplistic to capture the underlying patterns in the training data, leading to poor performance on both the training and testing datasets.
- The bias-variance tradeoff is a central issue in supervised learning, balancing model complexity and predictive accuracy. High bias refers to errors due to overly simplistic models that cannot capture the complexities of the data (underfitting), while high variance refers to errors due to models that are too complex and sensitive to the noise in the training data (overfitting). The goal is to find a balance where both bias and variance are minimized.
- Regularization techniques are employed to prevent overfitting by discouraging overly complex models. Common regularization methods include L1 regularization (Lasso), which adds an absolute value of the magnitude of coefficients as a penalty term, and L2 regularization (Ridge), which adds the squared magnitude of coefficients as a penalty term to the loss function.

The following Python example demonstrates linear regression with L2 regularization using Scikit-learn:

```
from sklearn.linear_model import Ridge
from sklearn.model_selection import train_test_split
from sklearn.metrics import mean_squared_error

# Assume X and y are predefined as data and target variables
X_train, X_test, y_train, y_test = train_test_split(X, y, test_size=0.2,
    random_state=42)

model = Ridge(alpha=1.0)
model.fit(X_train, y_train)

predictions = model.predict(X_test)
mse = mean_squared_error(y_test, predictions)
print(f"Mean Squared Error: {mse}")
```

When executed, this code produces:

```
Mean Squared Error: 25.1234
```

Hyperparameter tuning refers to the process of optimizing the parameters that govern the training process of an algorithm, which are not learned from the data. These parameters might include the learning rate, the number of trees in a random forest, or the penalty term in regularization methods. Techniques such as Grid Search and Random Search are often employed to find the optimal combination of hyperparameters.

Cross-validation, introduced in a subsequent section, allows for a more reliable model evaluation by ensuring that the model's performance is assessed across multiple subsets of the data. Common techniques include k-fold cross-validation and leave-one-out cross-validation.

The learning rate represents how much the model's parameters are adjusted with each iteration of the training process. In gradient-based optimization algorithms, such as Gradient Descent, the learning rate is crucial for whether the model converges to a minimum or oscillates around it.

The concept of a validation set is vital for hyperparameter tuning and model assessment. By setting apart a portion of the training data to validate the model's performance, it is possible to ensure that the hyperparameters are not simply being tuned to the training set, thus avoiding overfitting.

A confusion matrix is used to evaluate the performance of a classification model. It provides a comprehensive view of how well the model distinguishes between different classes by counting true positives, true negatives, false positives, and false negatives.

Model evaluation metrics for regression tasks, such as Mean Squared Error (MSE) and R-squared, quantify how well the predictions match the actual data. MSE measures the average squared difference between predictions and actual outcomes, while R-squared indicates the proportion of the variance in the dependent variable that is predictable from the independent variables.

Ensemble methods, which involve combining multiple machine learning models to improve performance, include techniques like bagging, boosting, and stacking. Bagging methods, such as Random Forest, reduce variance by averaging predictions of multiple models trained on different samples of the data. Boosting methods, like AdaBoost and Gradient Boosting, sequentially train models to correct the errors of the previous model, enhancing performance.

Clustering algorithms like K-means and hierarchical clustering fall under unsupervised learning, aiming to group data points into clusters based on similarity. K-means requires pre-specification of the number of clusters, while hierarchical clustering builds a tree of clusters without needing to specify the number.

Reinforcement learning involves training agents to make sequences of decisions by rewarding desirable actions and penalizing undesirable ones. This learning paradigm is markedly different in how it handles the interaction of the agent with the environment.

These concepts collectively build a robust foundation for understanding and mastering machine learning techniques, serving as the groundwork upon which more specific methodologies and algorithms are developed. Understanding each concept thoroughly is essential to effectively apply machine learning to real-world problems.

6.4 Machine Learning Workflow

The machine learning workflow encompasses a series of well-defined steps necessary to develop a robust predictive model. These steps ensure that the model not only performs well on the training data but also generalizes effectively to new, unseen data. Here, the workflow will be elaborated upon, detailing each stage from problem definition to model deployment.

Problem Definition and Objective Setting: The initial stage involves defining the problem clearly and setting a specific objective. This includes identifying the type of problem (e.g., classification or regression) and the desired outcome. A well-defined problem helps in selecting appropriate algorithms and evaluation metrics.

Data Collection: Data collection is critical as the quality and quantity of data significantly impact the model's performance. Data can be gathered from various sources such as databases, APIs, or web scraping. Ensuring that the data is relevant, sufficient, and representative of the problem domain is essential.

Data Preprocessing and Cleaning: Raw data often contains noise, missing values, and inconsistencies. Data preprocessing involves cleaning the data to remove or correct such issues. This stage may include techniques such as handling missing values, removing duplicates, correcting errors, and normalizing or standardizing data.

Exploratory Data Analysis (EDA): EDA is the process of analyzing the data sets to summarize their main characteristics. Visualization techniques and summary statistics are employed to understand data distributions, relationships among variables, and detect potential outliers or anomalies. Tools like histograms, scatter plots, or correlation matrices are commonly used.

Feature Engineering: Feature engineering involves creating new features or modifying existing ones to improve model performance. This can include techniques like encoding categorical variables, deriving new features from existing ones, or selecting a subset of relevant features. Feature scaling may also be applied to ensure that all features contribute equally to the model training.

Data Splitting: Splitting the data into training, validation, and test sets is a critical step to evaluate the model's performance at different stages. Typically, the data is divided as follows:

- **Training Set:** Used to train the model.
- **Validation Set:** Used for model selection and hyperparameter tuning.
- **Test Set:** Used to evaluate the final model's performance.

Model Selection: Choosing the appropriate model involves understanding the problem requirements and selecting an algorithm that suits those needs. Various factors such as model complexity, interpretability, and computational efficiency are considered. Common algorithms include linear regression, decision trees, and support vector machines, among others.

Model Training: During this stage, the selected model is trained on the training data. This involves feeding the data into the algorithm and adjusting its parameters to minimize the error between the predicted and actual outcomes. The training process may vary depending on the complexity of the algorithm and the size of the dataset.

Hyperparameter Tuning: Hyperparameters are settings that cannot be learned directly from the data but are set prior to the training process. Tuning these parameters is critical for optimizing model performance. Techniques such as grid search, random search, or Bayesian optimization can be employed to find the best hyperparameters.

Model Evaluation: Evaluating the model's performance involves using the validation and test sets to measure how well the model generalizes to new data. Key metrics such as accuracy, precision, recall, F1 score (for classification), or mean squared error (MSE) and R-squared (for regression) are used. Evaluation helps identify any overfitting or underfitting of the model.

Model Optimization: Based on the evaluation results, further modifications may be required to improve the model. This could involve tweaking the feature engineering process, selecting different algorithms, or adjusting the hyperparameters. The optimization process is iterative and aims to enhance model performance progressively.

Model Deployment: Once a satisfactory model is obtained, it is deployed into a production environment where it can make predictions on new data. Model deployment involves integrating the model into existing systems, ensuring scalability, and setting up monitoring mechanisms to track its performance over time.

Monitoring and Maintenance: Continuous monitoring of the deployed model is essential to ensure its performance remains consistent. Regular maintenance, including retraining the model with new data, addressing any concept drift, and updating features as necessary, ensures the model adapts to changes in the data distribution.

Below is a sample Python code demonstrating a simplified machine learning workflow using a decision tree classifier:

```
# Import necessary libraries
import pandas as pd
from sklearn.model_selection import train_test_split
from sklearn.preprocessing import StandardScaler
from sklearn.tree import DecisionTreeClassifier
from sklearn.metrics import accuracy_score

# Load data
data = pd.read_csv('dataset.csv')

# Data preprocessing
# Handle missing values
data.fillna(method='ffill', inplace=True)

# Feature engineering
features = pd.get_dummies(data.drop(['target'], axis=1))
target = data['target']

# Data splitting
X_train, X_test, y_train, y_test = train_test_split(features, target, test_size=0.2,
    random_state=42)

# Feature scaling
scaler = StandardScaler()
X_train = scaler.fit_transform(X_train)
X_test = scaler.transform(X_test)

# Model selection and training
model = DecisionTreeClassifier(max_depth=3, random_state=42)
model.fit(X_train, y_train)
```

```
# Model evaluation
y_pred = model.predict(X_test)
accuracy = accuracy_score(y_test, y_pred)

print(f'Accuracy: {accuracy:.2f}')
```

And an example of the output from the above code might be:

```
Accuracy: 0.85
```

The outlined workflow ensures a comprehensive approach to building machine learning models, facilitating improved performance and reliable deployment.

6.5 Data Splitting: Training, Validation, and Testing

Effective data management is an essential component of machine learning, where appropriate data splitting ensures unbiased evaluation and generalizability of models. This section delves into the importance and methodology of data splitting into training, validation, and testing subsets.

- **Training Set:** The primary function of the training set is model learning. This consists of input-output pairs used by the algorithm to learn data patterns. The model adjusts its parameters by minimizing the loss function on the training set, iteratively improving performance using techniques like gradient descent.
- **Validation Set:** The validation set serves as a proxy for prediction performance evaluation during the model building phase. It facilitates hyperparameter tuning and model selection by monitoring performance on unseen data, helping prevent overfitting. Hyperparameters, unlike model parameters, are set prior to the learning process and include regularization terms (λ for ridge regression), learning rates, and depths of trees in decision forests.
- **Test Set:** The test set is reserved for final evaluation. It acts as an unbiased dataset to assess the generalization capability of the model. Performance metrics such as accuracy, precision, recall, or mean squared error are calculated on this set to deliver an objective evaluation of the model before deployment in real-world applications.

- **Splitting Ratios:** Common data splitting ratios include 70-15-15, 60-20-20, or 80-10-10 for training, validation, and test sets respectively. The choice of ratio often depends on data availability and application-specific constraints.

- **Implementation:** Below is an example of data splitting using Python's scikit-learn library, which provides utilities for creating robust training, validation, and test sets.

```
from sklearn.model_selection import train_test_split

# Assume data and target contain our dataset and corresponding labels
X_train, X_temp, y_train, y_temp = train_test_split(data, target, test_size=0.3,
    random_state=42)
X_val, X_test, y_val, y_test = train_test_split(X_temp, y_temp, test_size=0.5,
    random_state=42)
```

- **Explanation:** The train_test_split function first partitions the data into training (70%) and a temporary subset (30%). Subsequently, the temporary subset is split equally into validation (15%) and test (15%) sets to complete the stratified dataset. The random_state parameter ensures reproducibility.

- **Output:**

```
Training set size: len(X_train)
Validation set size: len(X_val)
Test set size: len(X_test)
```

- **Cross-Validation:** A more robust alternative to a fixed validation set is *cross-validation*. It divides the dataset into *k* subsets (folds), and iteratively trains and validates the model *k* times. Each iteration uses *k-1* subsets for training and the remaining subset for validation. In *k-fold* cross-validation, commonly set to *k*=10, each iteration yields insights into the model's variability and average performance, mitigating overfitting risks.

  Below is an illustration of *k-fold* cross-validation using scikit-learn's *cross_val_score* function:

```
from sklearn.model_selection import cross_val_score
from sklearn.linear_model import LinearRegression

model = LinearRegression()
scores = cross_val_score(model, data, target, cv=10)

print("Cross-validation scores: ", scores)
print("Average cross-validation score: ", scores.mean())
```

The iterative process enables the evaluation of model performance metrics across different validation sets, ensuring a comprehensive assessment.

In summary, the partitioning of data into training, validation, and test sets, augmented with techniques like cross-validation, is crucial for developing reliable machine learning models that generalize well to unseen data. Implementing these techniques systematically ensures the integrity of the machine learning pipeline, leading to robust and dependable predictions.

6.6 Linear Regression

Linear regression is one of the simplest and most commonly used algorithms in machine learning. Its primary objective is to model the linear relationship between a dependent variable, usually denoted as y, and one or more independent variables, denoted as X. The fundamental assumption in linear regression is that there exists a linear association between the predictors X and the response y.

The mathematical representation of linear regression can be written as:

$$y = \beta_0 + \beta_1 x_1 + \beta_2 x_2 + \cdots + \beta_n x_n + \epsilon$$

where β_0 is the intercept, $\beta_1, \beta_2, \ldots, \beta_n$ are the coefficients or weights corresponding to each predictor $x_1, x_2, \ldots, x_n$, and ϵ is the error term which accounts for the variability in y that cannot be explained by the linear relationship with X.

To estimate the parameters β (i.e., $\beta_0, \beta_1, \ldots, \beta_n$), the most commonly used method is Ordinary Least Squares (OLS) which aims to minimize the sum of the squared residuals. The residual for a data point i is the difference between the observed value y_i and the predicted value $\hat{y}_i$:

$$\text{Residual}_i = y_i - \hat{y}_i$$

The sum of squared residuals is given by:

$$\text{SSE} = \sum_{i=1}^{m} (y_i - \hat{y}_i)^2$$

Our objective is therefore to minimize SSE. This problem can be expressed in matrix notation. Let $\mathbf{y}$ be the vector of observed responses, $\mathbf{X}$ be the matrix of input features with rows representing training samples and columns representing features, β be the vector of coefficients, and ϵ be the vector of errors. The OLS estimation problem becomes:

$$\mathbf{y} = \mathbf{X}\beta + \epsilon$$

The OLS solution for β can be derived by setting the derivative of the SSE with respect to β to zero and solving for β:

$$\hat{\beta} = (\mathbf{X}^T\mathbf{X})^{-1}\mathbf{X}^T\mathbf{y}$$

The matrix $(\mathbf{X}^T\mathbf{X})^{-1}\mathbf{X}^T$ is referred to as the Moore-Penrose pseudo-inverse of $\mathbf{X}$, and it effectively projects $\mathbf{y}$ onto the column space of $\mathbf{X}$.

Here is an example in Python illustrating the implementation of linear regression using NumPy:

```
import numpy as np

# Generate some example data
X = np.array([[1, 1], [1, 2], [2, 2], [2, 3]])
y = np.dot(X, np.array([1, 2])) + 3

# Adding the intercept term
X = np.hstack([np.ones((X.shape[0], 1)), X])

# Calculate the coefficients using OLS
beta_hat = np.linalg.inv(X.T @ X) @ X.T @ y
print(beta_hat)
```

and its expected output:

```
[3. 1. 2.]
```

This output indicates that the estimated intercept (β_0) is 3, and the coefficients (β_1) and (β_2) are 1 and 2, respectively. These match the underlying relationship we used to generate our data.

The assumptions of linear regression are vital to the performance and interpretation of the model:

- Linearity: The relationship between predictors and the response is linear.
- Independence: The residuals (errors) are independent.
- Homoscedasticity: The residuals have constant variance.

- Normality: The residuals are normally distributed.

Violations of these assumptions can lead to inefficiencies and biases in the parameter estimates. Diagnostic plots and statistical tests can help evaluate these assumptions in practice.

Regularization techniques such as Ridge regression (L2 regularization) and Lasso regression (L1 regularization) address some limitations of OLS by imposing a penalty on the size of the coefficients, which can lead to more robust models especially in settings with multicollinearity or high-dimensional data.

Linear regression provides a strong foundation for understanding more complex models in machine learning, offering both a simple implementation and strong interpretability when the underlying assumptions hold true.

6.7 Logistic Regression

Logistic regression is a quintessential algorithm used for classification tasks in machine learning. It is particularly effective for binary classification problems, where the goal is to assign one of two possible classes to each observation. The term "regression" in its name may be misleading; logistic regression is a classification technique, not a regression technique as in predicting continuous values.

At its core, logistic regression models the probability that a given instance belongs to a particular class. This probability is bounded between 0 and 1, making it suitable for categorical outcomes. The logistic function, also known as the sigmoid function, is used to map the output of a linear equation to this probability range.

The hypothesis function $h_\theta(x)$ in logistic regression is defined as follows:

$$h_\theta(x) = \frac{1}{1 + e^{-\theta^T x}}$$

Here, θ represents the parameters of the model, x is the feature vector, and e is the base of the natural logarithm. The output of this function represents the estimated probability that the observation belongs to the positive class.

For logistic regression, the decision boundary is defined by setting a threshold probability, typically 0.5. If $h_\theta(x) \geq 0.5$, the model predicts the positive class (usually labeled as 1). Otherwise, it predicts the negative class (usually labeled as 0).

The cost function for logistic regression is derived from the likelihood function, with its derivation rooted in the principle of maximum likelihood estimation (MLE). The cost function $J(\theta)$ is given by:

$$J(\theta) = -\frac{1}{m} \sum_{i=1}^{m} \left[y^{(i)} \log(h_\theta(x^{(i)})) + (1 - y^{(i)}) \log(1 - h_\theta(x^{(i)})) \right]$$

In this equation, m is the number of training examples, $y^{(i)}$ is the actual label of the i-th training example, and $h_\theta(x^{(i)})$ is the predicted probability for the i-th training example.

To minimize the cost function and find the optimal parameters θ, we use gradient descent. The gradient descent algorithm updates the parameters iteratively as follows:

$$\theta := \theta - \alpha \frac{\partial}{\partial \theta} J(\theta)$$

where α is the learning rate, a hyperparameter that controls the size of each step in the gradient descent process. The partial derivative of $J(\theta)$ with respect to θ_j is:

$$\frac{\partial}{\partial \theta_j} J(\theta) = \frac{1}{m} \sum_{i=1}^{m} \left(h_\theta(x^{(i)}) - y^{(i)} \right) x_j^{(i)}$$

By repeatedly updating the parameter vector θ according to this rule, we can minimize the cost function and find the best-fit model.

Logistic regression can be easily extended to multi-class classification problems through techniques like One-vs-Rest (OvR) or One-vs-One (OvO). In OvR, for example, we train one classifier per class, with the samples of that class as positive examples and all other samples as negative examples.

Below is an example of how logistic regression can be implemented in Python using the popular library, scikit-learn:

```
from sklearn.linear_model import LogisticRegression
```

```
from sklearn.model_selection import train_test_split
from sklearn.metrics import accuracy_score

# Sample data
X = [[0.5, 1.2], [1.3, 3.4], [3.8, 2.5], [5.5, 4.6], [6.8, 3.1]]
y = [0, 0, 1, 1, 1]

# Split data into training and test sets
X_train, X_test, y_train, y_test = train_test_split(X, y, test_size=0.2,
    random_state=42)

# Initialize the Logistic Regression model
model = LogisticRegression()

# Fit the model to the training data
model.fit(X_train, y_train)

# Make predictions on the test data
y_pred = model.predict(X_test)

# Evaluate the model
accuracy = accuracy_score(y_test, y_pred)
print(f'Accuracy: {accuracy:.2f}')
```

The output of the above script would be:

```
Accuracy: 1.00
```

In this example, the LogisticRegression class from scikit-learn is used to create a logistic regression model. The dataset is split into training and test sets using train_test_split. The model is trained with the fit method, and predictions are made with the predict method. Finally, the model's accuracy is evaluated using the accuracy_score function.

Evaluating logistic regression models extends beyond accuracy, especially in imbalanced datasets. Metrics like precision, recall, F1-score, and the area under the Receiver Operating Characteristic (ROC) curve provide more insights into a model's performance.

The applications of logistic regression are diverse, spanning fields like medicine, social sciences, marketing, and more. It remains a fundamental and valuable tool in a machine learning practitioner's toolkit.

6.8 Decision Trees

Decision Trees are a type of supervised learning algorithm that can be used for both classification and regression tasks. They are intuitive and easy to visualize, making them one of the most popular and powerful tools in a data scientist's arsenal. A decision tree is a flowchart-like structure where an internal node represents a feature (or attribute), a branch represents a decision rule, and each leaf node represents the outcome.

The construction of a decision tree includes selecting the best splits at each node, which is done based on certain criteria to optimize the learning process. For classification tasks, commonly used criteria for split include Gini impurity and entropy. For regression tasks, the mean squared error (MSE) is often used.

The algorithm recursively splits the dataset into subsets based on the feature that results in the best split, continuing until it reaches a stopping condition, such as the maximum depth of the tree or until no further improvement can be made.

Algorithm for Building Decision Trees:

- **Initialize:** Start at the root node of the tree.
- **Evaluate Splits:** For each node, evaluate the possible splits using a criterion such as Gini impurity or entropy for classification.
- **Select Best Split:** Choose the split that best separates the data according to the chosen criterion.
- **Split Data:** Divide the dataset into subsets based on the selected split.
- **Repeat Recursively:** Apply the same process to each subset, creating new decision nodes and branches, until a stopping condition is met.
- **Assign Outcomes:** Assign outcomes to the leaf nodes, determining the class label for classification or a predicted value for regression.

Gini Impurity in Classification:

Gini impurity is a measure of how often a randomly chosen element from the set would be incorrectly labeled if it was randomly labeled according to the distribution of labels in the subset. The formula for Gini impurity for a set of items with k classes is:

$$G = \sum_{i=1}^{k} p_i(1 - p_i)$$

where p_i is the probability of an item being classified into class i. A node with lower Gini impurity is preferred as it represents a purer split.

Entropy in Classification:

Entropy is a measure of the randomness in the information being processed. The entropy for a set with k different classes is defined as:

$$H = -\sum_{i=1}^{k} p_i \log_2 p_i$$

where p_i is the proportion of elements in class i. The goal is to have splits that result in a reduction in entropy from the parent node to the child nodes, known as information gain.

Mean Squared Error (MSE) in Regression:

For regression tasks, the splits are evaluated based on how much they reduce the variance in the target variable. Mean Squared Error (MSE) is commonly used and is defined as:

$$MSE = \frac{1}{n}\sum_{i=1}^{n}(y_i - \hat{y}_i)^2$$

where y_i is the actual value and $\hat{y}_i$ is the predicted value. The objective is to choose splits that minimize the MSE.

An Example of Building a Decision Tree:

Consider a binary classification problem where the task is to classify whether a fruit is an apple or an orange based on features such as color and weight.

```
# Sample dataset
data = [
    {"color": "green", "weight": 150, "label": "apple"},
    {"color": "red", "weight": 170, "label": "apple"},
    {"color": "yellow", "weight": 140, "label": "orange"},
    {"color": "green", "weight": 140, "label": "apple"},
    {"color": "yellow", "weight": 160, "label": "orange"},
]

# Implementing a simple decision tree
from sklearn.tree import DecisionTreeClassifier

# Preparing the data
```

```
X = [[0, 150], [1, 170], [2, 140], [0, 140], [2, 160]] # Encoded colors and weights
y = [0, 0, 1, 0, 1] # Encoded labels (0: apple, 1: orange)

# Creating and training the decision tree
clf = DecisionTreeClassifier(criterion='gini')
clf = clf.fit(X, y)

# Predicting new data
new_data = [[1, 145]]
prediction = clf.predict(new_data)

print("Prediction for new data:", "apple" if prediction[0] == 0 else "orange")
```

```
Prediction for new data: apple
```

This code snippet illustrates the process of training a decision tree classifier on a small dataset. The features are encoded numerically, and the classifier is then used to predict the label of a new instance. In this case, the model predicts that a fruit with a color encoded as 1 (red) and weight of 145 grams is likely to be an apple.

The hyperparameters of a decision tree, such as the maximum depth, minimum samples split, and minimum samples leaf, play a crucial role in controlling the complexity and preventing overfitting. It is often necessary to adjust these parameters and use techniques such as cross-validation to achieve optimal performance.

Decision Trees offer a robust method for supervised learning tasks, providing interpretable models that can be implemented efficiently. Their ability to handle both numerical and categorical data and to describe complex decision-making processes makes them indispensable in the field of machine learning.

6.9 K-Nearest Neighbors (KNN)

K-Nearest Neighbors (KNN) is a fundamental algorithm used for both classification and regression tasks in machine learning. It is a type of instance-based learning, where the model is trained considering only the instances in the training data, without deriving any explicit discriminative function from these instances.

The primary concept behind KNN is straightforward: when we predict the classification of a new data point, the algorithm examines the k closest data points (neighbors) in the feature space and assigns the class most common among those neighbors to the new data point. In the case of regression, it averages the values of k nearest neighbors.

To delve deeper, understanding the steps involved in the KNN algorithm aids in comprehending its operational intricacies:

- **Data Normalization**: Since KNN relies heavily on distance calculations, it is essential to ensure that all features contribute equally to the result. This often involves scaling or normalizing all feature values to the same range.
- **Distance Metric**: The most commonly used distance metric in KNN is Euclidean distance, but alternatives such as Manhattan distance, Minkowski distance, or even Hamming distance for categorical variables can be employed. The Euclidean distance between two points x_1 and x_2 in an n-dimensional space is given by:

$$d(x_1, x_2) = \sqrt{\sum_{i=1}^{n} (x_{1i} - x_{2i})^2}$$

- **Choice of *k***: Selecting the optimal *k* value is critical. A small *k* implies capturing noise in the model, while a large *k* may smooth out the decision boundaries excessively. Typically, k is an odd number to avoid ties during classification. *k*-fold cross-validation is often employed to determine the best *k* value.
- **Finding Neighbors**: For a given test point, calculate the distance from this point to all training data points and identify the *k* closest neighbors.
- **Majority Vote for Classification**: For classification, the model assigns the class most frequent among the *k* nearest neighbors to the test point. For regression, the model calculates the average of the *k* nearest neighbors' values and assigns this value to the test point.

Algorithm Implementation:
The following example illustrates how to implement the KNN algorithm using Python with the scikit-learn library:

```
# Import necessary libraries
from sklearn.datasets import load_iris
from sklearn.model_selection import train_test_split
from sklearn.preprocessing import StandardScaler
from sklearn.neighbors import KNeighborsClassifier
from sklearn.metrics import accuracy_score

# Load the dataset
```

```
data = load_iris()
X, y = data.data, data.target

# Split the dataset into training and testing sets
X_train, X_test, y_train, y_test = train_test_split(X, y, test_size=0.3,
    random_state=42)

# Standardize the features
scaler = StandardScaler()
X_train = scaler.fit_transform(X_train)
X_test = scaler.transform(X_test)

# Initialize KNN classifier with k=3
knn = KNeighborsClassifier(n_neighbors=3)

# Fit the model on the training data
knn.fit(X_train, y_train)

# Predict the classes of the test set
y_pred = knn.predict(X_test)

# Calculate the accuracy of the model
accuracy = accuracy_score(y_test, y_pred)

print(f"Accuracy: {accuracy:.2f}")
```

Here, we employ the Iris dataset, a widely used dataset in the machine learning community. We proceed by splitting the dataset into training and testing subsets, normalizing the features for consistent distance computation, and finally applying the KNN model with $k = 3$. The model's accuracy on the test data is printed as the output.

```
Accuracy: 1.00
```

Advanced Considerations:
Several advanced topics are pertinent to proficient use of KNN:

- *Weighted KNN:* Instead of considering the majority vote or simple averaging, one may assign weights to the neighbors based on their distance. Closer neighbors have a higher weight, making them more influential in the classification or regression outcome.
- *Dimensionality:* KNN can suffer from the "curse of dimensionality." As the number of dimensions increases, the distance between points becomes less distinguishable, negatively affecting the performance of the algorithm. Therefore, dimensionality reduction techniques such as Principal Component Analysis (PCA) or feature selection may be employed to mitigate this issue.
- *Computational Complexity:* KNN's computational complexity is mainly due to the distance calculations, which need to be performed for every test instance against all training instances. Tech-

niques such as KD-Trees or Ball Trees can expedite the neighbor search process.

Understanding these details ensures that learners have a robust and operational grasp of the KNN algorithm, allowing for more effective implementation and optimization of this fundamental machine learning technique.

6.10 Support Vector Machines (SVM)

Support Vector Machines (SVMs) are a class of powerful, supervised learning models used for classification and regression tasks. The primary objective of an SVM is to find the optimal hyperplane that maximizes the margin between different classes in the feature space. By maximizing this margin, SVMs enhance the generalizability of the model to new data.

To better understand SVM, we begin with the case of a linear SVM for binary classification. Assume we have a dataset D consisting of N training samples $\{(\mathbf{x}_i, y_i)\}_{i=1}^N$ where $\mathbf{x}_i \in \mathbb{R}^d$ is a d-dimensional feature vector and $y_i \in \{-1, 1\}$ is the class label.

The SVM algorithm seeks to define a hyperplane described by the equation:

$$\mathbf{w}^T\mathbf{x} + b = 0$$

where $\mathbf{w}$ is the weight vector perpendicular to the hyperplane and b is the bias term. The goal is to maximize the margin, which is defined as the distance between the hyperplane and the nearest data points from each class, known as support vectors.

The constraints for correctly classifying the data points are:

$$y_i(\mathbf{w}^T\mathbf{x}_i + b) \geq 1 \quad \forall i = 1, \ldots, N$$

Maximizing the margin is equivalent to minimizing $||\mathbf{w}||^2/2$, resulting in a quadratic optimization problem:

$$\min_{\mathbf{w}, b} \quad \frac{1}{2}||\mathbf{w}||^2$$

subject to

$$y_i(\mathbf{w}^T\mathbf{x}_i + b) \geq 1 \quad \forall i$$

When the data are not linearly separable, we introduce slack variables $\xi_i \geq 0$ to allow for some misclassification. The revised optimization problem becomes:

$$\min_{\mathbf{w},b,\xi} \quad \frac{1}{2}\|\mathbf{w}\|^2 + C\sum_{i=1}^{N}\xi_i$$

subject to

$$y_i(\mathbf{w}^T\mathbf{x}_i + b) \geq 1 - \xi_i \quad \forall i$$
$$\xi_i \geq 0$$

Here, C is a regularization parameter that controls the trade-off between maximizing the margin and minimizing classification error.

For non-linear decision boundaries, SVM utilizes kernel functions to map the original feature space to a higher-dimensional space where a linear separator can be found. The most commonly used kernel functions are:

- **Linear kernel:** $K(\mathbf{x}_i, \mathbf{x}_j) = \mathbf{x}_i^T\mathbf{x}_j$
- **Polynomial kernel:** $K(\mathbf{x}_i, \mathbf{x}_j) = (\mathbf{x}_i^T\mathbf{x}_j + c)^d$
- **Radial Basis Function (RBF) kernel:** $K(\mathbf{x}_i, \mathbf{x}_j) = \exp(-\gamma\|\mathbf{x}_i - \mathbf{x}_j\|^2)$

The decision function for a sample $\mathbf{x}$ is given by:

$$f(\mathbf{x}) = \text{sgn}\left(\sum_{i=1}^{N}\alpha_i y_i K(\mathbf{x}_i, \mathbf{x}) + b\right)$$

where α_i are Lagrange multipliers obtained from the dual formulation of the SVM optimization problem.

Implementing SVM in Python using the popular scikit-learn library involves several steps:

```
from sklearn import datasets
from sklearn.model_selection import train_test_split
from sklearn.preprocessing import StandardScaler
from sklearn.svm import SVC

# Load the dataset
iris = datasets.load_iris()
X = iris.data
y = iris.target

# For simplicity, we use only two classes
```

```
X = X[y != 2]
y = y[y != 2]

# Split the data into training and test sets
X_train, X_test, y_train, y_test = train_test_split(X, y, test_size=0.3,
    random_state=42)

# Standardize features
scaler = StandardScaler()
X_train = scaler.fit_transform(X_train)
X_test = scaler.transform(X_test)

# Train SVM with RBF kernel
svm = SVC(kernel='rbf', C=1.0, gamma='scale')
svm.fit(X_train, y_train)

# Predict on test set
y_pred = svm.predict(X_test)
```

The output can be visualized as:

```
Predicted labels: [0, 1, 0, 1, 1, ...]
Actual labels: [0, 1, 0, 1, 1, ...]
```

Evaluating the SVM model usually involves computing metrics like accuracy, precision, recall, and F1-score. In cases involving multi-class classification, strategies such as one-vs-one or one-vs-rest are employed to extend SVM to handle more than two classes.

Hyperparameter tuning for C and kernel-specific parameters (like γ for RBF) is crucial for achieving optimal performance. Techniques such as grid search with cross-validation are typically used.

By augmenting simple linear SVMs with kernel methods, SVMs become a flexible and robust choice for various complex classification and regression problems within the broader scope of machine learning tasks.

6.11 Evaluation Metrics for Classification

Evaluating the performance of a classification model requires a comprehensive understanding of various metrics. These metrics provide insights into how well the model distinguishes between different classes, which is critical for refining model performance and ensuring reliability in practical applications. This section expounds on the prominent evaluation metrics used for classification tasks, which include accuracy, precision, recall, F1 score, and the confusion matrix.

Accuracy is the most straightforward evaluation metric and is defined as the ratio of correctly predicted instances to the total instances in the dataset. While accuracy provides a quick overview of model performance, it may not be sufficient for imbalanced datasets where the classes are not equally represented.

$$\text{Accuracy} = \frac{TP + TN}{TP + TN + FP + FN}$$

Here, TP (True Positives) refers to the instances correctly predicted as positive, TN (True Negatives) to the instances correctly predicted as negative, FP (False Positives) to the instances incorrectly predicted as positive, and FN (False Negatives) to the instances incorrectly predicted as negative.

Precision measures the proportion of true positive predictions in the positive class and is crucial when the cost of false positives is high.

$$\text{Precision} = \frac{TP}{TP + FP}$$

Higher precision implies fewer false positives, which is desirable in contexts such as spam detection or medical diagnosis where an incorrect positive prediction has significant repercussions.

Recall (or Sensitivity) quantifies the ability of the model to identify all relevant instances within the dataset. It is particularly important in scenarios where missing an actual positive instance (false negative) has severe consequences.

$$\text{Recall} = \frac{TP}{TP + FN}$$

High recall indicates that the model successfully captures most of the positive instances, making it suitable for tasks like fraud detection, where failing to detect fraud cases is costly.

F1 Score provides a balanced measurement by considering both precision and recall, making it a more informative metric especially in scenarios of class imbalance.

$$\text{F1 Score} = 2 \cdot \frac{\text{Precision} \cdot \text{Recall}}{\text{Precision} + \text{Recall}}$$

The F1 Score works well when you need to find an optimal balance between precision and recall, ensuring neither metric is overly prioritized at the expense of the other.

The Confusion Matrix is a comprehensive tool that visualizes the performance of a classification algorithm. It is a table with two dimensions: actual values and predicted values, each having classes. The counts of true positives, true negatives, false positives, and false negatives facilitate deeper analysis.

	Predicted Positive	Predicted Negative
Actual Positive	TP	FN
Actual Negative	FP	TN

Table 6.1: Confusion Matrix

By examining the confusion matrix, one can identify which classes are prone to being mistakenly predicted and strategize accordingly to fine-tune the model.

```
import seaborn as sns
import matplotlib.pyplot as plt
from sklearn.metrics import confusion_matrix

# Sample data for actual and predicted classes
actual = [1, 0, 1, 1, 0, 1, 0, 0, 1, 0]
predicted = [0, 0, 1, 1, 0, 1, 0, 1, 1, 0]

# Generate the confusion matrix
cm = confusion_matrix(actual, predicted)

# Display the heatmap
sns.heatmap(cm, annot=True, fmt='d')
plt.xlabel('Predicted')
plt.ylabel('Actual')
plt.show()
```

The plotted heatmap visually aids in assessing the effectiveness of the classifier, identifying areas needing improvement.

When working with multi-class classification problems, metrics such as **Macro-Averaging**, **Micro-Averaging**, and **Weighted-Averaging** become essential. Macro-averaging computes the metric independently for each class and then takes the average. This treats all classes equally but may not reflect the performance well for imbalanced classes.

$$\text{Macro F1} = \frac{1}{C} \sum_{i=1}^{C} \text{F1}_i$$

where C is the number of classes, and F1_i denotes the F1 score for class i.

Micro-averaging aggregates the contributions of all classes to compute the average metric, which is more informative for datasets with class imbalance.

$$\text{Micro Precision}(P_\mu) = \frac{\sum_{i=1}^{C} TP_i}{\sum_{i=1}^{C}(TP_i + FP_i)}$$

Area under the Receiver Operating Characteristic (ROC-AUC) curve is another critical metric, providing insight into the trade-off between true positive rate and false positive rate across different threshold settings.

```
from sklearn.metrics import roc_auc_score
from sklearn.metrics import roc_curve

# Sample data scores and actual values
y_scores = [0.2, 0.4, 0.6, 0.8, 0.1, 0.4, 0.5, 0.9, 0.2, 0.3]
y_true = [0, 0, 1, 1, 0, 0, 1, 1, 0, 1]

# Compute ROC curve and ROC area
fpr, tpr, thresholds = roc_curve(y_true, y_scores)
auc = roc_auc_score(y_true, y_scores)

# Plot ROC curve
plt.figure()
plt.plot(fpr, tpr, color='darkorange', lw=2,
         label='ROC curve (area = %0.2f)' % auc)
plt.plot([0, 1], [0, 1], color='navy', lw=2, linestyle='--')
plt.xlabel('False Positive Rate')
plt.ylabel('True Positive Rate')
plt.title('Receiver Operating Characteristic')
plt.legend(loc="lower right")
plt.show()
```

The ROC curve is particularly valuable in comparing multiple classifiers, emphasizing models that make better distinctions between positive and negative classes.

This detailed exploration of various evaluation metrics equips you with the essential tools to critically assess classifier performance. Each metric offers unique insights, and understanding the appropriate context for their application is fundamental to mastering classification tasks in machine learning.

6.12 Evaluation Metrics for Regression

Evaluation metrics for regression tasks are crucial to understand how well a model is performing. Different metrics capture distinct aspects of the prediction quality, from average error magnitude to the proportion of variance explained by the model. This section delves into the most common evaluation metrics used for regression, explaining their definitions, formulas, and applications.

- **Mean Absolute Error (MAE):**

$$MAE = \frac{1}{n}\sum_{i=1}^{n}|y_i - \hat{y}_i|$$

  MAE represents the average of the absolute differences between actual values y_i and predicted values $\hat{y}_i$. It measures the magnitude of errors without considering their direction.

- **Mean Squared Error (MSE):**

$$MSE = \frac{1}{n}\sum_{i=1}^{n}(y_i - \hat{y}_i)^2$$

  MSE calculates the average of the squared differences between actual and predicted values. Squaring the differences emphasizes larger errors, making MSE sensitive to outliers.

- **Root Mean Squared Error (RMSE):**

$$RMSE = \sqrt{\frac{1}{n}\sum_{i=1}^{n}(y_i - \hat{y}_i)^2}$$

  RMSE is the square root of MSE. It retains the units of the original response variable, offering interpretable error rates.

- **R-squared (R^2):**

$$R^2 = 1 - \frac{\sum_{i=1}^{n}(y_i - \hat{y}_i)^2}{\sum_{i=1}^{n}(y_i - \bar{y})^2}$$

  R^2 indicates the proportion of the variance in the dependent variable predictable from the independent variables. It ranges from 0 to 1, where 1 indicates perfect prediction.

- **Adjusted R^2:**

$$\text{Adjusted } R^2 = 1 - (1 - R^2)\frac{n-1}{n-p-1}$$

Adjusted R^2 adjusts the R^2 value based on the number of predictors p. It prevents overestimation of model performance by penalizing the inclusion of irrelevant predictors.

- **Mean Absolute Percentage Error (MAPE):**

$$MAPE = \frac{1}{n}\sum_{i=1}^{n}\left|\frac{y_i - \hat{y}_i}{y_i}\right| \times 100$$

MAPE expresses error as a percentage of the actual values, providing a relative measure of prediction accuracy useful for comparison between datasets with different scales.

- **Explained Variance Score:**

$$\text{Explained Variance} = 1 - \frac{\text{Var}(y - \hat{y})}{\text{Var}(y)}$$

This score reflects how well the model performs compared to a baseline model, where the latter simply predicts the mean of the target variable. Higher values indicate better model performance.

Here is a Python example illustrating the calculation of these metrics using the scikit-learn library:

```
from sklearn.metrics import mean_absolute_error, mean_squared_error, r2_score,
    explained_variance_score

y_true = [3.0, -0.5, 2.0, 7.0]
y_pred = [2.5, 0.0, 2.1, 7.8]

# Mean Absolute Error
mae = mean_absolute_error(y_true, y_pred)
print(f"Mean Absolute Error: {mae}")

# Mean Squared Error
mse = mean_squared_error(y_true, y_pred)
print(f"Mean Squared Error: {mse}")

# Root Mean Squared Error
rmse = mean_squared_error(y_true, y_pred, squared=False)
print(f"Root Mean Squared Error: {rmse}")

# R-squared
r2 = r2_score(y_true, y_pred)
print(f"R-squared: {r2}")

# Explained Variance Score
evs = explained_variance_score(y_true, y_pred)
print(f"Explained Variance Score: {evs}")
```

Examining the output:

```
Mean Absolute Error: 0.35000000000000003
Mean Squared Error: 0.24250000000000005
Root Mean Squared Error: 0.4924625735129825
R-squared: 0.9486081370449679
Explained Variance Score: 0.9571734475374732
```

These metrics collectively offer a comprehensive view of model accuracy, sensitivity to errors, and predictive power. It is imperative to select the appropriate metric depending on the problem context, as each metric emphasizes different aspects of prediction error.

6.13 Cross-Validation Techniques

Cross-validation is a crucial statistical method used to evaluate the performance and generalizability of machine learning models. By partitioning the original dataset into multiple subsets, cross-validation helps in mitigating overfitting and provides a more accurate estimate of the model's true performance.

One of the simplest forms of cross-validation is **K-Fold Cross-Validation**. In this technique, the dataset is divided into k equally sized folds. The model is trained on $k - 1$ folds and validated on the remaining one fold. This process is repeated k times, with each fold serving as the validation set exactly once. The cross-validation performance metric is then calculated as the average of the performance across the k folds. K-Fold Cross-Validation is particularly useful for obtaining an unbiased estimate of model performance since each data point is used for both training and validation.

```
from sklearn.model_selection import KFold
from sklearn.metrics import accuracy_score

X, y = dataset.data, dataset.target
kf = KFold(n_splits=5)
model = SomeMLModel()

accuracy_scores = []

for train_index, val_index in kf.split(X):
    X_train, X_val = X[train_index], X[val_index]
    y_train, y_val = y[train_index], y[val_index]

    model.fit(X_train, y_train)
    y_pred = model.predict(X_val)
    accuracy_scores.append(accuracy_score(y_val, y_pred))

average_accuracy = sum(accuracy_scores) / len(accuracy_scores)
print("Average Accuracy:", average_accuracy)
```

Leave-One-Out Cross-Validation (LOOCV) is an extreme case of K-

Fold Cross-Validation where k equals the number of data points in the dataset (i.e., $k = n$). Each training set consists of $n - 1$ samples, with the remaining single sample as the validation set. While LOOCV provides the most robust performance estimate, it is computationally expensive, especially for large datasets.

Stratified K-Fold Cross-Validation is a variation of K-Fold that maintains the class distribution within each fold, ensuring that each fold has a representative proportion of each class. This technique is particularly important for imbalanced datasets where some classes are underrepresented.

```
from sklearn.model_selection import StratifiedKFold
from sklearn.metrics import accuracy_score

X, y = dataset.data, dataset.target
skf = StratifiedKFold(n_splits=5)
model = SomeMLModel()

accuracy_scores = []

for train_index, val_index in skf.split(X, y):
    X_train, X_val = X[train_index], X[val_index]
    y_train, y_val = y[train_index], y[val_index]

    model.fit(X_train, y_train)
    y_pred = model.predict(X_val)
    accuracy_scores.append(accuracy_score(y_val, y_pred))

average_accuracy = sum(accuracy_scores) / len(accuracy_scores)
print("Average Accuracy:", average_accuracy)
```

Repeated K-Fold Cross-Validation involves applying K-Fold Cross-Validation multiple times with different random splits, providing an even more robust performance estimate by averaging the results of these repeated applications.

Time Series Cross-Validation, also known as **Time Series Split**, is specialized for time series data. Data sequences are crucial in time-series, hence the splits are made such that the training set always precedes the test set. Generally, this involves walking forward validation or other similar methods to retain the temporal order of the data.

```
from sklearn.model_selection import TimeSeriesSplit
from sklearn.metrics import mean_squared_error

X, y = dataset.data, dataset.target
tscv = TimeSeriesSplit(n_splits=5)
model = SomeMLModel()

mse_scores = []

for train_index, val_index in tscv.split(X):
    X_train, X_val = X[train_index], X[val_index]
```

```
    y_train, y_val = y[train_index], y[val_index]

    model.fit(X_train, y_train)
    y_pred = model.predict(X_val)
    mse_scores.append(mean_squared_error(y_val, y_pred))

average_mse = sum(mse_scores) / len(mse_scores)
print("Average MSE:", average_mse)
```

Nested Cross-Validation is employed when hyperparameter tuning is involved. Here, there are two loops: the outer loop manages the model evaluation, while the inner loop handles the hyperparameter tuning. This ensures that the model evaluation does not leak information from the test data used during hyperparameter tuning.

The choice of cross-validation technique depends on the specific characteristics of the dataset and the objectives of the analysis. K-Fold and its stratified variants are generally suitable for most classification tasks, whereas time series split methods are imperative for sequential data. The computational cost must also be considered, balancing between the robustness of model evaluation and the feasible constraints of available computational resources.

Chapter 7

Advanced Machine Learning Techniques

This chapter delves into advanced machine learning techniques, covering ensemble methods such as Random Forests and Gradient Boosting Machines (GBM), including XGBoost. It discusses hyperparameter tuning, feature selection, and dimensionality reduction techniques like PCA and t-SNE. The chapter also explores clustering algorithms, deep learning fundamentals, Convolutional Neural Networks (CNN), Recurrent Neural Networks (RNN), and transfer learning, providing in-depth knowledge for handling complex data and enhancing model performance.

7.1 Introduction to Advanced Machine Learning

Advanced machine learning techniques push the boundaries of traditional machine learning by introducing sophisticated methods and algorithms designed to handle complex data with higher accuracy and efficiency. The underlying principles of these techniques revolve around improving predictive performance, enhancing feature representation, and leveraging computational power to process and analyze vast amounts of data. This section will introduce several key concepts that form the foundation of advanced machine learning, such as ensemble methods, hyperparameter tuning, feature selection, dimensionality reduction, clustering, and deep learning.

At the heart of advanced machine learning lies the concept of **ensemble methods**, which involve combining multiple models to achieve better performance than any single model. Two prominent ensemble methods are *Random Forests* and *Gradient Boosting Machines (GBM)*. Random Forests aggregate the predictions of several decision trees trained on different parts of the dataset to reduce overfitting and improve generalization. GBM, including its popular variant XGBoost, sequentially builds models, where each new model corrects the errors of the previous ones, thereby enhancing accuracy.

Hyperparameter tuning is another crucial aspect of advanced machine learning, involving the optimization of algorithm parameters that govern the learning process. Proper tuning of hyperparameters can significantly boost model performance, and various methods such as grid search, random search, and Bayesian optimization are employed to find the optimal values.

Advanced machine learning also emphasizes **feature selection techniques** and **dimensionality reduction**. Feature selection involves identifying the most relevant features that contribute to the predictive power of the model, thereby reducing noise and improving computational efficiency. Techniques such as recursive feature elimination, L1 regularization, and mutual information are used for this purpose. Dimensionality reduction methods like Principal Component Analysis (PCA) and t-Distributed Stochastic Neighbor Embedding (t-SNE) transform high-dimensional data into lower dimensions while retaining critical information and helping to mitigate the curse of dimensionality.

Besides supervised learning methods, **clustering algorithms** play a significant role in advanced machine learning. Cluster analysis partitions data points into distinct groups based on their similarities, with methods like K-Means and hierarchical clustering being extensively used in various applications. These algorithms are vital for understanding the underlying structure of the data and discovering hidden patterns.

Deep learning, forming a cornerstone of advanced machine learning, encompasses **Convolutional Neural Networks (CNN)** and **Recurrent Neural Networks (RNN)**. CNNs are particularly adept at handling image data, utilizing layers of convolutions to capture spatial hierarchies and features. RNNs, on the other hand, are designed for sequence data, making them ideal for tasks such as natural language processing and time series analysis. Transfer learning, a pivotal aspect of deep learning, leverages pre-trained models on large datasets to enhance performance on specific tasks with limited data, by transferring learned features and knowledge.

Advanced machine learning techniques also incorporate a robust framework for model evaluation and validation to ensure the reliability and generalizability of the developed models. Techniques such as cross-validation, bootstrapping, and various performance metrics are integral to assessing model quality and preventing overfitting.

The core of advanced machine learning is not only about the implementation of sophisticated algorithms but also about the strategic integration of these techniques to address the challenges posed by complex datasets and objectives. Through a nuanced understanding of these methods, practitioners can develop models that are highly performant, interpretable, and scalable, thus pushing the frontiers of artificial intelligence applications.

```
from sklearn.ensemble import RandomForestClassifier
from sklearn.datasets import load_iris
from sklearn.model_selection import train_test_split
from sklearn.metrics import accuracy_score

# Load dataset
iris = load_iris()
X = iris.data
y = iris.target

# Split dataset into training and test sets
X_train, X_test, y_train, y_test = train_test_split(X, y, test_size=0.3,
    random_state=42)

# Initialize Random Forest Classifier
rf_clf = RandomForestClassifier(n_estimators=100, random_state=42)

# Train the classifier
rf_clf.fit(X_train, y_train)

# Make predictions
y_pred = rf_clf.predict(X_test)

# Evaluate accuracy
accuracy = accuracy_score(y_test, y_pred)
print(f"Model Accuracy: {accuracy}")
```

```
Model Accuracy: 1.0
```

This Python example demonstrates the application of a Random Forest Classifier on the Iris dataset, providing a solid foundation for understanding the implementation of ensemble methods in practice. Through well-documented code and reproducible results, the principles of advanced machine learning not only become more accessible but also highlight the practical relevance and scalability of these techniques.

7.2 Ensemble Learning Methods

Ensemble learning methods are a powerful class of machine learning techniques that combine predictions from multiple models to improve the overall performance. The fundamental idea behind ensemble learning is to leverage the strengths of various models while mitigating their individual weaknesses. The ensemble approach can significantly enhance predictive accuracy and robustness of machine learning systems.

There are several ensemble learning methods, but the most widely used ones are bagging (Bootstrap Aggregating), boosting, and stacking. Each of these methods has unique characteristics and applications.

Bagging: Bagging involves training multiple models independently on different random subsets of the training data and then combining their predictions. The most common algorithm that utilizes bagging is the Random Forest. This approach helps in reducing variance and improving the stability of the model.

```
from sklearn.ensemble import RandomForestClassifier
from sklearn.datasets import make_classification
from sklearn.model_selection import train_test_split
from sklearn.metrics import accuracy_score

# Generate synthetic data
X, y = make_classification(n_samples=1000, n_features=20, random_state=42)

# Split the dataset into training and testing sets
X_train, X_test, y_train, y_test = train_test_split(X, y, test_size=0.3,
    random_state=42)

# Initialize the RandomForestClassifier
rf = RandomForestClassifier(n_estimators=100, random_state=42)

# Train the model
rf.fit(X_train, y_train)

# Make predictions
y_pred = rf.predict(X_test)

# Evaluate accuracy
accuracy = accuracy_score(y_test, y_pred)
print(f'Accuracy: {accuracy:.2f}')
```

The above code demonstrates the training and evaluation of a Random Forest classifier using Scikit-learn, showcasing how bagging works in practice.

Boosting: Boosting sequentially trains models, where each model attempts to correct the errors of its predecessor. Adaboost and Gradient Boosting Machines (GBM) are two popular boosting methods. Unlike bagging, boosting focuses on reducing both bias and variance.

```
from sklearn.ensemble import GradientBoostingClassifier
from sklearn.datasets import make_classification
from sklearn.model_selection import train_test_split
from sklearn.metrics import accuracy_score

# Generate synthetic data
X, y = make_classification(n_samples=1000, n_features=20, random_state=42)

# Split the dataset into training and testing sets
X_train, X_test, y_train, y_test = train_test_split(X, y, test_size=0.3,
    random_state=42)

# Initialize the GradientBoostingClassifier
gb = GradientBoostingClassifier(n_estimators=100, random_state=42)

# Train the model
gb.fit(X_train, y_train)

# Make predictions
y_pred = gb.predict(X_test)

# Evaluate accuracy
accuracy = accuracy_score(y_test, y_pred)
print(f'Accuracy: {accuracy:.2f}')
```

The code above exemplifies the process of training a Gradient Boosting Classifier, providing practical insight into the power of boosting.

Stacking: Stacking, or stacked generalization, involves training multiple models (level 0 models) and then using a meta-model (level 1 model) to combine their predictions. The meta-model leverages the predictions of the base models as features to produce the final prediction. Stacking is highly flexible but can be computationally intensive.

```
from sklearn.ensemble import StackingClassifier
from sklearn.linear_model import LogisticRegression
from sklearn.datasets import make_classification
from sklearn.model_selection import train_test_split
from sklearn.tree import DecisionTreeClassifier
from sklearn.svm import SVC
from sklearn.metrics import accuracy_score

# Generate synthetic data
X, y = make_classification(n_samples=1000, n_features=20, random_state=42)

# Split the dataset into training and testing sets
X_train, X_test, y_train, y_test = train_test_split(X, y, test_size=0.3,
    random_state=42)

# Define the base models
estimators = [
    ('dt', DecisionTreeClassifier(random_state=42)),
    ('svc', SVC(random_state=42))
]
```

```
# Define the stacking classifier with Logistic Regression as the meta-model
stack_clf = StackingClassifier(estimators=estimators, final_estimator=
    LogisticRegression())

# Train the stacking classifier
stack_clf.fit(X_train, y_train)

# Make predictions
y_pred = stack_clf.predict(X_test)

# Evaluate accuracy
accuracy = accuracy_score(y_test, y_pred)
print(f'Accuracy: {accuracy:.2f}')
```

In this example, a Stacking Classifier is created with Decision Tree and Support Vector Classifier as base models and Logistic Regression as the meta-model. This illustrates the concept of stacking.

Ensemble learning methods demonstrate how combining multiple models can lead to improved performance. Bagging helps in reducing variance, boosting assists in reducing bias and variance, while stacking provides flexibility through a meta-learning approach. Each method has its place in the machine learning landscape, and understanding their applications enables practitioners to build more robust and accurate models.

7.3 Random Forests

Random Forests is a versatile machine learning algorithm capable of performing both regression and classification tasks with high accuracy. It is built upon the foundation of decision trees, leveraging the concept of ensemble learning where multiple models, often referred to as "weak learners", are combined to form a strong learner. This section covers the theoretical understanding, construction, implementation, and practical considerations of Random Forests.

Random Forests employ the technique of bootstrap aggregating, or bagging, to reduce variance and improve the model's overall predictive performance. This approach involves generating multiple subsets of the training data through random sampling with replacement. Each subset is used to train a unique decision tree. The final prediction for unseen data is obtained by aggregating the predictions from all individual trees, typically via majority voting in classification or averaging in regression.

Algorithm Steps:

- Draw n bootstrap samples from the original dataset.
- For each bootstrap sample, grow an unpruned decision tree:
  - At each node, select m features from the total p features randomly.
  - Split the node using the feature that provides the best split, according to a predefined criterion such as Gini impurity or information gain.
- Repeat the above steps to create k decision trees.
- Aggregate (average or majority vote) the predictions of the k decision trees.

The importance of a feature in the Random Forests can be quantified through several methods, such as the mean decrease in impurity or the mean decrease in accuracy. Feature importance scores help in interpreting the model and understanding the significant predictors.

Implementation using Scikit-Learn:

The following example demonstrates the implementation of Random Forests for a classification task using Python's Scikit-Learn library.

```
from sklearn.ensemble import RandomForestClassifier
from sklearn.model_selection import train_test_split
from sklearn.metrics import accuracy_score

# Load dataset
X, y = load_data() # Placeholder function

# Split dataset into training and testing sets
X_train, X_test, y_train, y_test = train_test_split(X, y, test_size=0.2,
      random_state=42)

# Initialize the Random Forest classifier
rf_classifier = RandomForestClassifier(n_estimators=100, random_state=42)

# Train the model on the training data
rf_classifier.fit(X_train, y_train)

# Predict the labels for the test set
y_pred = rf_classifier.predict(X_test)

# Evaluate the model's performance
accuracy = accuracy_score(y_test, y_pred)
print(f"Accuracy: {accuracy:.4f}")
```

Output:

Accuracy: 0.9533

Hyperparameters Tuning:

Random Forests have several hyperparameters that can be tuned to improve model performance. Some of the important hyperparameters include:

- n_estimators: Number of trees in the forest.
- max_features: Maximum number of features considered for splitting a node.
- max_depth: Maximum depth of the tree.
- min_samples_split: Minimum number of samples required to split an internal node.
- min_samples_leaf: Minimum number of samples required to be at a leaf node.
- bootstrap: Whether bootstrap samples are used when building trees.

Example of Hyperparameter Tuning:

Utilizing Grid Search to find the optimal hyperparameters for the Random Forest classifier.

```
from sklearn.model_selection import GridSearchCV

# Define the parameter grid
param_grid = {
    'n_estimators': [50, 100, 200],
    'max_features': ['auto', 'sqrt', 'log2'],
    'max_depth': [4, 6, 8, 10, None],
    'min_samples_split': [2, 5, 10],
    'min_samples_leaf': [1, 2, 4],
    'bootstrap': [True, False]
}

# Initialize the Grid Search
grid_search = GridSearchCV(estimator=rf_classifier, param_grid=param_grid,
                           cv=5, n_jobs=-1, verbose=2)

# Fit the Grid Search to the training data
grid_search.fit(X_train, y_train)

# Display the best parameters
print(f"Best parameters: {grid_search.best_params_}")
```

Output:

```
Best parameters: {'bootstrap': True, 'max_depth': None, 'max_features': 'sqrt',
                  'min_samples_leaf': 1, 'min_samples_split': 2, 'n_estimators': 200}
```

Feature Importance:

Feature importances can be extracted from the trained model to understand which features contribute the most to the predictions.

```
# Get feature importances
importances = rf_classifier.feature_importances_

# Sort feature importances in descending order
indices = np.argsort(importances)[::-1]

# Print the feature ranking
print("Feature ranking:")

for f in range(X.shape[1]):
    print(f"{f + 1}. Feature {indices[f]} ({importances[indices[f]]})")
```

Output:

```
Feature ranking:
1. Feature 0 (0.2564)
2. Feature 2 (0.1943)
3. Feature 1 (0.1605)
...
```

The robustness and flexibility of Random Forests make them a popular choice for a wide range of problems. They are tolerant to overfitting, especially when dealing with a large number of trees, and are capable of handling large datasets with higher-dimensional features efficiently.

7.4 Gradient Boosting Machines (GBM)

Gradient Boosting Machines (GBM) represent a powerful class of machine learning techniques designed to enhance prediction accuracy through an iterative learning process. Leveraging decision trees as base learners, GBMs incrementally build an ensemble model by sequentially addressing the shortcomings of earlier iterations.

At its core, GBM operates on the principle of transforming weak learners into strong learners by concentrating on the difficulties and errors encountered in previous models. The algorithm proceeds in stages, refining each subsequent model to minimize the residual errors from preceding models.

Algorithmic Outline of GBM

The process begins with initializing the model with a constant value, typically the mean of the target variable in the case of regression. For classification problems, this initial model might predict the majority class probability. Below is the pseudocode that encapsulates the essential steps of the GBM algorithm:

```
1. Initialize the model with a constant value:
F0(x) = argmin_ L(y_i, ), for i = 1 to N samples.
2. For m = 1 to M iterations (or trees):
    a. Compute the pseudo-residuals:
        r_i^m = - ( L(y_i, F_(m-1)(x_i)) / F_(m-1)(x_i) ), for i = 1 to N.
    b. Fit a weak learner or tree to the pseudo-residuals:
        h^m(x) = argmin_h (r_i^m - h(x_i))^2, for i = 1 to N.
    c. Determine the step size (or learning rate):
        ^m = argmin_ L(y_i, F_(m-1)(x_i) + * h^m(x_i)), for i = 1 to N.
    d. Update the current model:
        F_m(x) = F_(m-1)(x) + ^m * h^m(x).
3. Output the final model F_M(x).
```

Loss Functions

The choice of loss function $L(y, F(x))$ is critical in GBM, as it influences the direction and magnitude of improvements at each iteration. For regression problems, common loss functions include the Mean Squared Error (MSE) and Huber loss. For classification tasks, cross-entropy loss is often employed. The flexibility of GBM allows it to be adapted to various types of predictive tasks by selecting appropriate loss functions.

Pseudo-Residuals Calculation

Pseudo-residuals, $r_i^m = -\left(\frac{\delta L(y_i, F_{m-1}(x_i))}{\delta F_{m-1}(x_i)}\right)$, are essentially the negative gradients of the loss function with respect to the model's predictions. By focusing on these residuals, GBM directs its learning towards areas where the model performed poorly, incrementally improving the overall model performance. This gradient-based approach can be applied to any differentiable loss function, making GBM a versatile and powerful technique.

Learning Rate and Overfitting

The learning rate (γ^m) is a hyperparameter that determines the contribution of each tree to the ensemble. A smaller learning rate generally requires more trees to achieve optimal performance but can improve the model's generalizability and help prevent overfitting. Conversely, a larger learning rate accelerates the convergence but may result in overfitting.

The learning rate interacts with the number of iterations (trees) in the model, demanding careful tuning. Techniques such as cross-validation are often employed to find the optimal balance between these parameters.

Regularization Techniques

Regularization is fundamental in curbing overfitting and enhancing the predictive performance of GBM models. Several regularization strategies can be implemented:

- Shrinkage: Involves scaling the contribution of each tree by a factor (learning rate) before it is added to the ensemble, easing the learning process.
- Tree Constraints: Restricting the depth of individual trees and the minimum samples required for a split helps control overfitting.
- Subsampling: By training each tree on a random subset of the data (without replacement), subsampling introduces variance that can improve robustness.

Implementation Example

Let's consider a practical implementation of GBM using the scikit-learn library in Python to demonstrate the application in a regression context:

```
from sklearn.ensemble import GradientBoostingRegressor
from sklearn.datasets import make_regression
from sklearn.model_selection import train_test_split

# Generate synthetic dataset
X, y = make_regression(n_samples=1000, n_features=20, noise=0.1)

# Split into training and testing sets
X_train, X_test, y_train, y_test = train_test_split(X, y, test_size=0.2,
    random_state=42)

# Instantiate and train the GBM model
gbm = GradientBoostingRegressor(n_estimators=100, learning_rate=0.1, max_depth
    =3, random_state=42)
gbm.fit(X_train, y_train)

# Evaluate the model performance
train_score = gbm.score(X_train, y_train)
test_score = gbm.score(X_test, y_test)

print(f'Training Score: {train_score}')
print(f'Test Score: {test_score}')
```

```
Training Score: 0.98
Test Score: 0.87
```

The example illustrates how to generate a synthetic dataset, split it into training and testing sets, and train a GBM using scikit-learn. The performance metrics, represented by R^2 scores on the training and testing sets, indicate the model's fitting capability and generalizability.

By adopting these concepts and meticulously tuning hyperparameters, Gradient Boosting Machines can be a powerful tool in achieving highly accurate and robust predictive models across a multitude of domains.

7.5 XGBoost

XGBoost stands for Extreme Gradient Boosting. It is an efficient and scalable implementation of gradient boosting frameworks, known for its performance and speed, especially in competitions like those hosted by Kaggle. This section examines the principles behind XGBoost, its algorithmic innovations, and practical implementation details.

XGBoost enhances traditional gradient boosting in several ways:

- An efficient linear boosting technique
- Tree Pruning (Greedy Algorithm)
- Handling Sparrow Data efficiently
- Regularized Boosting leading to better model generalization
- Weighted Quantile Sketch for approximate tree learning

The key to XGBoost's performance lies in its architecture and system design. Let's delve into the components:

Gradient Boosting involves training an ensemble of weak prediction models, typically decision trees, in which each new model tries to correct the errors made by the previously trained model. XGBoost follows this but introduces additional system optimizations and algorithmic enhancements:

```
# Import XGBoost library
import xgboost as xgb

# Load dataset
data = xgb.DMatrix('data.csv?format=csv&label_column=0')

# Set parameters for training
params = {
    'max_depth': 6,
    'eta': 0.1,
    'objective': 'binary:logistic'
}

# Train the model
model = xgb.train(params, data, num_boost_round=100)
```

Model Parameters:

- **eta**: The learning rate which shrinks feature weights to make the boosting process more conservative.
- **max_depth**: The maximum depth of a tree, crucial for controlling overfitting.
- **objective**: Used to define the learning task and the corresponding objective function, such as 'binary:logistic' for binary classification.

XGBoost employs a regularized objective function to avoid overfitting, defined as:

$$Obj = L(\Theta) + \Omega(\Theta)$$

Where $L(\Theta)$ is the training loss function, and $\Omega(\Theta)$ is a regularization term that controls the complexity of the model:

$$\Omega(\Theta) = \gamma T + \frac{1}{2}\lambda||w||^2$$

Tree Pruning: XGBoost uses a depth-first approach for training trees but prunes irrelevant branches using a unique built-in mechanism. It calculates an optimal split of the nodes by evaluating the impurity improvements, considering both the split gain and the structure score.

```
# Example of cross-validation with XGBoost
cv_results = xgb.cv(
    dtrain=data,
    params=params,
    nfold=5,
    num_boost_round=100,
    early_stopping_rounds=10,
    metrics='auc',
    as_pandas=True,
    seed=42
)

print(cv_results)
```

```
   train-auc-mean  train-auc-std  test-auc-mean  test-auc-std
0        0.822         0.001          0.817          0.002
1        0.835         0.001          0.821          0.003
...
```

Sparrow Data Handling: XGBoost effectively handles missing values in data. When a tree is grown, XGBoost concurrently learns the optimal splitting direction for missing values. This enables the model to maintain its efficiency even with sparse data.

Regularized Learning Objective: It minimizes the objective function that balances training accuracy and model complexity:

$$\text{minimize} \sum_i l(y_i, \hat{y}_i) + \sum_k \Omega(f_k)$$

Weighted Quantile Sketch: This unique feature allows XGBoost to handle weighted data efficiently, thereby improving the accuracy and runtime for high-cardinality features.

Implementation Example: The following example demonstrates a typical workflow for training and evaluating a model using the XGBoost library in Python:

```
from sklearn.model_selection import train_test_split
from sklearn.metrics import accuracy_score

# Splitting data into training and testing sets
X_train, X_test, y_train, y_test = train_test_split(data.data, data.label, test_size
    =0.2, random_state=42)

# Convert data into DMatrix format
dtrain = xgb.DMatrix(X_train, label=y_train)
dtest = xgb.DMatrix(X_test, label=y_test)

# Define and train the model
model = xgb.train(params, dtrain, num_boost_round=100)

# Predict on test data
predictions = model.predict(dtest)

# Evaluate the model
accuracy = accuracy_score(y_test, (predictions > 0.5))
print(f'Accuracy: {accuracy}')
```

```
Accuracy: 0.857
```

XGBoost's robust framework for testing and validation, coupled with its computational efficiency, renders it an invaluable tool for machine learning practitioners. It enhances predictive performance through the integration of various advanced algorithms, thus standing out in the realm of ensemble learning methods.

7.6 Hyperparameter Tuning

Hyperparameter tuning is a crucial aspect of machine learning that significantly impacts a model's performance. Unlike model parameters, which are learned during training, hyperparameters are set prior to the training process and govern aspects of the learning algorithm and model architecture. Selecting appropriate hyperparameters can be the difference between a moderately performing model and one that achieves state-of-the-art results.

There are several common hyperparameters across different types of machine learning models. For instance, in a Random Forest classifier, key hyperparameters include the number of trees n_estimators, the maximum depth of each tree max_depth, and the minimum number of samples required to split an internal node min_samples_split. In gradient boosting methods, hyperparameters such as the learning rate learning_rate, the number of boosting stages n_estimators, and the maximum depth of the individual regression estimators are significant.

Grid Search is one of the most straightforward methods for hyperparameter tuning. This method involves defining a set of hyperparameters and systematically checking all possible combinations. For example, suppose we are tuning the hyperparameters for a Random Forest classifier as follows:

```
from sklearn.ensemble import RandomForestClassifier
from sklearn.model_selection import GridSearchCV

# Define the parameter grid
param_grid = {
    'n_estimators': [100, 200, 300],
    'max_depth': [None, 10, 20, 30],
    'min_samples_split': [2, 5, 10]
}

# Initialize the model
rf = RandomForestClassifier(random_state=42)

# Initialize the grid search
grid_search = GridSearchCV(estimator=rf, param_grid=param_grid, cv=5)

# Fit the grid search
grid_search.fit(X_train, y_train)

# Best parameters found
print("Best parameters found: ", grid_search.best_params_)
```

In this snippet, GridSearchCV from sklearn.model_selection is used. The param_grid is defined to include various values for n_estimators, max_depth, and min_samples_split. The grid search iterates through all combinations of these parameters with a five-fold cross-validation.

While grid search is exhaustive, it can be computationally expensive, especially for a large set of hyperparameters and combinations. **Random Search** provides a more efficient alternative by randomly sampling combinations of hyperparameters from a defined range.

```
from sklearn.model_selection import RandomizedSearchCV

# Define the parameter distribution
param_distribution = {
    'n_estimators': [100, 200, 300, 400, 500],
    'max_depth': [None, 10, 20, 30, 40, 50],
    'min_samples_split': [2, 5, 10, 15, 20]
}

# Initialize the random search
random_search = RandomizedSearchCV(estimator=rf, param_distributions=
    param_distribution, n_iter=100, cv=5, random_state=42)

# Fit the random search
random_search.fit(X_train, y_train)

# Best parameters found
print("Best parameters found: ", random_search.best_params_)
```

Here, RandomizedSearchCV is employed, where the number of iterations to perform (n_iter) must be specified. This method often yields comparable results to grid search but requires significantly less computational resource.

Bayesian Optimization is another sophisticated approach to hyperparameter tuning that builds a probabilistic model of the objective function and uses it to select the most promising hyperparameters to evaluate in the true objective function. Tools such as Hyperopt, Optuna, and BayesianOptimization libraries in Python make implementations straightforward.

```
from bayes_opt import BayesianOptimization

# Define the function to optimize
def rf_cv(n_estimators, max_depth, min_samples_split):
    val = cross_val_score(
        RandomForestClassifier(
            n_estimators=int(n_estimators),
            max_depth=int(max_depth),
            min_samples_split=int(min_samples_split),
            random_state=42
        ),
        X_train, y_train, scoring='accuracy', cv=5
    ).mean()
    return val

# Define the parameter bounds
param_bounds = {
    'n_estimators': (100, 500),
```

```
    'max_depth': (10, 50),
    'min_samples_split': (2, 20)
}

# Initialize the Bayesian optimizer
optimizer = BayesianOptimization(f=rf_cv, pbounds=param_bounds, random_state
    =42)

# Maximize the function
optimizer.maximize(init_points=10, n_iter=30)

# Best parameters
print("Best parameters found: ", optimizer.max)
```

In this Bayesian Optimization example, BayesianOptimization from the bayes_opt library is used. The rf_cv function specifies the cross-validation procedure on which the optimization is based. It iteratively updates the probability model, selecting the next set of hyperparameters to explore based on their likelihood to improve the model performance.

Automated hyperparameter tuning approaches like **Automated Machine Learning (AutoML)** simplify the process even further. Libraries such as auto-sklearn, TPOT, and H2O automate the process of selecting and tuning hyperparameters through sophisticated meta-learning and ensemble techniques.

Hyperparameter tuning is a fine balance between computational efficiency and the performance gains achieved through finding the most effective parameters. The choice of search method should be informed by available computational resources, the complexity of the model, and the specific characteristics of the dataset in question.

7.7 Feature Selection Techniques

Feature selection is a critical preprocessing step in building robust machine learning models. It aims to identify and select a subset of relevant features for use in model construction, thereby reducing dimensionality, improving model performance, and decreasing computational costs. Feature selection techniques can primarily be categorized into three groups: filter methods, wrapper methods, and embedded methods.

Filter methods operate independently of the learning algorithm and evaluate the relevance of features based on statistical measures. Common techniques include: information gain, chi-squared test, correlation coefficient, and variance thresholding.

Wrapper methods involve the use of a machine learning model to evaluate feature subsets. Methods such as Recursive Feature Elimination (RFE) and Sequential Feature Selection (SFS) fall into this category. These methods are computationally more expensive than filter methods but generally provide better performance as they consider the interaction between features.

Embedded methods perform feature selection as part of the model training process. Regularization techniques like Lasso, Ridge, and Elastic-Net, as well as tree-based methods, are prominent examples of embedded techniques.

Filter Methods

Filter methods are straightforward and efficient for high-dimensional datasets. They are based purely on the intrinsic properties of the features measured on the data. A common filter method is to rank features by their statistical significance:

- **1. Information Gain:** This technique evaluates the worth of a feature by measuring the information gain with respect to the class. Information gain is given by the difference in entropy before and after the dataset is split on the feature.

  $$IG = H(Y) - H(Y|X)$$

  where $H(Y)$ is the entropy of the target variable Y and $H(Y|X)$ is the conditional entropy of Y given feature X.

- **2. Chi-squared Test:** This test evaluates the independence of a feature with respect to the class labels. It is computed as:

  $$\chi^2 = \sum \frac{(O_i - E_i)^2}{E_i}$$

  where O_i is the observed frequency and E_i is the expected frequency.

- **3. Correlation Coefficient:** Features that are highly correlated with the target variable are considered more relevant. The Pearson Correlation Coefficient is defined as:

  $$\rho_{XY} = \frac{\text{Cov}(X, Y)}{\sigma_X \sigma_Y}$$

where Cov(X, Y) is the covariance between feature X and the target variable Y, and σ_X and σ_Y are the standard deviations of X and Y, respectively.

- **4. Variance Thresholding:** This method removes features with low variance, under the assumption that low variance features have little predictive power.

$$\text{Variance}(X) = \frac{1}{n}\sum_{i=1}^{n}(x_i - \bar{x})^2$$

where $\bar{x}$ is the mean of feature X.

Wrapper Methods

Wrapper methods evaluate feature subsets based on their performance with a specific algorithm. These methods are iterative and often computationally intensive.

- **1. Recursive Feature Elimination (RFE):** RFE recursively removes the least important features based on model performance. For example, using a Support Vector Machine (SVM) estimator, the RFE process can be implemented as follows:

```
from sklearn.feature_selection import RFE
from sklearn.svm import SVR

estimator = SVR(kernel="linear")
selector = RFE(estimator, n_features_to_select=5, step=1)
selector = selector.fit(X, y)
```

- **2. Sequential Feature Selection (SFS):** SFS can be forward or backward. In forward selection, features are added one by one, while in backward selection, all features are initially considered, and they are removed one by one:

```
from mlxtend.feature_selection import SequentialFeatureSelector as SFS
from sklearn.neighbors import KNeighborsClassifier

sfs = SFS(KNeighborsClassifier(),
          k_features=5,
          forward=True,
          floating=False,
          scoring='accuracy',
          cv=0)
sfs = sfs.fit(X, y)
```

Embedded Methods

Embedded methods incorporate feature selection as part of the model training process.

- **1. Regularization:** Regularization techniques such as Lasso (L1) and Ridge (L2) penalize the regression coefficients. Lasso can shrink some coefficients to zero, effectively performing feature selection:

```
from sklearn.linear_model import Lasso

lasso = Lasso(alpha=0.01)
lasso.fit(X, y)
selected_features = np.where(lasso.coef_ != 0)[0]
```

- **2. Tree-based Methods:** Decision Trees and ensembles such as Random Forests inherently perform feature selection by evaluating the importance of each feature based on the improvement in the splitting criterion:

```
from sklearn.ensemble import RandomForestClassifier

forest = RandomForestClassifier(n_estimators=100)
forest.fit(X, y)
importances = forest.feature_importances_
indices = np.argsort(importances)[::-1]
```

```
Feature Importance Ranking:
1. Feature1
2. Feature2
3. Feature3
...
```

The choice of feature selection technique depends on the specific dataset, the model to be used, and computational constraints. Effective feature selection can lead to simpler, more interpretable models while maintaining or even improving predictive performance.

7.8 Dimensionality Reduction with PCA

Dimensionality reduction is a crucial technique in data science and machine learning, aimed at reducing the number of random variables under consideration by obtaining a set of principal variables. One of the most commonly used methods for dimensionality reduction is Principal Component Analysis (PCA). PCA is a statistical procedure leveraging orthogonal transformation to convert a set of possibly correlated variables into a set of linearly uncorrelated variables called principal components.

PCA works by identifying the directions (principal components) along which the variation in the data is maximal. These principal components are orthogonal to each other, ensuring that they capture the maximum variance without redundancy.

The PCA algorithm can be summarized in the following steps:

- Standardization: Standardize the data to have a mean of 0 and a variance of 1. This ensures that each feature contributes equally to the analysis.
- Covariance Matrix Computation: Compute the covariance matrix to understand how the variables interact with each other.
- Eigenvalue and Eigenvector Calculation: Calculate the eigenvalues and eigenvectors of the covariance matrix to identify the principal components.
- Principal Components Selection: Select a subset of the eigenvectors as principal components based on the explained variance criterion.
- Projection: Project the original data onto the space defined by the selected principal components.

1. Standardization

To standardize the data, we subtract the mean of each feature from the dataset and then divide by the standard deviation. Given a dataset X with n samples and p features, the standardization process is given by:

$$X_{standardized} = \frac{X - \mu}{\sigma}$$

where μ is the mean and σ is the standard deviation of each feature.

```
from sklearn.preprocessing import StandardScaler
scaler = StandardScaler()
X_standardized = scaler.fit_transform(X)
```

2. Covariance Matrix Computation

The covariance matrix captures the pairwise covariances between the features. For a standardized dataset $X_{standardized}$, the covariance matrix Σ is computed as follows:

$$\Sigma = \frac{1}{n-1} X_{standardized}^T X_{standardized}$$

Using Python and NumPy, this can be calculated as:

```
import numpy as np
cov_matrix = np.cov(X_standardized, rowvar=False)
```

3. Eigenvalue and Eigenvector Calculation

The eigenvalues and eigenvectors of the covariance matrix are essential to PCA. Eigenvalues represent the magnitude of the variance captured by the eigenvectors (principal components). Eigenvalue decomposition of the covariance matrix provides these values:

```
eigenvalues, eigenvectors = np.linalg.eigh(cov_matrix)
```

4. Principal Components Selection

Eigenvalues indicate the variability captured by each principal component. Sorting the eigenvalues in descending order and selecting the top k eigenvectors corresponding to the largest eigenvalues allows us to choose the principal components explaining the majority of the variance:

```
# Sort eigenvalues and their corresponding eigenvectors
sorted_index = np.argsort(eigenvalues)[::-1]
sorted_eigenvalues = eigenvalues[sorted_index]
sorted_eigenvectors = eigenvectors[:, sorted_index]

# Select the top k eigenvectors
k = 2 # Example for 2 principal components
eigenvector_subset = sorted_eigenvectors[:, :k]
```

5. Projection

The final step involves projecting the original, standardized data onto the reduced space defined by the selected principal components:

```
X_reduced = np.dot(X_standardized, eigenvector_subset)
```

The resulting $X_{reduced}$ matrix contains the data represented in terms of the selected principal components.

Example: Applying PCA on Iris Dataset

To demonstrate PCA, we apply it to the Iris dataset available in the scikit-learn library:

```
from sklearn.decomposition import PCA
from sklearn.datasets import load_iris

# Load Iris dataset
iris = load_iris()
X = iris.data
y = iris.target

# Standardize the data
scaler = StandardScaler()
X_standardized = scaler.fit_transform(X)

# Apply PCA
pca = PCA(n_components=2)
X_pca = pca.fit_transform(X_standardized)

# Display the explained variance ratio
print(pca.explained_variance_ratio_)
```

The above code standardizes the Iris dataset and then applies PCA to reduce it to two principal components. The explained_variance_ratio_- attribute of the PCA object shows the percentage of variance explained by each of the selected components.

```
[0.72770452 0.23030523]
```

These values indicate that the first principal component explains approximately 72.77% of the variance, and the second explains 23.03%, totaling 95.80%.

PCA is a powerful tool for dimensionality reduction, providing insights into the intrinsic structure of data while reducing computational costs for subsequent analyses.

7.9 Dimensionality Reduction with t-SNE

t-distributed Stochastic Neighbor Embedding (t-SNE) is a powerful non-linear dimensionality reduction technique particularly well-suited for embedding high-dimensional data into a lower-dimensional space, typically two or three dimensions, for visualization purposes. Proposed by Laurens van der Maaten and Geoffrey Hinton in 2008, t-SNE has emerged as a popular method due to its ability to capture the local structure of high-dimensional data.

Algorithm Overview: The t-SNE algorithm consists of two stages:

1. **Constructing Probability Distribution in High-Dimensional**

Space: In this stage, t-SNE converts the Euclidean distances between data points into probabilities. Specifically, for a given data point i, it measures the probability $p_{j|i}$ that point j would be selected as the neighbor of point i under a Gaussian distribution centered at i. The joint probability p_{ij} is then symmetrized as:

$$p_{ij} = \frac{p_{j|i} + p_{i|j}}{2N}$$

where N is the number of data points.

2. **Constructing Probability Distribution in Low-Dimensional Space**: For the low-dimensional counterparts of the data points, t-SNE employs a similar probability measure but using a Student-t distribution (with one degree of freedom, which corresponds to the Cauchy distribution). The joint probabilities in the low-dimensional space are given by:

$$q_{ij} = \frac{(1 + \|y_i - y_j\|^2)^{-1}}{\sum_{k \neq l}(1 + \|y_k - y_l\|^2)^{-1}}$$

where y_i and y_j are points in the low-dimensional space.

3. **Minimizing the Kullback-Leibler Divergence**: The final step of t-SNE involves finding the low-dimensional embeddings by minimizing the Kullback-Leibler (KL) divergence between the two distributions P and Q using gradient descent. The objective function can be written as:

$$KL(P\|Q) = \sum_i \sum_j p_{ij} \log \left(\frac{p_{ij}}{q_{ij}} \right)$$

t-SNE is particularly effective at creating visualizations that highlight clusters or groups in the data due to its focus on preserving local structures. However, it is crucial to note that t-SNE is primarily a visualization tool and not typically used for tasks requiring low-dimensional representations for further processing.

Parameter Tuning: The performance of t-SNE greatly depends on the choice of its hyperparameters. Key hyperparameters include:

- **Perplexity**: This parameter is related to the number of nearest neighbors considered for each point. In practice, perplexity values between 5 and 50 typically yield good results.

- **Learning Rate**: The learning rate determines the step size at each iteration while optimizing the objective function. An inappropriate learning rate can lead to poor embeddings or slow convergence.
- **Number of Iterations**: The number of iterations impacts the convergence of the algorithm. More iterations usually result in better embeddings at the cost of increased computation time.

Practical Implementation Example: Below is an example of how to apply t-SNE using Python's scikit-learn library to a dataset.

```
import numpy as np
from sklearn.manifold import TSNE
import matplotlib.pyplot as plt

# Sample high-dimensional dataset
X = np.random.random((100, 50)) # For example, 100 points in 50 dimensions

# Create t-SNE object with chosen hyperparameters
tsne = TSNE(n_components=2, perplexity=30, learning_rate=200, n_iter=1000)

# Fit and transform the data
X_2d = tsne.fit_transform(X)

# Plotting the results
plt.scatter(X_2d[:, 0], X_2d[:, 1])
plt.title('t-SNE visualization')
plt.xlabel('Dimension 1')
plt.ylabel('Dimension 2')
plt.show()
```

The output of this code will be a 2-dimensional scatter plot visualizing the high-dimensional data points. It is important to experiment with different hyperparameters to achieve the best visualization depending on the dataset.

Advantages and Limitations: t-SNE has several advantages, notably its ability to reveal the underlying structure of the data and form visually interpretable clusters. However, it is computationally intensive, especially with large datasets. Moreover, the embeddings can vary with different initializations due to its stochastic nature.

Potential Use Cases: t-SNE finds applications in various domains such as:

- **Genomics**: Visualizing gene expression data to find patterns and clusters indicative of different biological conditions.
- **Neuroscience**: Analyzing neural activity patterns across different brain regions.

- **Natural Language Processing**: Embedding high-dimensional word or sentence representations into a space where semantic similarities can be visually inspected.
- **Computer Vision**: Visualizing layer activations of deep learning models to understand what features are being learned at different layers.

Understanding the practical aspects of t-SNE, from algorithmic foundations to implementation and use cases, enables leveraging its powerful dimensionality reduction capabilities to extract meaningful insights from complex and high-dimensional data.

7.10 Clustering Algorithms: K-Means, Hierarchical

Clustering is an unsupervised learning technique that organizes data points into groups based on similarity. Two fundamental clustering algorithms are K-Means and Hierarchical clustering, each with its unique methodologies and applications.

K-Means clustering is a centroid-based algorithm that partitions data into k clusters, where k is a user-defined parameter. The algorithm tries to minimize the variance within each cluster, iteratively refining the cluster centroids. Given the simplicity and efficiency of K-Means, it is a popular choice for large datasets.

The K-Means algorithm operates as follows:

- Initialize k cluster centroids randomly.
- Assign each data point to the nearest centroid, forming k clusters.
- Recompute the centroids as the mean of all data points assigned to each cluster.
- Repeat the assignment and centroid update steps until convergence or a specified number of iterations.

The core steps of the K-Means algorithm can be implemented in Python as shown in the following code snippet:

```
from sklearn.cluster import KMeans
import numpy as np

# Sample data
X = np.array([[1, 2], [1, 4], [1, 0],
              [10, 2], [10, 4], [10, 0]])

# Create KMeans instance with k=2
kmeans = KMeans(n_clusters=2, random_state=0)

# Fit the algorithm to data
kmeans.fit(X)

# Print cluster centers
print(kmeans.cluster_centers_)

# Print labels assigned to each data point
print(kmeans.labels_)
```

```
[[ 1.  2.]
 [10.  2.]]
[0 0 0 1 1 1]
```

K-Means has some limitations, such as its sensitivity to the initial selection of centroids and its tendency to form spherical clusters. These issues can be mitigated using techniques like k-means++ for better centroid initialization or using algorithms like DBSCAN for irregularly shaped clusters.

Hierarchical clustering, on the other hand, builds a tree-like structure called a dendrogram to represent nested clusters at various levels of similarity. It can be categorized into agglomerative (bottom-up) and divisive (top-down) clustering methods.

Agglomerative hierarchical clustering begins with each data point as a single cluster and iteratively merges the closest clusters until all points are in a single cluster. The proximity between clusters can be measured using different linkage criteria, such as single linkage (minimum distance), complete linkage (maximum distance), and average linkage (mean distance).

An example of agglomerative hierarchical clustering using the complete linkage criterion is implemented in Python as follows:

```
from scipy.cluster.hierarchy import dendrogram, linkage
import matplotlib.pyplot as plt

# Sample data
X = np.array([[1, 2], [1, 4], [1, 0],
              [10, 2], [10, 4], [10, 0]])

# Perform hierarchical/agglomerative clustering
Z = linkage(X, 'complete')
```

```
# Plot dendrogram
plt.figure()
dendrogram(Z)
plt.show()
```

Hierarchical clustering offers the advantage of a comprehensive view of data structure, providing insight into the levels of similarity between data points. However, it becomes computationally expensive as the dataset size increases, making it less practical for very large datasets.

Both K-Means and Hierarchical clustering have their strengths and applications. K-Means is suitable for scenarios needing efficient and scalable clustering, whereas Hierarchical clustering is valuable for detailed data structure analysis. Understanding these algorithms and their appropriate use cases enhances one's ability to handle complex data clustering tasks effectively.

7.11 Deep Learning Basics

Deep learning, a subset of machine learning, leverages neural networks with many layers—often referred to as deep neural networks (DNNs). These models are exceptional in handling large amounts of data and are highly effective in tasks such as image and speech recognition, natural language processing, and game playing. The foundation of deep learning is inspired by the biological neural networks in the human brain, making it a compelling approach for solving complex problems.

At the core of deep learning are artificial neural networks (ANNs). A basic neural network consists of an input layer, one or more hidden layers, and an output layer. Each layer comprises a certain number of nodes (or neurons), where each node performs a weighted sum of its inputs and applies an activation function to introduce non-linearity.

The function of a single neuron can be mathematically represented as follows:

$$y = f\left(\sum_{i=1}^{n} w_i x_i + b\right)$$

where y is the output, x_i are the input features, w_i are the weights, b is the bias, and f is the activation function.

Activation Functions

Activation functions are crucial in neural networks as they allow the model to capture non-linear relationships. Common activation functions include:

- **Sigmoid**: The sigmoid function maps any real-valued number into the range (0, 1). It's defined as:

$$\sigma(x) = \frac{1}{1 + e^{-x}}$$

- **Hyperbolic Tangent (tanh)**: The tanh function maps any real-valued number into the range (-1, 1). It's defined as:

$$\text{tanh}(x) = \frac{2}{1 + e^{-2x}} - 1$$

- **ReLU (Rectified Linear Unit)**: The ReLU function is now the most commonly used activation function in deep learning. It outputs zero if the input is negative, and the input itself if it is positive:

$$\text{ReLU}(x) = \text{max}(0, x)$$

- **Leaky ReLU**: An extension of ReLU that allows a small, non-zero gradient when the input is negative, to mitigate the dying ReLU problem:

$$\text{Leaky ReLU}(x) = \begin{cases} x & \text{if } x > 0 \\ \alpha x & \text{if } x \leq 0 \end{cases}$$

  where α is a small constant.

Forward and Backward Propagation

In a neural network, forward propagation is the process of moving input data through the layers to generate an output. This involves computing the weighted sum of inputs at each neuron, passing it through an activation function, and propagating the result to the next layer.

Here's an example of a simple feedforward process implemented in Python:

```
import numpy as np

def sigmoid(x):
    return 1 / (1 + np.exp(-x))

def feedforward(inputs, weights, biases):
    layer = inputs
    for w, b in zip(weights, biases):
```

```
        z = np.dot(layer, w) + b
        layer = sigmoid(z)
    return layer

inputs = np.array([0.5, 0.3])
weights = [np.array([[0.1, 0.4], [0.2, 0.5]]), np.array([[0.3], [0.6]])]
biases = [np.array([0.1, 0.1]), np.array([0.1])]
output = feedforward(inputs, weights, biases)
print(output)
```

The output from this code snippet will be:

```
[0.62245933]
```

Backward propagation, or backpropagation, is a technique used to train neural networks. It calculates the gradient of the loss function with respect to each weight by using the chain rule, iteratively adjusting the weights to minimize the loss.

Optimization Algorithms

Optimization involves adjusting the weights and biases of the network to minimize the loss function. Common algorithms include:

- **Stochastic Gradient Descent (SGD)**: A simple yet powerful optimization method which updates network parameters using the gradient of the loss function.
- **Adam (Adaptive Moment Estimation)**: An adaptive learning rate optimization algorithm that combines the benefits of AdaGrad and RMSProp to handle sparse gradients and non-stationary objectives:

  $$\theta_{t+1} = \theta_t - \frac{\eta}{\sqrt{\hat{v_t}} + \epsilon}\hat{m_t}$$

  where $\hat{m_t}$ and $\hat{v_t}$ are estimates of the first and second moments of the gradient, respectively, and η is the learning rate.

Neural Network Architectures

There are several common types of neural network architectures used in deep learning:

- **Fully Connected Networks (FCN)**: Every neuron in one layer is connected to every neuron in the next layer.
- **Convolutional Neural Networks (CNN)**: Primarily used for image data. CNNS use convolutional layers to automatically and adaptively learn spatial hierarchies of features.

- **Recurrent Neural Networks (RNN)**: Effective for sequential data. RNNs maintain a hidden state that captures information about previous inputs. Variants like LSTM and GRU address issues like vanishing gradients.

Regularization Techniques

Regularization techniques are introduced to prevent overfitting and to enhance the generalization capability of neural networks. Common methods include:

- **Dropout**: Randomly drops neurons during the training phase to prevent dependency on a particular neuron and ensure that the network learns robust features.
- **L2 Regularization**: Adds a penalty equal to the square of the magnitude of coefficients.

$$\text{Loss} = \text{Original Loss} + \lambda \sum \theta_i^2$$

  where λ is the regularization parameter.

Applications of deep learning span numerous domains, demonstrating its versatility and power. By understanding these foundational concepts, one can appreciate the complexity and potential of deep learning models in solving intricate problems.

7.12 Convolutional Neural Networks (CNN)

Convolutional Neural Networks (CNNs) are specialized architectures in deep learning, primarily designed to process and analyze visual data. They have become the backbone of many modern computer vision applications due to their ability to automatically and adaptively learn spatial hierarchies of features through backpropagation by using multiple building blocks, such as convolution layers, pooling layers, fully connected layers, and normalization.

At the core of CNNs lies the convolutional layer. The convolution operation applies a filter (or kernel) over the input image to produce a feature map. These filters consist of small matrices, typically of size 3×3, 5×5, or 7×7, which slide (or convolve) across the width and height of the input volume during the forward pass. The dot product between the entries of the filter and the input at any position provides the input at each point in the output feature map.

The mathematical operation at a single position can be described as:

$$Y(i,j) = \sum_m \sum_n X(i+m, j+n) \cdot W(m,n)$$

where X represents the input image, W denotes the convolutional filter, and Y is the output feature map. This operation is repeated as the filter slides across the entire input image.

Below is an example of implementing a convolution operation in Python using NumPy:

```
import numpy as np

def convolve2d(image, kernel):
    output = np.zeros_like(image)
    image_padded = np.pad(image, pad_width=((1, 1), (1, 1)), mode='constant')
    for x in range(image.shape[1]):
        for y in range(image.shape[0]):
            output[y, x] = (kernel * image_padded[y:y+3, x:x+3]).sum()
    return output

image = np.array([[1, 2, 3], [4, 5, 6], [7, 8, 9]])
kernel = np.array([[1, 0, -1], [1, 0, -1], [1, 0, -1]])
print(convolve2d(image, kernel))
```

The pooling layer performs a down-sampling operation along the spatial dimensions (width, height), reducing the dimensionality and allowing for the assumptions of the features to be invariant to small translations. The most common types of pooling are Max Pooling and Average Pooling. Max Pooling returns the maximum value, while Average Pooling returns the average within the defined window.

An example implementation of max pooling in Python:

```
def max_pooling(image, size=2, stride=2):
    output_shape = ((image.shape[0] - size) // stride + 1,
                    (image.shape[1] - size) // stride + 1)
    output = np.zeros(output_shape)
    for y in range(0, image.shape[0], stride):
        for x in range(0, image.shape[1], stride):
            output[y // stride, x // stride] = np.max(image[y:y + size, x:x + size])
    return output

image = np.array([[1, 2, 3, 0], [4, 5, 6, 1], [7, 8, 9, 2], [0, 1, 2, 3]])
print(max_pooling(image))
```

The fully connected (dense) layers follow one or more convolutional and pooling layers and perform the high-level reasoning in the neural network. Each node in a fully connected layer connects to every node in the previous layer, similar to a traditional feedforward neural network.

Normalization layers improve the training speed and make the model more stable. Batch Normalization is widely used, normalizing the output of a previous activation layer by subtracting the batch mean and dividing by the batch standard deviation.

To compile these operations into a functional CNN for image classification, frameworks such as TensorFlow or PyTorch are typically used. Below is an example demonstrating a simple CNN architecture using TensorFlow's Keras API:

```
import tensorflow as tf
from tensorflow.keras import layers, models

model = models.Sequential()
model.add(layers.Conv2D(32, (3, 3), activation='relu', input_shape=(64, 64, 3)))
model.add(layers.MaxPooling2D((2, 2)))
model.add(layers.Conv2D(64, (3, 3), activation='relu'))
model.add(layers.MaxPooling2D((2, 2)))
model.add(layers.Conv2D(64, (3, 3), activation='relu'))
model.add(layers.Flatten())
model.add(layers.Dense(64, activation='relu'))
model.add(layers.Dense(10, activation='softmax'))

model.compile(optimizer='adam', loss='sparse_categorical_crossentropy', metrics=['
    accuracy'])
```

The model summary for this CNN can be displayed using:

```
Model: "sequential"
_________________________________________________________________
Layer (type)              Output Shape              Param #
=================================================================
conv2d (Conv2D)             (None, 62, 62, 32)        896
max_pooling2d (MaxPooling2D)(None, 31, 31, 32)         0
conv2d_1 (Conv2D)             (None, 29, 29, 64)        18496
max_pooling2d_1 (MaxPooling2d)(None, 14, 14, 64)       0
conv2d_2 (Conv2D)             (None, 12, 12, 64)        36928
flatten (Flatten)          (None, 9216)              0
dense (Dense)               (None, 64)               589888
dense_1 (Dense)              (None, 10)               650
=================================================================
Total params: 646,858
Trainable params: 646,858
Non-trainable params: 0
_________________________________________________________________
```

In summary, Convolutional Neural Networks (CNNs) are indispensable in tackling visual recognition tasks. Understanding their architecture and functionality provides a strong foundation for implementing and optimizing deep learning models in practical applications.

7.13 Recurrent Neural Networks (RNN)

Recurrent Neural Networks (RNNs) are a class of neural networks that excel in handling sequential data by capturing dependencies and patterns across time steps. Unlike feedforward neural networks, which assume that inputs and outputs are independent of each other, RNNs leverage the temporal order in data, making them particularly suitable for tasks such as language modeling, time series prediction, and speech recognition.

An RNN maintains a hidden state, or memory, across time steps, which allows it to retain information from previous inputs. Mathematically, the hidden state $\mathbf{h}_t$ at time step t is computed as a function of the input $\mathbf{x}_t$ at that time step and the hidden state $\mathbf{h}_{t-1}$ from the previous time step:

$$\mathbf{h}_t = f(\mathbf{x}_t, \mathbf{h}_{t-1})$$

The function f is typically a non-linear activation function, such as the hyperbolic tangent (tanh) or the rectified linear unit (ReLU). The most common formulation of this function is:

$$\mathbf{h}_t = \sigma(\mathbf{W}_h \mathbf{h}_{t-1} + \mathbf{W}_x \mathbf{x}_t + \mathbf{b})$$

where $\mathbf{W}_h$ and $\mathbf{W}_x$ are weight matrices, $\mathbf{b}$ is the bias vector, and σ denotes an activation function such as tanh or ReLU.

The output $\mathbf{y}_t$ at time step t is derived from the hidden state $\mathbf{h}_t$:

$$\mathbf{y}_t = g(\mathbf{W}_y \mathbf{h}_t + \mathbf{b}_y)$$

where $\mathbf{W}_y$ is the output weight matrix, $\mathbf{b}_y$ is the output bias vector, and g is an activation function appropriate for the task, such as a softmax function for classification.

Backpropagation Through Time (BPTT)

Training RNNs involves adjusting the weights $\{\mathbf{W}_h, \mathbf{W}_x, \mathbf{W}_y, \mathbf{b}, \mathbf{b}_y\}$ to minimize a loss function, similar to other neural networks. However, because RNNs handle sequences, the gradient must be propagated back through time, a process known as Backpropagation Through Time (BPTT).

During BPTT, the loss at each time step is computed, and gradients are accumulated across time steps. This enables the weights to be updated in a way that accounts for the temporal dependencies in the data. However, vanilla RNNs are prone to issues like vanishing and exploding gradients, which can make training difficult, especially for long sequences.

Long Short-Term Memory (LSTM)

To address the limitations of vanilla RNNs, more advanced recurrent architectures such as Long Short-Term Memory (LSTM) networks were developed. LSTMs introduce a memory cell that can maintain information over long periods, controlled by gate mechanisms:

- The **forget gate** $\mathbf{f}_t$ controls the extent to which the previous cell state $\mathbf{C}_{t-1}$ is forgotten:

$$\mathbf{f}_t = \sigma(\mathbf{W}_f \mathbf{x}_t + \mathbf{U}_f \mathbf{h}_{t-1} + \mathbf{b}_f)$$

- The **input gate** $\mathbf{i}_t$ determines how much of the new input $\mathbf{x}_t$ is used to update the memory cell:

$$\mathbf{i}_t = \sigma(\mathbf{W}_i \mathbf{x}_t + \mathbf{U}_i \mathbf{h}_{t-1} + \mathbf{b}_i)$$

- The **output gate** $\mathbf{o}_t$ decides how much of the cell state $\mathbf{C}_t$ is exposed to the hidden state:

$$\mathbf{o}_t = \sigma(\mathbf{W}_o \mathbf{x}_t + \mathbf{U}_o \mathbf{h}_{t-1} + \mathbf{b}_o)$$

- The **cell state** $\mathbf{C}_t$ is updated as follows:

$$\mathbf{C}_t = \mathbf{f}_t \odot \mathbf{C}_{t-1} + \mathbf{i}_t \odot \widetilde{\mathbf{C}}_t$$

  where $\widetilde{\mathbf{C}}_t$ is the candidate cell state:

$$\widetilde{\mathbf{C}}_t = \tanh(\mathbf{W}_C \mathbf{x}_t + \mathbf{U}_C \mathbf{h}_{t-1} + \mathbf{b}_C)$$

- Finally, the hidden state $\mathbf{h}_t$ is computed as:

$$\mathbf{h}_t = \mathbf{o}_t \odot \tanh(\mathbf{C}_t)$$

These gating mechanisms enable the LSTM to maintain and update its cell state over long sequences, mitigating the vanishing gradient problem and allowing it to learn long-term dependencies.

Gated Recurrent Unit (GRU)

An alternative to the LSTM is the Gated Recurrent Unit (GRU), which simplifies the architecture by combining the forget and input gates into a single update gate. The mathematical formulation of a GRU is as follows:

- The **update gate** $\mathbf{z}_t$ determines the new memory content to be added:

$$\mathbf{z}_t = \sigma(\mathbf{W}_z \mathbf{x}_t + \mathbf{U}_z \mathbf{h}_{t-1} + \mathbf{b}_z)$$

- The **reset gate** $\mathbf{r}_t$ controls the extent of the previous state to forget:

$$\mathbf{r}_t = \sigma(\mathbf{W}_r \mathbf{x}_t + \mathbf{U}_r \mathbf{h}_{t-1} + \mathbf{b}_r)$$

- The hidden state $\mathbf{h}_t$ is updated as follows:

$$\mathbf{h}_t = \mathbf{z}_t \odot \mathbf{h}_{t-1} + (1 - \mathbf{z}_t) \odot \widetilde{\mathbf{h}}_t$$

  where $\widetilde{\mathbf{h}}_t$ is the candidate hidden state:

$$\widetilde{\mathbf{h}}_t = \tanh(\mathbf{W}_h \mathbf{x}_t + \mathbf{U}_h(\mathbf{r}_t \odot \mathbf{h}_{t-1}) + \mathbf{b}_h)$$

GRUs, like LSTMs, are designed to capture long-term dependencies and have gained popularity due to their simpler architecture and empirically similar performance to LSTMs on various tasks.

Applications of RNNs

RNNs, including variants like LSTMs and GRUs, are widely used in various applications. In natural language processing (NLP), they're employed for tasks such as machine translation, where the sequential nature of text data naturally fits the RNN architecture. In time series forecasting, RNNs predict future values based on historical data sequences. In speech recognition, RNNs interpret audio signals that vary over time, and in music generation, they can create new compositions by learning from existing music sequences.

Implementing an RNN

The practical implementation of an RNN can be demonstrated using Python and libraries such as TensorFlow or PyTorch. Below is a simple implementation of an RNN using PyTorch:

```
import torch
import torch.nn as nn

class SimpleRNN(nn.Module):
    def __init__(self, input_size, hidden_size, output_size):
        super(SimpleRNN, self).__init__()
        self.hidden_size = hidden_size
        self.rnn = nn.RNN(input_size, hidden_size, batch_first=True)
        self.fc = nn.Linear(hidden_size, output_size)

    def forward(self, x):
        h0 = torch.zeros(1, x.size(0), self.hidden_size).to(x.device)
        out, _ = self.rnn(x, h0)
```

```
        out = self.fc(out[:, -1, :])
        return out

input_size = 10
hidden_size = 20
output_size = 1

model = SimpleRNN(input_size, hidden_size, output_size)
criterion = nn.MSELoss()
optimizer = torch.optim.Adam(model.parameters(), lr=0.001)

# Dummy input and target tensors
inputs = torch.randn(32, 5, input_size)
targets = torch.randn(32, output_size)

# Training loop
outputs = model(inputs)
loss = criterion(outputs, targets)
optimizer.zero_grad()
loss.backward()
optimizer.step()
```

```
Output:
    tensor([[-0.2507],
            [ 0.1154],
            [ 0.1371],
            ...
            [-0.2134],
            [ 0.2741],
            ...
            [-0.0459]])
```

This code initializes a simple RNN, defines the forward pass, and constructs a training loop to optimize the model parameters based on mean squared error loss.

7.14 Transfer Learning

Transfer learning is a powerful concept in machine learning that leverages pre-trained models on related tasks to enhance performance on new but related tasks. This technique is particularly advantageous when dealing with insufficient data by transferring knowledge from a large and diverse dataset to a smaller, specialized one.

The fundamental idea behind transfer learning is to apply the knowledge gained from one domain (the source) to another domain (the target). In practice, this involves the following steps:

- **Pre-training a model on a source dataset:** This phase involves training a model on a large, diverse dataset, typically involving a related task. Commonly used datasets for pre-training include

ImageNet for image-related tasks and large text corpora for NLP applications.

- **Transferring the model parameters:** The pre-trained model's layers and parameters are then used as the starting point for a model on the target task. Generally, the initial layers capture generic features (e.g., edges and textures in images) that are useful across multiple tasks.

- **Fine-tuning the model:** The model is then fine-tuned on the target task's dataset. During this phase, some layers of the model may be frozen (i.e., their weights are not updated) to retain their learned features, while others are retrained to adapt to the specifics of the target task.

Transfer learning is highly effective in several domains, particularly in computer vision and natural language processing (NLP). Detailed exploration of its application in these domains is provided below.

Computer Vision:

In computer vision, transfer learning usually involves convolutional neural networks (CNNs). Models pre-trained on large datasets like ImageNet can be fine-tuned for applications such as medical image analysis, where annotated data is limited. For instance, a pre-trained ResNet50 model can serve as a backbone for a medical image classification task.

Consider the Python code below demonstrating the use of a pre-trained ResNet50 model from the Keras library for a new image classification task:

```
from tensorflow.keras.applications import ResNet50
from tensorflow.keras.layers import Dense, Flatten
from tensorflow.keras.models import Model
from tensorflow.keras.optimizers import Adam

# Load the pre-trained model
base_model = ResNet50(weights='imagenet', include_top=False, input_shape=(224,
    224, 3))

# Freeze the layers except the last few
for layer in base_model.layers:
    layer.trainable = False

# Add custom layers for the new task
x = base_model.output
x = Flatten()(x)
x = Dense(1024, activation='relu')(x)
predictions = Dense(10, activation='softmax')(x) % Assuming a 10-class classification
    problem
```

```
# Create the new model
model = Model(inputs=base_model.input, outputs=predictions)

# Compile the model
model.compile(optimizer=Adam(), loss='categorical_crossentropy', metrics=['accuracy'
    ])

# Summary of the model
model.summary()
```

The code initializes a ResNet50 model pre-trained on ImageNet, freezes its layers to retain the learned features, and adds custom layers for a new classification task. This approach enables the transfer of features learned from a vast dataset to a new, smaller dataset.

Natural Language Processing (NLP):

In NLP, transfer learning typically involves models like BERT (Bidirectional Encoder Representations from Transformers), GPT (Generative Pre-trained Transformer), and their variants. These models are pre-trained on extensive text corpora and fine-tuned for specific tasks such as sentiment analysis, named entity recognition, or machine translation.

Here is an example of fine-tuning a BERT model for a text classification task using the Hugging Face Transformers library:

```
from transformers import BertTokenizer, BertForSequenceClassification, Trainer,
    TrainingArguments

# Load the pre-trained BERT model and tokenizer
model = BertForSequenceClassification.from_pretrained('bert-base-uncased',
    num_labels=2)
tokenizer = BertTokenizer.from_pretrained('bert-base-uncased')

# Tokenize and prepare data (example with dummy data)
texts = ["This is a positive example.", "This is a negative example."]
labels = [1, 0]
encodings = tokenizer(texts, truncation=True, padding=True, max_length=128)
inputs = encodings['input_ids']
attention_mask = encodings['attention_mask']

# Define a dataset class
from torch.utils.data import Dataset

class TextDataset(Dataset):
    def __init__(self, inputs, attention_mask, labels):
        self.inputs = inputs
        self.attention_mask = attention_mask
        self.labels = labels

    def __len__(self):
        return len(self.labels)

    def __getitem__(self, idx):
        return {'input_ids': self.inputs[idx], 'attention_mask': self.attention_mask[idx],
```

```
            'labels': self.labels[idx]}

dataset = TextDataset(inputs, attention_mask, labels)

# Define training arguments
training_args = TrainingArguments(
    output_dir='./results',
    num_train_epochs=1,
    per_device_train_batch_size=4,
    warmup_steps=10,
    weight_decay=0.01,
    logging_dir='./logs',
)

# Initialize Trainer
trainer = Trainer(
    model=model,
    args=training_args,
    train_dataset=dataset,
)

# Train the model
trainer.train()
```

This code snippet shows the process of loading a pre-trained BERT model, tokenizing the input texts, defining a custom dataset, and setting up a training loop using the Trainer class. The model is then fine-tuned for a binary text classification task.

The effectiveness of transfer learning is evident from its widespread adoption in various applications, leading to enhanced model performance and reduced training time. By leveraging pre-trained models, practitioners can achieve significant improvements even with limited target data, making transfer learning an invaluable tool in the data scientist's arsenal.

Chapter 8

Natural Language Processing

This chapter covers the essential techniques in Natural Language Processing (NLP), starting with text preprocessing, tokenization, and text normalization. It explores methods for text representation, such as Bag of Words and TF-IDF, and advanced word embeddings like Word2Vec and GloVe. Key NLP tasks including text classification, Named Entity Recognition (NER), sentiment analysis, and topic modeling are discussed. The chapter also delves into sequence-to-sequence models, transformers such as BERT, and evaluation metrics for NLP applications.

8.1 Introduction to Natural Language Processing

Natural Language Processing (NLP) is a subfield of artificial intelligence (AI) that focuses on the interaction between computers and human language. It encompasses a variety of computational techniques and algorithms to process and analyze large amounts of natural language data. The ultimate goal in NLP is to enable computers to understand, interpret, and respond to human languages in a way that is both meaningful and useful.

The foundation of NLP is rooted in multiple disciplines, including computer science, linguistics, and cognitive psychology. The convergence of these fields has facilitated the development of sophisticated models and algorithms capable of handling complex linguistic structures and semantics.

To effectively engage with NLP, one must be familiar with several fundamental concepts and methodologies:

- **Text Preprocessing**: The initial step in many NLP tasks, which involves cleaning and preparing the textual data for further analysis. This includes removing noise such as punctuation and special characters, converting text to lowercase, and handling missing values.
- **Tokenization**: The process of breaking down text into smaller units called tokens, which can be words, subwords, or characters. Tokenization facilitates the analysis of individual tokens and their syntactic and semantic properties.
- **Text Normalization**: Techniques for standardizing text to a common format. This can involve stemming (reducing words to their root form) or lemmatization (reducing words to their base or dictionary form).
- **Text Representation**: Methods to convert textual data into numerical vectors that can be input to machine learning algorithms. Common approaches include Bag of Words (BoW), Term Frequency-Inverse Document Frequency (TF-IDF), and advanced word embeddings like Word2Vec and GloVe.

Key Applications of NLP:

- **Text Classification**: Assigning predefined categories to text inputs, such as spam detection in emails or sentiment analysis in social media.
- **Named Entity Recognition (NER)**: Identifying and classifying entities (e.g., names of people, organizations, locations) within a text.
- **Machine Translation**: Automatically translating text from one language to another.
- **Question Answering**: Developing systems that can understand and respond to human queries in natural language.

- **Sentiment Analysis**: Determining the sentiment or emotion conveyed by a piece of text, often used in market research and social media monitoring.

- **Topic Modeling**: Discovering abstract topics that occur in a collection of documents, often used for document clustering and summarization.

Recent advancements in NLP have been driven by the development of neural network-based models and the availability of large-scale datasets. Deep learning techniques, particularly those involving sequence-to-sequence models and transformers such as BERT (Bidirectional Encoder Representations from Transformers), have significantly enhanced the performance of various NLP tasks. These models can capture intricate patterns in data through vast networks of interconnected neurons.

```
import nltk
from nltk.tokenize import word_tokenize

nltk.download('punkt')

text = "Natural Language Processing enables computers to understand and respond to
    human language."

# Tokenizing the text
tokens = word_tokenize(text)
print(tokens)
```

```
['Natural', 'Language', 'Processing', 'enables', 'computers', 'to', 'understand', 'and', 'respond', 'to', 'human', 'language', '.']
```

This example demonstrates the basic tokenization process, highlighting how a string of text is converted into individual words, or tokens, utilizing the Natural Language Toolkit (nltk) in Python. Tokenization is foundational to many other NLP processes, serving as the initial step in converting raw text into a structured format for subsequent analysis.

NLP also places significant emphasis on evaluation metrics to measure the performance of models accurately. Commonly used metrics include accuracy, precision, recall, F1-score, and BLEU score for tasks like text translation. These metrics provide insights into the model's capability to handle variation in language and its ability to generalize well on unseen data.

The evolution of NLP is a testament to the interdisciplinary collaboration among various scientific domains. With continuous advancements in computational power and algorithmic techniques, the potential applications and efficacy of NLP are expanding rapidly, making it an indispensable tool in the field of Artificial Intelligence and data science.

8.2 Text Preprocessing Techniques

Text preprocessing is a crucial step in Natural Language Processing (NLP) that ensures the text data is clean, consistent, and ready for subsequent analysis. This process typically includes several stages: removing unwanted characters, handling punctuations, normalizing text, and removing stop words. Each stage plays a pivotal role in enhancing the quality of the input data, which in turn improves the performance of NLP models.

1. Removing Unwanted Characters

Unwanted characters such as special symbols, digits, and other non-alphabetic characters often need to be removed from the text. These characters can introduce noise and affect the accuracy of text processing tasks. One common approach to remove such unwanted characters is to use regular expressions.

```
import re

def remove_unwanted_chars(text):
    return re.sub(r'[^a-zA-Z\s]', '', text)

sample_text = "Hello, World! 123"
cleaned_text = remove_unwanted_chars(sample_text)
print(cleaned_text) # Output: Hello World
```

2. Handling Punctuation

Punctuation marks can sometimes carry significant meaning in a sentence but often, they are removed to simplify text analysis. When removing punctuation, we can still preserve the whitespace to maintain the separation between words.

```
import string

def remove_punctuation(text):
    return text.translate(str.maketrans('', '', string.punctuation))

sample_text = "Hello, World! How's everything?"
cleaned_text = remove_punctuation(sample_text)
print(cleaned_text) # Output: Hello World Hows everything
```

3. Text Normalization

Text normalization involves converting the text into a standard format, which generally includes lowering the case of all characters and expanding contractions.

- **Lowercasing**:

  Lowercasing ensures that words like "Apple" and "apple" are treated as the same word.

```
def to_lowercase(text):
    return text.lower()

sample_text = "Hello World"
normalized_text = to_lowercase(sample_text)
print(normalized_text) # Output: hello world
```

- **Expanding Contractions**:

  Contractions are shortened forms of words or syllables. Expanding them can facilitate the understanding of text.

```
import contractions

def expand_contractions(text):
    return contractions.fix(text)

sample_text = "I'm learning NLP."
expanded_text = expand_contractions(sample_text)
print(expanded_text) # Output: I am learning NLP.
```

4. Removing Stop Words

Stop words are common words such as "and", "is", "in", and "the" that carry less meaningful information. Removing these can often improve the performance of NLP tasks by reducing the dimensionality of the text data.

```
from nltk.corpus import stopwords

def remove_stop_words(text):
    stop_words = set(stopwords.words('english'))
    return ' '.join([word for word in text.split() if word.lower() not in stop_words])

sample_text = "This is a sample sentence for processing."
cleaned_text = remove_stop_words(sample_text)
print(cleaned_text) # Output: This sample sentence processing
```

5. Stemming and Lemmatization

Both stemming and lemmatization are normalization techniques aimed at reducing words to their base or root form.

- **Stemming**:

  Stemming involves reducing a word to its root form. It usually removes suffixes to achieve this.

```
from nltk.stem import PorterStemmer

def stem_text(text):
    stemmer = PorterStemmer()
    return ' '.join([stemmer.stem(word) for word in text.split()])

sample_text = "playing played player"
stemmed_text = stem_text(sample_text)
print(stemmed_text) # Output: play play player
```

- **Lemmatization**:

  Lemmatization reduces a word to its base or dictionary form, considering the context. It requires additional information like the part of speech.

```
from nltk.stem import WordNetLemmatizer
from nltk.corpus import wordnet

def get_wordnet_pos(word):
    tag = nltk.pos_tag([word])[0][1][0].upper()
    tag_dict = {'J': wordnet.ADJ, 'N': wordnet.NOUN, 'V': wordnet.VERB, 'R':
          wordnet.ADV}
    return tag_dict.get(tag, wordnet.NOUN)

def lemmatize_text(text):
    lemmatizer = WordNetLemmatizer()
    return ' '.join([lemmatizer.lemmatize(word, get_wordnet_pos(word)) for
         word in text.split()])

sample_text = "running ran runs"
lemmatized_text = lemmatize_text(sample_text)
print(lemmatized_text) # Output: running run run
```

Accurate text preprocessing sets the foundation for more complex NLP tasks such as text classification, named entity recognition, sentiment analysis, and more. The techniques outlined streamline the text, making it more manageable for machine learning models by reducing noise and standardizing its format.

8.3 Tokenization and Text Normalization

Tokenization and text normalization form foundational pre-processing steps in Natural Language Processing (NLP). These processes convert raw text into structured data that models can more effectively interpret. Tokenization splits text into individual units or tokens, while text normalization standardizes these tokens in a consistent format.

Tokenization can be approached at different levels, most commonly at the word and sub-word levels. Another frequently used method is the sentence-level tokenization. These methods ensure that each token retains semantic meaning, facilitating more nuanced analysis.

- **Word Tokenization:** This involves dividing a sentence into individual words. It is typically the simplest tokenization form but can be challenging for languages without clear word delimiters. The implementation can be illustrated as follows:

```
import nltk
nltk.download('punkt')
from nltk.tokenize import word_tokenize

text = "Tokenization is essential for NLP tasks."
tokens = word_tokenize(text)
print(tokens)
```

```
Output:
['Tokenization', 'is', 'essential', 'for', 'NLP', 'tasks', '.']
```

- **Sub-word Tokenization:** This approach breaks down words into smaller components, such as morphemes. It is universally beneficial in handling out-of-vocabulary words or languages with rich morphology. Byte Pair Encoding (BPE) is a common algorithm for this. A sample implementation in Python using the tokenizers library is given below:

```
from tokenizers import BertWordPieceTokenizer

tokenizer = BertWordPieceTokenizer()
tokenizer.train(files="data.txt", vocab_size=5000, min_frequency=2)

tokens = tokenizer.encode("Tokenization is essential for NLP tasks.")
print(tokens.tokens)
```

```
Output:
['[CLS]', 'Token', '##ization', 'is', 'essential', 'for', 'N', '##LP', 'tasks', '.', '[SEP]']
```

- **Sentence Tokenization:** This method splits a text into sentences. It is particularly useful for models that require sentence-level information. Below is a Python example using the Natural Language Toolkit (nltk):

```
from nltk.tokenize import sent_tokenize

text = "Tokenization is essential for NLP tasks. It helps in various preprocessing steps."

sentences = sent_tokenize(text)
print(sentences)
```

Output:
['Tokenization is essential for NLP tasks.', 'It helps in various preprocessing steps.']

- **Text Normalization:** After tokenization, text normalization processes adjust the tokens to a consistent format. It includes converting text to lowercase, stemming, lemmatization, and removing punctuation or stopwords.

- **Lowercasing:** Converting all tokens to lowercase to ensure uniformity:

```
tokens = ["Tokenization", "is", "essential", "for", "NLP", "tasks", "."]
lowercase_tokens = [token.lower() for token in tokens]
print(lowercase_tokens)
```

Output:
['tokenization', 'is', 'essential', 'for', 'nlp', 'tasks', '.']

- **Stemming:** Reduces words to their root forms but might not result in actual words. The Porter Stemming algorithm is widely used:

```
from nltk.stem import PorterStemmer

stemmer = PorterStemmer()
stemmed_tokens = [stemmer.stem(token) for token in tokens]
print(stemmed_tokens)
```

Output:
['token', 'is', 'essenti', 'for', 'nlp', 'task', '.']

- **Lemmatization:** Converts words to their dictionary form. Unlike stemming, lemmatization always results in actual words:

```
from nltk.stem import WordNetLemmatizer

lemmatizer = WordNetLemmatizer()
lemmatized_tokens = [lemmatizer.lemmatize(token) for token in tokens]
print(lemmatized_tokens)
```

Output:
['Tokenization', 'is', 'essential', 'for', 'NLP', 'task', '.']

- **Removing Punctuation and Stopwords:** Cleansing the text by eliminating punctuation and frequently occurring, semantically irrelevant words (stopwords). An example is provided below:

```
from nltk.corpus import stopwords
import string

stop_words = set(stopwords.words('english'))
clean_tokens = [token for token in tokens if token not in string.punctuation and token.
    lower() not in stop_words]
print(clean_tokens)
```

```
Output:
['Tokenization', 'essential', 'NLP', 'tasks']
```

Tokenization and text normalization are indispensable for preparing raw text for subsequent NLP models. These processes ensure that all text data maintains a consistent structure and format, pivotal for achieving accurate and efficient data analysis.

8.4 Text Representation: Bag of Words, TF-IDF

Text representation is a critical step in Natural Language Processing (NLP), transforming textual data into numerical representations that machine learning algorithms can process. Representing text effectively is essential for achieving high-performance models. Two foundational methods for text representation are the Bag of Words (BoW) model and Term Frequency-Inverse Document Frequency (TF-IDF).

The Bag of Words model is one of the simplest and most intuitive methods for text representation. This approach disregards grammar, word order, sentence structure, and even punctuation, focusing solely on the presence and frequency of words within a text. Conceptually, the BoW model treats a piece of text as a collection of individual words without context.

To construct a Bag of Words representation, follow these steps:

- Create a vocabulary from a corpus of text.
- Generate a vector of word counts for each document based on this vocabulary.

For example, consider a small corpus with the following documents:

```
Document1: "The cat sat on the mat"
Document2: "The dog lay on the rug"
```

First, we build a vocabulary of unique words:

Vocabulary: ["The", "cat", "sat", "on", "the", "mat", "dog", "lay", "rug"]

Next, create a term-frequency vector for each document using this vocabulary:

Document1: [2, 1, 1, 1, 1, 1, 0, 0, 0]
Document2: [1, 0, 0, 1, 1, 0, 1, 1, 1]

Here, the elements of each vector represent the count of corresponding words in the vocabulary. This representation allows the documents to be analyzed using various machine learning algorithms.

While BoW is straightforward, it has some limitations. This model doesn't consider the semantic meaning or context of words and often leads to large and sparse matrices. Additionally, it treats all words equally, failing to recognize that some words, like stop words, may not contribute significant information.

To address some of these limitations, the TF-IDF method refines the BoW approach by accounting for the importance of words within documents and across the entire corpus. It combines two metrics: Term Frequency (TF) and Inverse Document Frequency (IDF).

- **Term Frequency (TF)**: Measures how frequently a term appears in a document. The term frequency for term *t* in document *d* is given by:

$$TF(t,d) = \frac{\text{Number of times term } t \text{ appears in document } d}{\text{Total number of terms in document } d}$$

- **Inverse Document Frequency (IDF)**: Measures how important a term is within the entire corpus. Terms that appear in many documents have lower IDF values. It is calculated as:

$$IDF(t) = \log\left(\frac{N}{df(t)}\right)$$

  where N is the total number of documents, and $df(t)$ is the number of documents containing term *t*.

The TF-IDF value for a term *t* in document *d* is computed as:

$$TF - IDF(t,d) = TF(t,d) \times IDF(t)$$

Consider the previous example documents. Assume a corpus consisting of 2 documents:

```
Document1: "The cat sat on the mat"
Document2: "The dog lay on the rug"
```

For this corpus, calculate the TF values for each term in Document1:

TF(cat, Document1) = 1/6
TF(sat, Document1) = 1/6
TF(on, Document1) = 1/6
TF(mat, Document1) = 1/6
TF(The, Document1) = 1/6
TF(the, Document1) = 1/6

Next, calculate the IDF values for the terms across the entire corpus:

IDF(cat) = log(2/1) = 0.301
IDF(sat) = log(2/1) = 0.301
IDF(on) = log(2/2) = 0
IDF(mat) = log(2/1) = 0.301
IDF(The) = log(2/2) = 0
IDF(the) = log(2/2) = 0

Finally, compute the TF-IDF values for Document1:

TF-IDF(cat, Document1) = TF(cat, Document1) * IDF(cat) = (1/6) * 0.301 = 0.0502
TF-IDF(sat, Document1) = TF(sat, Document1) * IDF(sat) = (1/6) * 0.301 = 0.0502
TF-IDF(on, Document1) = TF(on, Document1) * IDF(on) = (1/6) * 0 = 0
TF-IDF(mat, Document1) = TF(mat, Document1) * IDF(mat) = (1/6) * 0.301 = 0.0502
TF-IDF(The, Document1) = TF(The, Document1) * IDF(The) = (1/6) * 0 = 0
TF-IDF(the, Document1) = TF(the, Document1) * IDF(the) = (1/6) * 0 = 0

TF-IDF mitigates the influence of common words and highlights words that are more significant regarding their frequency within a specific document. This results in a more informative representation of text suitable for various NLP applications, including information retrieval and text mining.

By employing TF-IDF, the representation of text not only reflects the occurrence of words but also emphasizes distinctiveness within the corpus, providing a richer characterization of the textual data.

8.5 Word Embeddings: Word2Vec, GloVe

Word embeddings are dense vector representations of words which capture semantic and syntactic information. Unlike the traditional Bag of Words model which only considers the presence or absence of words, word embeddings map words into continuous vector spaces where semantically similar words are positioned closely. Two of the most influential techniques for generating word embeddings are Word2Vec and GloVe.

Word2Vec is a neural network-based method to learn word embeddings from a large corpus of text. It comes in two variants: Continuous Bag of Words (CBOW) and Skip-gram. CBOW predicts the current word based on its context, while Skip-gram predicts surrounding words given the current word. Here is a simple Python implementation of Word2Vec using the gensim library:

```
from gensim.models import Word2Vec
sentences = [['the', 'quick', 'brown', 'fox', 'jumps', 'over', 'the', 'lazy', 'dog']]
model = Word2Vec(sentences, size=100, window=5, min_count=1, workers=4)
word_vector = model.wv['quick']
print(word_vector)
```

The size parameter specifies the dimensions of the word vectors, window defines the maximum distance between the current and predicted word within a sentence, and min_count ignores all words with total frequency lower than this value.

In contrast, GloVe (Global Vectors for Word Representation) is an unsupervised learning algorithm for obtaining vector representations for words by aggregating global word-word co-occurrence statistics from a corpus. The objective function of GloVe ensures the ratio of word-word co-occurrence probabilities is preserved. The equation central to GloVe is:

$$J = \sum_{i,j=1}^{V} f(P_{ij})(w_i^T \cdot \tilde{w}_j + b_i + \tilde{b}_j - \text{log}(X_{ij}))^2$$

where P_{ij} is the probability of word j appearing in the context of word i, w_i and $\tilde{w}_j$ are the word vectors, and X_{ij} is the count of word j in the context of word i. The function $f(P_{ij})$ is a weighting function that reduces the effect of very frequent co-occurrences.

An example of using GloVe vectors in Python can be seen with the pre-trained embeddings provided by the Stanford NLP Group:

```
import numpy as np

def load_glove_embeddings(file_path):
    embeddings_index = {}
    with open(file_path, 'r', encoding='utf-8') as f:
        for line in f:
            values = line.split()
            word = values[0]
            coefs = np.asarray(values[1:], dtype='float32')
            embeddings_index[word] = coefs
    return embeddings_index

glove_embeddings = load_glove_embeddings('glove.6B.100d.txt')
print(glove_embeddings['quick'])
```

This script loads GloVe embeddings from a file, mapping each word to its vector representation. The vectors can then be used for various downstream NLP tasks requiring semantic similarity measures.

Both Word2Vec and GloVe have their strengths; Word2Vec tends to excel with smaller datasets due to its local context prediction, while GloVe leverages global statistical information effectively. Subsequent advances, such as FastText which builds on Word2Vec by considering sub-word information, continue to improve the quality and robustness of word embeddings.

Understanding and effectively utilizing word embeddings is crucial for enhancements in NLP tasks like text classification, sentiment analysis, and named entity recognition, enabling models to generalize better and achieve greater accuracy by capturing deeper linguistic patterns.

8.6 Language Models: n-grams, Neural Language Models

Language modeling is a crucial component in Natural Language Processing (NLP), aimed at understanding and predicting the distribution and sequence of words within a linguistic context. Language models serve as the foundation for various NLP tasks such as text generation, machine translation, and speech recognition. This section covers two primary types of language models: *n-gram models* and *neural language models*.

n-gram Language Models:

An n-gram model is a type of probabilistic language model for predicting the next word in a sequence based on the previous n-1 words. An n-gram is a contiguous sequence of n items from a given sample of text or speech. In this context, items are typically words or characters. The simplest form of an n-gram model is the unigram model (n=1).

The probability of a word sequence $W = w_1, w_2, ..., w_n$ in an n-gram model is calculated based on the product of the conditional probabilities of each word given the previous $n - 1$ words:

$$P(W) = P(w_1, w_2, ..., w_n) \approx \prod_{i=1}^{n} P(w_i \mid w_{i-(n-1)}, ..., w_{i-1})$$

For example, in a bigram model (n=2), the probability of the sequence is approximated as:

$$P(W) \approx P(w_1) \cdot P(w_2 \mid w_1) \cdot P(w_3 \mid w_2) \cdot ... \cdot P(w_n \mid w_{n-1})$$

This model's effectiveness depends on the size of n. Larger n can capture more context but suffer from data sparsity, while smaller n are computationally efficient but may lack context sensitivity.

```
from collections import defaultdict
import random

# Sample corpus
corpus = [
    "the quick brown fox",
    "jumps over the lazy dog",
    "the quick blue cat",
]

# Tokenize corpus
tokens = []
for sentence in corpus:
    tokens.extend(sentence.lower().split())

# Build bigram model
bigrams = list(zip(tokens, tokens[1:]))
bigram_model = defaultdict(lambda: defaultdict(lambda: 0))

# Calculate frequencies
for w1, w2 in bigrams:
    bigram_model[w1][w2] += 1

# Convert frequencies to probabilities
for w1 in bigram_model:
    total_count = float(sum(bigram_model[w1].values()))
    for w2 in bigram_model[w1]:
        bigram_model[w1][w2] /= total_count

# Generate text using the bigram model
current_word = random.choice(tokens)
output = [current_word]
for _ in range(15):
    next_word_candidates = list(bigram_model[current_word].keys())
    next_word_probabilities = list(bigram_model[current_word].values())
    current_word = random.choices(next_word_candidates, next_word_probabilities)
        [0]
    output.append(current_word)

print(' '.join(output))
```

Neural Language Models:

With the advent of deep learning, neural language models have become the state-of-the-art approach for language modeling tasks. These models leverage neural networks to capture the complex dependencies within language data.

One fundamental neural language model is the *Recurrent Neural Network* (RNN). RNNs are particularly suited for sequence data because of their ability to maintain a hidden state that captures information about previous elements in the sequence. The key computation in an RNN for modeling the probability of a word sequence $W = w_1, w_2, ..., w_n$ is:

$$h_t = \sigma(W_h h_{t-1} + W_x x_t)$$

$$P(w_t \mid w_1, w_2, ..., w_{t-1}) = \text{softmax}(W_o h_t)$$

where h_t is the hidden state at time t, W_h and W_x are weight matrices, σ is a nonlinear activation function, and x_t is the input word embedding at time t.

Recurrent neural networks can be prone to issues such as vanishing and exploding gradients. To address these, advanced architectures like Long Short-Term Memory (LSTM) and Gated Recurrent Unit (GRU) have been developed. These architectures include gating mechanisms that help in learning long-term dependencies.

```
import torch
import torch.nn as nn
import torch.optim as optim

# Define the RNN model
class RNNLanguageModel(nn.Module):
    def __init__(self, vocab_size, embedding_dim, hidden_dim):
        super(RNNLanguageModel, self).__init__()
        self.embeddings = nn.Embedding(vocab_size, embedding_dim)
        self.rnn = nn.RNN(embedding_dim, hidden_dim, batch_first=True)
        self.fc = nn.Linear(hidden_dim, vocab_size)

    def forward(self, x, hidden):
        embeds = self.embeddings(x)
        out, hidden = self.rnn(embeds, hidden)
        out = self.fc(out)
        return out, hidden

# Hyperparameters
vocab_size = 5000
embedding_dim = 100
hidden_dim = 256
lr = 0.001

# Initialize model, loss function, optimizer
model = RNNLanguageModel(vocab_size, embedding_dim, hidden_dim)
criterion = nn.CrossEntropyLoss()
optimizer = optim.Adam(model.parameters(), lr=lr)

# Sample training loop (assuming preprocessed data in 'data_loader')
num_epochs = 10
for epoch in range(num_epochs):
    hidden = None
```

```
for inputs, targets in data_loader:
    # Zero the gradients
    optimizer.zero_grad()
    # Forward pass
    outputs, hidden = model(inputs, hidden)
    # Compute loss
    loss = criterion(outputs.view(-1, vocab_size), targets.view(-1))
    # Backward pass and optimization
    loss.backward()
    optimizer.step()

print(f'Epoch {epoch+1}/{num_epochs}, Loss: {loss.item()}')
```

Other neural language models include the *Transformer*, which employs self-attention mechanisms to capture dependencies irrespective of their distance in the sequence. Transformers have revolutionized the field of NLP, leading to the development of pre-trained models like BERT and GPT, which showcase significant improvements in various NLP tasks.

8.7 Text Classification

Text classification is a fundamental task in Natural Language Processing (NLP) that involves assigning predefined categories to textual data. This is prevalent in various applications such as spam detection, sentiment analysis, and document categorization. The process of text classification typically encompasses several stages: preprocessing the text, extracting features, and deploying a machine learning algorithm to accomplish the classification.

Text preprocessing is a critical initial step that ensures the textual data is in a suitable format for subsequent analysis. This stage commonly includes tasks such as tokenization, lowercasing, removal of stopwords, stemming, and lemmatization. For example, converting all text to lowercase ensures uniformity, while removing stopwords eliminates common but insignificant words.

To illustrate, consider the task of classifying email messages as either spam or non-spam. The preprocessing stage may look like this:

```
import nltk
from nltk.corpus import stopwords
from nltk.stem import PorterStemmer
import string

nltk.download('stopwords')
ps = PorterStemmer()

def preprocess_text(text):
```

```
    # Tokenize the text into words
    words = nltk.word_tokenize(text)
    # Convert to lowercase
    words = [word.lower() for word in words]
    # Remove punctuation
    words = [word for word in words if word not in string.punctuation]
    # Remove stopwords
    words = [word for word in words if word not in stopwords.words('english')]
    # Apply stemming
    words = [ps.stem(word) for word in words]
    return ' '.join(words)
```

After preprocessing, the next stage is feature extraction. Common methods of feature extraction include Bag of Words (BoW), Term Frequency-Inverse Document Frequency (TF-IDF), and word embeddings. Each approach has its strengths and suits different scenarios.

The BoW model represents text by the frequency of words in the document. While simple and intuitive, BoW can result in high-dimensional vectors and does not capture semantic information. In contrast, the TF-IDF method enhances BoW by weighing terms based on their significance across the corpus, and thus can provide better results for many applications. Word embeddings like Word2Vec and GloVe capture semantic relationships between words but require substantial computational resources and data.

An example of feature extraction using TF-IDF can be implemented as follows:

```
from sklearn.feature_extraction.text import TfidfVectorizer

documents = ["This is a sample document.", "This document is another example."]
# Initialize the TF-IDF Vectorizer
tfidf_vectorizer = TfidfVectorizer()
# Fit and transform the documents
tfidf_matrix = tfidf_vectorizer.fit_transform(documents)

# Display the resulting TF-IDF matrix
print(tfidf_matrix)
```

```
(0, 2)    0.46979128775362933
(0, 3)    0.5802858236844358
(0, 1)    0.46979128775362933
(0, 0)    0.46979128775362933
(1, 2)    0.0
(1, 3)    0.417075736706406
(1, 1)    0.8170784211407311
(1, 0)    0.0
```

Once features are extracted, a machine learning algorithm is used to perform the classification. Common algorithms employed for text classification include Naive Bayes, Support Vector Machines (SVM), and neural networks.

The Naive Bayes classifier is particularly pertinent for text classification due to its efficiency and the fact that it performs well even with a relatively small amount of training data. It relies on Bayes' theorem, assuming independence between features. The Support Vector Machine algorithm, on the other hand, is effective in high-dimensional spaces and is versatile owing to its ability to employ various kernel functions.

For instance, implementing a Naive Bayes classifier using the Scikit-learn library is straightforward:

```
from sklearn.naive_bayes import MultinomialNB
from sklearn.model_selection import train_test_split
from sklearn.metrics import accuracy_score

# Sample documents and labels
documents = ["Free money", "Hi, how are you?", "Congratulations, you've won!", "Let'
    s have a meeting tomorrow."]
labels = [1, 0, 1, 0] # 1 for spam, 0 for non-spam

# Preprocess the documents
documents = [preprocess_text(doc) for doc in documents]

# Extract TF-IDF features
X = tfidf_vectorizer.fit_transform(documents)
y = labels

# Split the data into training and testing sets
X_train, X_test, y_train, y_test = train_test_split(X, y, test_size=0.25,
    random_state=42)

# Initialize and train the Naive Bayes classifier
clf = MultinomialNB()
clf.fit(X_train, y_train)

# Predict and evaluate the model
y_pred = clf.predict(X_test)
print("Accuracy:", accuracy_score(y_test, y_pred))
```

```
Accuracy: 1.0
```

Neural networks, including Convolutional Neural Networks (CNNs) and Recurrent Neural Networks (RNNs), have proven to be exceptionally powerful in text classification tasks, particularly with the advent of transformers and BERT models. CNNs can capture local features through convolutional filters, while RNNs are adept at handling sequential data, making them suitable for tasks where word order is crucial.

Consider a simple neural network for text classification using TensorFlow:

```
import tensorflow as tf
from tensorflow.keras.preprocessing.text import Tokenizer
from tensorflow.keras.preprocessing.sequence import pad_sequences
from tensorflow.keras.models import Sequential
from tensorflow.keras.layers import Embedding, Flatten, Dense
```

```
# Sample documents and labels
documents = ["Free money", "Hi, how are you?", "Congratulations, you've won!", "Let'
    s have a meeting tomorrow."]
labels = [1, 0, 1, 0] # 1 for spam, 0 for non-spam

# Tokenize and pad sequences
tokenizer = Tokenizer(num_words=100)
tokenizer.fit_on_texts(documents)
sequences = tokenizer.texts_to_sequences(documents)
padded_sequences = pad_sequences(sequences, maxlen=5)

# Define the neural network model
model = Sequential()
model.add(Embedding(input_dim=100, output_dim=8, input_length=5))
model.add(Flatten())
model.add(Dense(1, activation='sigmoid'))

# Compile and train the model
model.compile(optimizer='adam', loss='binary_crossentropy', metrics=['accuracy'])
model.fit(padded_sequences, labels, epochs=10, verbose=1)

# Predicting and evaluating the model (for simplicity, using the training data)
accuracy = model.evaluate(padded_sequences, labels, verbose=0)
print("Accuracy:", accuracy[1])
```

```
Accuracy: 1.0
```

Each of these methods has its unique advantages and trade-offs, and the optimal algorithm largely depends on the specifics of the classification task, the nature of the textual data, and available computational resources. By carefully preprocessing the text, extracting meaningful features, and selecting appropriate machine learning models, robust and accurate text classification systems can be developed.

8.8 Named Entity Recognition (NER)

Named Entity Recognition (NER) is a fundamental task in Natural Language Processing (NLP) that involves locating and classifying named entities in unstructured text into predefined categories such as the names of persons, organizations, locations, expressions of times, quantities, monetary values, percentages, etc. This task is crucial for many higher-level applications, including question answering systems, machine translation, and information retrieval.

The process of NER can be broken down into two main tasks: entity detection and entity classification. Entity detection involves identifying the spans of text that constitute the entities, whereas entity classification determines the type of the detected entities.

Sequence Labeling Approach

One common method for NER is treating the task as a sequence labeling problem, where each word in a sentence is assigned a label indicating whether it is part of a named entity and what type of entity it is. A popular labeling scheme is the BIO format, where each tag is labeled as Beginning, Inside, or Outside of an entity. For example:

```
[("Barack", "B-PER"), ("Obama", "I-PER"), ("was", "O"), ("born", "O"), ("in", "O"),
    ("Hawaii", "B-LOC")]
```

Here, B-PER denotes the beginning of a person entity, I-PER denotes the continuation of that person entity, and B-LOC signifies the beginning of a location entity.

Feature Engineering

Successful NER relies heavily on the features extracted from the text. Traditional approaches often use handcrafted features, including:

- **Orthographic Features**: Character-level features such as capitalization, presence of digits, and special characters.
- **Word Shape Features**: Patterns of the character sequences (e.g., "Xxxxx" for capitalized words).
- **Contextual Features**: The words surrounding a given token to capture local dependencies.
- **Lexical Features**: Usage of predefined lexicons or gazetteers for names, locations, organizations, etc.

An example of feature extraction code:

```
def extract_features(sentence):
    features = []
    for i, word in enumerate(sentence):
        word_features = {
            "word.lower()": word.lower(),
            "word[-3:]": word[-3:], # Suffix
            "word.isupper()": word.isupper(),
            "word.istitle()": word.istitle(),
            "word.isdigit()": word.isdigit(),
        }
        if i > 0:
            word_features.update({
                "prev_word.lower()": sentence[i-1].lower()
            })
        else:
            word_features.update({
                "BOS": True # Beginning of Sentence
            })
        if i < len(sentence) - 1:
```

```
            word_features.update({
                "next_word.lower()": sentence[i+1].lower()
            })
        else:
            word_features.update({
                "EOS": True # End of Sentence
            })
        features.append(word_features)
    return features
```

Machine Learning Models

Various machine learning models have been employed for NER, ranging from rule-based systems to probabilistic models and deep learning approaches.

Hidden Markov Models (HMMs): Hidden Markov Models are probabilistic models that can capture the sequence nature of text by modeling the probabilities of transitions between tags and the probabilities of observing words given the tags.

Conditional Random Fields (CRFs): Conditional Random Fields are another probabilistic model that surpasses the capabilities of HMMs by directly modeling the conditional probability of sequences of labels given a sequence of observations. This allows CRFs to consider the entire sequence of input when making a decision, providing robustness in labeling tasks.

```
import sklearn_crfsuite
from sklearn_crfsuite import metrics

# Training data: sentences represented as sequences of dicts (features)
X_train, y_train = [extract_features(s) for s in sentences], labels

crf = sklearn_crfsuite.CRF(
    algorithm='lbfgs',
    c1=0.1, # Coefficients for L1 and L2 regularization
    c2=0.1,
    max_iterations=100,
    all_possible_transitions=True
)
crf.fit(X_train, y_train)

# Predicting on new data
y_pred = crf.predict(X_test)
```

Neural Network Models: Recent advances leverage deep learning models for NER. Approaches like Recurrent Neural Networks (RNNs), Long Short-Term Memory networks (LSTMs), and more recently, Transformers, have shown significant improvements due to their ability to capture longer-range dependencies in text.

An LSTM-based model might use word embeddings as input features, capturing semantic information encoded in the embeddings. A common setup includes Bidirectional LSTMs (BiLSTMs) to capture contextual information from both directions in the text.

```
import tensorflow as tf
from tensorflow.keras import layers

model = tf.keras.Sequential([
    layers.Input(shape=(max_seq_length, embedding_dim)),
    layers.Bidirectional(layers.LSTM(units=64, return_sequences=True)),
    layers.TimeDistributed(layers.Dense(n_tags, activation='softmax'))
])
model.compile(optimizer='adam', loss='sparse_categorical_crossentropy')
model.fit(X_train, y_train, epochs=10, batch_size=32)
```

Transformer-based models, such as BERT, enhance NER performance by using self-attention mechanisms to weigh the importance of each word in the context. Such models are often fine-tuned on specific NER tasks to adapt their understanding to the particular domain and entity types.

Evaluation Metrics

Evaluating NER systems typically involves metrics such as precision, recall, and F1-score. Precision measures the ratio of correctly identified entities to the total entities identified by the model, while recall measures the ratio of correctly identified entities to the total actual entities in the data. The F1-score is the harmonic mean of precision and recall.

```
Precision:  P = \frac{TP}{TP + FP}
Recall:     R = \frac{TP}{TP + FN}
F1-Score:   F1 = 2 \cdot \frac{P \cdot R}{P + R}
```

These evaluations can be calculated and reported using libraries such as sklearn.

```
from sklearn.metrics import classification_report

print(classification_report(y_test, y_pred))
```

8.9 Sentiment Analysis

Sentiment Analysis, also known as opinion mining, is a Natural Language Processing (NLP) task that involves the classification of textual data based on the sentiment it conveys. This sentiment can be broadly categorized as positive, negative, or neutral, although more fine-grained classifications are also possible, depending on the application. Sentiment Analysis has numerous practical applications, including social media monitoring, customer feedback analysis, and market research.

At a fundamental level, sentiment analysis involves several key steps: text preprocessing, feature extraction, model selection, and evaluation. Each of these steps plays a crucial role in building a robust and accurate sentiment analysis system.

Text Preprocessing: Text preprocessing is the initial stage that transforms raw text into a format suitable for analysis. Preprocessing involves several steps:

- **Tokenization:** Splitting text into individual words or tokens.
- **Lowercasing:** Converting all characters in the text to lowercase to ensure uniformity.
- **Removal of Stop Words:** Eliminating common words such as "and", "is", and "the" that do not contribute meaningful information for sentiment analysis.
- **Stemming and Lemmatization:** Reducing words to their base or root form.

```
import nltk
from nltk.tokenize import word_tokenize
from nltk.corpus import stopwords
from nltk.stem import PorterStemmer, WordNetLemmatizer

# Sample text
text = "Natural Language Processing is fascinating!"

# Tokenization
tokens = word_tokenize(text)

# Lowercasing
tokens = [word.lower() for word in tokens]

# Removal of Stop Words
stop_words = set(stopwords.words('english'))
tokens = [word for word in tokens if word not in stop_words]

# Stemming
ps = PorterStemmer()
tokens_stemmed = [ps.stem(word) for word in tokens]

# Lemmatization
lemmatizer = WordNetLemmatizer()
tokens_lemmatized = [lemmatizer.lemmatize(word) for word in tokens]

print(tokens_lemmatized)
```

```
[ 'natural', 'language', 'processing', 'fascinating', '!' ]
```

Feature Extraction: Once the text is preprocessed, it needs to be transformed into a numerical representation suitable for machine learning models. Several techniques are commonly used for feature extraction in sentiment analysis:

- **Bag of Words (BoW):** Represents text as a collection of words with their respective frequencies.
- **Term Frequency-Inverse Document Frequency (TF-IDF):** Enhances the BoW approach by considering the importance of words in the context of the entire corpus.
- **Word Embeddings:** Provides dense vector representations for words capturing semantic similarity.

```
from sklearn.feature_extraction.text import TfidfVectorizer

# Sample corpus
corpus = [
    "I love machine learning",
    "I love coding",
    "I enjoy learning new things"
]

# TF-IDF Vectorization
vectorizer = TfidfVectorizer()
X = vectorizer.fit_transform(corpus)

# Converting to array for better visualization
print(X.toarray())
```

```
[[0.         0.         0.47107781 0.62276601 0.62276601]
 [0.         0.         0.861037   0.         0.50854232]
 [0.52640543 0.66767854 0.         0.52640543 0.        ]]
```

Model Selection: With features extracted, the next step is to select and train a suitable model for sentiment analysis. Commonly used models include:

- **Naive Bayes:** A probabilistic model that is particularly effective for text classification.
- **Support Vector Machines (SVM):** A powerful discriminative classifier that works well with high-dimensional data.
- **Deep Learning Models:** Recurrent Neural Networks (RNNs), Long Short-Term Memory (LSTM) networks, and Transformer-based models like BERT.

```
from sklearn.naive_bayes import MultinomialNB
from sklearn.model_selection import train_test_split
from sklearn.metrics import accuracy_score, classification_report

# Sample data and labels
texts = ["I love this product", "I hate this product", "This product is okay"]
labels = [1, 0, 1] # 1 for positive, 0 for negative

# TF-IDF Vectorization
vectorizer = TfidfVectorizer()
X = vectorizer.fit_transform(texts)

# Train-test split
X_train, X_test, y_train, y_test = train_test_split(X, labels, test_size=0.33,
    random_state=42)

# Model Training
model = MultinomialNB()
model.fit(X_train, y_train)

# Model Prediction
y_pred = model.predict(X_test)

# Evaluation
print("Accuracy:", accuracy_score(y_test, y_pred))
print(classification_report(y_test, y_pred))
```

```
Accuracy: 1.0
              precision    recall  f1-score   support

           0       1.00      1.00      1.00         1
           1       1.00      1.00      1.00         1

    accuracy                           1.00         2
   macro avg       1.00      1.00      1.00         2
weighted avg       1.00      1.00      1.00         2
```

Evaluation Metrics: Evaluating the performance of sentiment analysis models involves using metrics such as accuracy, precision, recall, and F1-score. These metrics provide insights into the model's ability to correctly classify sentiments and are crucial for comparing different models and approaches.

For complex datasets and applications, more advanced techniques such as cross-validation, grid search for hyperparameter tuning, and ensembling multiple models can be applied to enhance the performance and robustness of sentiment analysis systems.

8.10 Topic Modeling

Topic modeling is a critical technique in Natural Language Processing (NLP) used to uncover the latent structure within a corpus of documents.

It provides a way to automatically discover the abstract topics that occur in a collection of text. This section delves into the foundational concepts and methodologies for topic modeling, focusing on the most commonly used algorithms such as Latent Dirichlet Allocation (LDA) and Non-negative Matrix Factorization (NMF).

Topic modeling algorithms aim to find patterns in the usage of words across documents, thereby identifying clusters of words that typically appear together and correspond to specific topics. These topics can then be used to understand, summarize, and organize large collections of text data.

Latent Dirichlet Allocation (LDA)

Latent Dirichlet Allocation (LDA) is a generative probabilistic model for collections of discrete data such as text corpora. The core idea of LDA is that documents are represented as random mixtures over latent topics, where each topic is characterized by a distribution over words.

The graphical model for LDA consists of a three-level hierarchical Bayesian model:

- **Document-Level Distribution**: Each document is modeled as a mixture of topics, where the mixture is drawn from a conjugate Dirichlet prior.
- **Topic-Level Distribution**: Each topic is characterized by a distribution over words, which is also drawn from a Dirichlet prior.
- **Word-Level Assignment**: For each word in a document, a topic is chosen according to the document's topic distribution, and then a word is generated from the corresponding topic's word distribution.

Mathematically, the generative process of LDA can be described as follows:

1. For each topic k, draw $\beta_k \sim \text{Dirichlet}(\eta)$.
2. For each document d:
   (a) Draw topic proportions $\theta_d \sim \text{Dirichlet}(\alpha)$.
   (b) For each word w_{dn}:
      i. Draw a topic $z_{dn} \sim \text{Multinomial}(\theta_d)$.
      ii. Draw a word $w_{dn} \sim \text{Multinomial}(\beta_{z_{dn}})$.

The key parameters of LDA include the document-topic distributions θ_d and the topic-word distributions β_k. Inference in LDA aims to estimate these distributions given a set of observed documents. Common methods for inference include Variational Inference and Gibbs Sampling.

Here is a Python example using the 'gensim' library to perform topic modeling with LDA:

```
import gensim
import gensim.corpora as corpora
from gensim.models import LdaModel

# Example corpus
documents = ["Human machine interface for lab abc computer applications",
             "A survey of user opinion of computer system response time",
             "The EPS user interface management system",
             ...]

# Preprocess the documents
texts = [[word for word in document.lower().split()] for document in documents]

# Create a dictionary and corpus
dictionary = corpora.Dictionary(texts)
corpus = [dictionary.doc2bow(text) for text in texts]

# Train the LDA model
lda_model = LdaModel(corpus=corpus, id2word=dictionary, num_topics=10, passes
    =10)

# Print the topics
topics = lda_model.print_topics(num_words=5)
for topic in topics:
    print(topic)
```

Non-negative Matrix Factorization (NMF)

Non-negative Matrix Factorization (NMF) is an alternative topic modeling technique that factors a given matrix into two matrices with the property that all three matrices have no negative elements. In the context of text data, the term-document matrix is factorized into matrices representing topics and their word distributions.

Given a term-document matrix **V**, NMF aims to find two matrices **W** and **H** such that:

$$\mathbf{V} \approx \mathbf{WH}$$

Where **W** is the topic-term matrix and **H** is the topic-document matrix. The goal is to minimize the reconstruction error, subject to the constraint that all elements of **W** and **H** are non-negative. This ensures that the resulting topics are interpretable, as probabilities must be non-negative.

The optimization problem for NMF can be formulated as:

$$\min_{\mathbf{W},\mathbf{H}} \|\mathbf{V} - \mathbf{WH}\|_F^2$$

Subject to $\mathbf{W} \geq 0$ and $\mathbf{H} \geq 0$, where $\|\cdot\|_F$ denotes the Frobenius norm. An example of NMF using the 'sklearn' library is shown below:

```
from sklearn.feature_extraction.text import TfidfVectorizer
from sklearn.decomposition import NMF

# Example corpus
documents = ["Human machine interface for lab abc computer applications",
             "A survey of user opinion of computer system response time",
             "The EPS user interface management system",
             ...]

# Create a TF-IDF vectorizer
vectorizer = TfidfVectorizer(stop_words='english')
tfidf = vectorizer.fit_transform(documents)

# Train the NMF model
nmf_model = NMF(n_components=10, random_state=1)
nmf_model.fit(tfidf)

# Print the topics
feature_names = vectorizer.get_feature_names_out()
for topic_idx, topic in enumerate(nmf_model.components_):
    print(f"Topic #{topic_idx}:")
    print(" ".join([feature_names[i] for i in topic.argsort()[:-6:-1]]))
```

These methodologies, LDA and NMF, offer robust frameworks for discovering hidden topics within text data, providing valuable insights in various applications such as document clustering, recommendation systems, and content analysis. Understanding and implementing these techniques equip practitioners with powerful tools for extracting meaning from large text corpora.

8.11 Sequence-to-Sequence Models

Sequence-to-Sequence (Seq2Seq) models are a class of models designed for transforming sequences from one domain to sequences in another domain. These models are highly effective for tasks such as machine translation, text summarization, and conversational agents. The central architecture of Seq2Seq models is composed of two core components: an encoder and a decoder, both of which are typically Recurrent Neural Networks (RNNs) such as Long Short-Term Memory (LSTM) or Gated Recurrent Unit (GRU).

Encoder-Decoder Architecture

The encoder's role is to process the input sequence and encapsulate its information into a fixed-length context vector. This is achieved by sequentially reading the input tokens and updating the internal hidden state. Mathematically, given an input sequence $X = (x_1, x_2, \ldots, x_n)$, the encoder produces a sequence of hidden states $H = (h_1, h_2, \ldots, h_n)$, where each hidden state h_t is computed as:

$$h_t = f_{\text{enc}}(x_t, h_{t-1})$$

Here, f_{enc} denotes the recurrent function, which can be an LSTM, GRU, or any other RNN variant.

The final hidden state h_n of the encoder is often used as the context vector c, encapsulating the entire input sequence into a single vector:

$$c = h_n$$

The decoder, on the other hand, utilizes this context vector c to generate the output sequence $Y = (y_1, y_2, \ldots, y_m)$. At each timestep t, the decoder generates an output token y_t based on the context vector and its previous hidden state s_{t-1}. The initial hidden state s_0 of the decoder is typically set to the context vector c. The process is defined as:

$$s_t = f_{\text{dec}}(y_{t-1}, s_{t-1}, c)$$

$$y_t = g(s_t)$$

Here, f_{dec} is the decoder's recurrent function and g is a function mapping the hidden state to an output token, often implemented as a softmax layer over the vocabulary.

Training the Seq2Seq Model

The Seq2Seq model is commonly trained using the Teacher Forcing algorithm. This involves feeding the actual target tokens as inputs to the decoder during training, rather than the tokens generated by the model itself. This approach helps accelerate convergence and stabilize training. The loss function used is typically the categorical cross-entropy between the predicted tokens and the actual tokens. The objective is to minimize this loss over all time steps.

The training process can be summarized in the following algorithmic format:

```
for epoch in range(num_epochs):
    for (input_sequence, target_sequence) in training_data:
        # Encode the input sequence
        encoder_hidden = encoder.init_hidden()
        for input_token in input_sequence:
            encoder_output, encoder_hidden = encoder(input_token, encoder_hidden)

        # Initialize the decoder with the context vector
        decoder_hidden = encoder_hidden
        decoder_input = <start_token>

        loss = 0
        for target_token in target_sequence:
            decoder_output, decoder_hidden = decoder(decoder_input,
                decoder_hidden)
            loss += loss_function(decoder_output, target_token)
            decoder_input = target_token # Teacher forcing

        # Backpropagation and optimization steps
        loss.backward()
        optimizer.step()
        optimizer.zero_grad()
```

Attention Mechanism

One limitation of the basic Seq2Seq model is the fixed-length context vector, which can be a bottleneck when dealing with long sequences. The Attention Mechanism addresses this by allowing the decoder to focus on different parts of the input sequence at each decoding step. Instead of relying solely on the final encoder hidden state, the decoder generates a context vector dynamically.

The attention mechanism computes a set of attention weights α_t, which measure the relevance of each encoder hidden state h_j to the current decoding step t:

$$\alpha_{tj} = \frac{\exp(e_{tj})}{\sum_{k=1}^{n} \exp(e_{tk})}$$
$$e_{tj} = \text{score}(s_{t-1}, h_j)$$

Here, score can be a variety of functions such as dot product, concatenation, or a learned feedforward network. The resulting context vector c_t for timestep t is a weighted sum of the encoder hidden states:

$$c_t = \sum_{j=1}^{n} \alpha_{tj} h_j$$

The decoder's hidden state and output are then conditioned on this dynamically computed context vector c_t:

$$s_t = f_{\text{dec}}(y_{t-1}, s_{t-1}, c_t)$$

$$y_t = g(s_t)$$

Application Example: Machine Translation

Consider a practical example of Seq2Seq models in machine translation. Suppose we want to translate the English sentence "I am a student" to its French equivalent "Je suis étudiant". The input sequence $(x_1, x_2, x_3, x_4) =$ ("I", "am", "a", "student") is processed by the encoder, producing a sequence of hidden states. The final encoder hidden state becomes the context vector for the decoder, which then generates the translated sequence by outputting tokens step-by-step, using the attention mechanism to focus on relevant parts of the input sequence at each step.

Given the input-output pair:

```
Input Sequence: ["I", "am", "a", "student"]
Output Sequence: ["Je", "suis", "étudiant", "<eos>"]
```

The encoder processes the input sequence and the decoder initializes with the encoder's final hidden state. For each token in the output sequence, the decoder generates one token at a time, adjusting its focus through attention if employed.

Machine Translation Example with Attention:

Encoder Outputs	**Attention Weights at $t = 1$ (for "Je")**
h_1 : [.....]	$\alpha_{11}, \alpha_{12}, \alpha_{13}, \alpha_{14}$
h_2 : [.....]	
h_3 : [.....]	
h_4 : [.....]	

Table 8.1: Encoder Outputs and Attention Weights

Decoder step $t = 1$:

```
Input: <start_token>
Context Vector: c_1 (computed using attention weights and encoder outputs)
Output: Je
```

This approach significantly enhances translation quality, especially for longer sentences, by leveraging the attention mechanism to dynamically utilize diverse parts of the input sequence.

Seq2Seq models with attention have demonstrated remarkable effectiveness across various applications in NLP, including but not limited to text summarization, dialogue systems, and more.

8.12 Transformers and BERT

Transformers have significantly advanced the field of NLP by providing a mechanism that handles long-range dependencies better than previous architectures like RNNs or LSTMs. Transformers leverage a key innovation called self-attention, allowing them to weigh the influence of different words in a sentence dynamically. This section delves into the architecture of transformers, followed by the intricacies of Bidirectional Encoder Representations from Transformers (BERT), which has set new benchmarks in various NLP tasks.

Transformer Architecture

The transformer model, introduced by Vaswani et al. (2017), has two main components: an encoder and a decoder. Each of these components is composed of multiple layers, often referred to as "blocks." The encoder processes the input sequence, while the decoder generates the output sequence. We will delve into the encoder structure, as BERT is based solely on the encoder mechanism.

Each encoder block consists of two primary sub-layers:

- A multi-head self-attention mechanism.
- A position-wise feed-forward neural network.

Both sub-layers are followed by layer normalization and residual connections to ensure better gradient flow during training.

The multi-head self-attention mechanism allows the model to focus on different parts of the input sequence simultaneously. Given an input sequence $x_1, x_2, \ldots, x_n$, the self-attention mechanism can be formally defined as follows:

$$\text{Attention}(Q, K, V) = \text{softmax}\left(\frac{QK^T}{\sqrt{d_k}}\right)V$$

where Q, K, and V are the query, key, and value matrices derived from the input embeddings X. The dimensions of these matrices are critical and follow the rules: $Q, K \in \mathbb{R}^{n \times d_k}$ and $V \in \mathbb{R}^{n \times d_v}$. The parameter d_k is the dimension of the key vectors, and the factor $\sqrt{d_k}$ scales the dot products to prevent them from becoming too large.

In the multi-head attention mechanism, several attention heads are computed in parallel:

$$\text{MultiHead}(Q, K, V) = \text{Concat}(\text{head}_1, \text{head}_2, \ldots, \text{head}_h)W^O$$

where each attention head is $\text{head}_i = \text{Attention}(QW_i^Q, KW_i^K, VW_i^V)$. The projection matrices W_i^Q, W_i^K, W_i^V transform the input into distinct subspaces, and W^O is the output projection matrix.

Position-Wise Feed-Forward Network

After the multi-head self-attention mechanism, which processes the sequence contextually, a position-wise feed-forward network (FFN) is applied. This network consists of two fully connected layers with a ReLU activation in between:

$$\text{FFN}(x) = \max(0, xW_1 + b_1)W_2 + b_2$$

The feed-forward layer is applied identically and independently to each position.

As the transformer model does not encode position information, positional encodings are added to the input embeddings to provide the model with information about the relative or absolute position of the tokens in the sequence. The positional encodings have the same dimension as the embeddings and are typically derived using sine and cosine functions of varying frequencies:

$$PE_{(pos,2i)} = \sin\left(\frac{pos}{10000^{2i/d_{model}}}\right) \quad PE_{(pos,2i+1)} = \cos\left(\frac{pos}{10000^{2i/d_{model}}}\right)$$

BERT: Bidirectional Encoder Representations from Transformers

BERT, introduced by Devlin et al. (2018), is a pre-trained transformer model that yields state-of-the-art performance on a wide array of NLP tasks. Unlike traditional models which are either unidirectional or shallowly bidirectional, BERT is deeply bidirectional. This bidirectionality enables BERT to consider the context from both left and right simultaneously, enhancing its understanding of the words' meaning in context.

BERT's architecture relies solely on the transformer encoder blocks and involves two critical steps: pre-training and fine-tuning.

The pre-training phase includes two main tasks:

- Masked Language Model (MLM): In this task, 15% of the tokens in each sequence are replaced with a $[\mathrm{MASK}]$ token. The objective is for the model to predict the original tokens based on the context provided by the non-masked tokens.
- Next Sentence Prediction (NSP): This task involves predicting whether a given sentence B follows a given sentence A. This is essential for tasks involving relationships between sentences, such as Question Answering and Natural Language Inference.

During pre-training, BERT's objective function is the sum of the masked language model probability and the next sentence prediction probability, denoted as:

$$L = -\sum_i \log P(w_i \mid [\mathrm{MASK}]) - \sum_j \log P(s_j \mid A_j)$$

After pre-training, which provides a robust representation of language, BERT can be fine-tuned on specific tasks. Fine-tuning involves adding a task-specific output layer to the pre-trained model and training it on the labeled data of the target task. This process requires significantly less time and computational resources than training from scratch.

Fine-tuning can be formalized as:

$$L_{\text{task}} = -\sum_k \log P(y_k \mid T)$$

where y_k is the label for the k-th instance and T is the input transformed by BERT's encoder.

Example of BERT Fine-Tuning for Text Classification

The workflow for fine-tuning BERT for a text classification task can be demonstrated with the following Python code using the PyTorch framework and the Hugging Face Transformers library. This example aims to classify sentences into positive or negative sentiments.

```
import torch
from transformers import BertForSequenceClassification, BertTokenizer
from torch.utils.data import DataLoader, RandomSampler, SequentialSampler
from torch.optim import AdamW
from tqdm import tqdm
```

```
# Load the BERT tokenizer
tokenizer = BertTokenizer.from_pretrained('bert-base-uncased')

# Load the dataset (example data)
train_texts = ["I love the new design!", "This is the worst product ever."]
train_labels = [1, 0]

# Tokenize the data
train_encodings = tokenizer(train_texts, truncation=True, padding=True)

# Convert to torch dataset
class TextDataset(torch.utils.data.Dataset):
    def __init__(self, encodings, labels):
        self.encodings = encodings
        self.labels = labels

    def __getitem__(self, idx):
        item = {key: torch.tensor(val[idx]) for key, val in self.encodings.items()}
        item['labels'] = torch.tensor(self.labels[idx])
        return item

    def __len__(self):
        return len(self.labels)

train_dataset = TextDataset(train_encodings, train_labels)

# Load BERT for sequence classification
model = BertForSequenceClassification.from_pretrained('bert-base-uncased')

# Initialize the data loader
train_loader = DataLoader(train_dataset, sampler=RandomSampler(train_dataset),
    batch_size=8)

# Initialize the optimizer
optimizer = AdamW(model.parameters(), lr=5e-5)

# Define the training loop
model.train()
for epoch in range(3):
    for batch in tqdm(train_loader):
        optimizer.zero_grad()
        outputs = model(**batch)
        loss = outputs.loss
        loss.backward()
        optimizer.step()
```

In the code above, the dataset is tokenized using the BERT tokenizer and converted into a format suitable for training with PyTorch. The BERT model is then fine-tuned for three epochs, optimizing the classification loss.

8.13 Evaluation Metrics for NLP

Evaluation metrics are essential in assessing the performance of Natural Language Processing (NLP) models. These metrics provide a quantitative method for gauging the effectiveness of algorithms and are critical for comparing different models and configurations.

Accuracy is a fundamental metric often used in classification tasks. It is defined as the ratio of correctly predicted instances to the total number of instances. Mathematically, accuracy can be expressed as:

$$\text{Accuracy} = \frac{\text{Number of correct predictions}}{\text{Total number of predictions}}$$

However, accuracy alone may not provide a full picture in the presence of class imbalance. Therefore, precision, recall, and F1-score are often used to give a more nuanced performance evaluation.

Precision measures the ratio of true positive predictions to the sum of true positives and false positives, thereby focusing on the accuracy of the positive predictions:

$$\text{Precision} = \frac{\text{True Positives}}{\text{True Positives} + \text{False Positives}}$$

Recall, also known as sensitivity or true positive rate, measures the ratio of true positives to the sum of true positives and false negatives. Recall gives an indication of how many actual positive cases were correctly identified:

$$\text{Recall} = \frac{\text{True Positives}}{\text{True Positives} + \text{False Negatives}}$$

The F1-score is the harmonic mean of precision and recall, providing a single metric that balances both concerns:

$$\text{F1-score} = \frac{2 \times \text{Precision} \times \text{Recall}}{\text{Precision} + \text{Recall}}$$

For multi-class classification tasks, these metrics are often extended using micro, macro, and weighted averages.

To provide a comprehensive performance evaluation, especially for tasks like Named Entity Recognition (NER) and text classification, confusion matrices are employed. A confusion matrix allows visualization of the performance of an algorithm:

	Predicted Positive	Predicted Negative
Actual Positive	True Positive (TP)	False Negative (FN)
Actual Negative	False Positive (FP)	True Negative (TN)

Another crucial metric is the Area Under the Receiver Operating Characteristic Curve (AUC-ROC). The ROC curve is a graphical plot that illustrates the diagnostic ability of a binary classifier system as its discrimination threshold is varied. The AUC-ROC value provides a scalar value summarizing the performance:

$$\text{AUC-ROC} = P(\text{score for a positive example} > \text{score for a negative example})$$

Perplexity is commonly used to evaluate language models. It is a measure of how well a probability distribution or probability model predicts a sample. A lower perplexity indicates that the model is better at predicting the sample:

$$\text{Perplexity}(P) = \exp\left(-\frac{1}{N}\sum_{i=1}^{N}\log P(w_i)\right)$$

When dealing with tasks like machine translation and summarization, metrics such as BLEU (Bilingual Evaluation Understudy) and ROUGE (Recall-Oriented Understudy for Gisting Evaluation) are used. BLEU measures the precision of n-grams (with a typically included brevity penalty) between the model output and reference translations:

$$\text{BLEU} = \text{BP} \cdot \exp\left(\sum_{n=1}^{N} w_n \log p_n\right)$$

Where BP is the brevity penalty, w_n is a weight, and p_n is the precision of n-grams.

ROUGE, particularly ROUGE-N and ROUGE-L, measures overlap in n-grams and the longest common subsequence (LCS) between the model's output and references, respectively:

$$\text{ROUGE-N} = \frac{\sum_{S\in\text{Reference summaries}}\sum_{n\text{-gram}\in S}\text{Matches}(n\text{-gram})}{\sum_{S\in\text{Reference summaries}}\sum_{n\text{-gram}\in S}\text{Count}(n\text{-gram})}$$

$$\text{ROUGE-L} = F_{LCS} = \frac{(1+\beta^2) \times \text{Precision}_{LCS} \times \text{Recall}_{LCS}}{\beta^2 \times \text{Precision}_{LCS} + \text{Recall}_{LCS}}$$

These evaluation metrics are crucial for ensuring that NLP models are both accurate and reliable across different tasks and datasets. They help in understanding the strengths and weaknesses of a model, guiding iterative improvements and optimizations.

To illustrate the practical implementation of these metrics, consider the following Python code snippets that calculate precision, recall, and F1-score using the Scikit-learn library:

```
from sklearn.metrics import precision_score, recall_score, f1_score

y_true = [0, 1, 1, 0, 1, 0, 1, 0] # Actual labels
y_pred = [0, 1, 0, 0, 0, 0, 1, 1] # Predicted labels

precision = precision_score(y_true, y_pred)
recall = recall_score(y_true, y_pred)
f1 = f1_score(y_true, y_pred)

print(f"Precision: {precision}")
print(f"Recall: {recall}")
print(f"F1-Score: {f1}")
```

The output for this script would be:

```
Precision: 0.6666666666666666
Recall: 0.5
F1-Score: 0.5714285714285715
```

Such implementations provide insight into the convenience and power of using specialized libraries for evaluating NLP models.

Chapter 9

Time Series Analysis

This chapter introduces time series analysis, focusing on the components of time series data and methods for decomposition. It covers the importance of stationarity, autocorrelation, and partial autocorrelation. The chapter discusses techniques such as moving averages, smoothing, ARIMA, and Seasonal ARIMA models. Advanced methods like exponential smoothing and Holt-Winters are explored, along with machine learning approaches for time series, model evaluation, and forecasting, providing a comprehensive framework for analyzing temporal data.

9.1 Introduction to Time Series Analysis

Time series analysis is a statistical technique that deals with time-ordered data points. These data points are typically collected or recorded at specific time intervals and are used to understand the underlying structure and function that produce the observations. The primary goals of time series analysis include understanding the underlying mechanisms, forecasting future values, and identifying patterns, trends, and seasonal variations.

A time series can be defined as a sequence of observations $y_1, y_2, y_3, \ldots, y_T$ where T denotes the number of observations. Each observation y_i is associated with a specific time t_i. Typically, the data points in a time series are spaced at uniform intervals—hourly, daily, weekly, monthly, etc.

For the purpose of analysis, it is often helpful to visualize the time series. We can draw a line plot where the x-axis represents time and the y-axis represents the observed values.

```
import matplotlib.pyplot as plt
import pandas as pd

# Assuming 'data' is a pandas DataFrame with a DateTime index and a 'value' column
data = pd.read_csv('time_series_data.csv', parse_dates=['date'], index_col='date')

plt.figure(figsize=(10, 6))
plt.plot(data.index, data['value'], label='Time Series Data')
plt.xlabel('Time')
plt.ylabel('Value')
plt.title('Time Series Plot')
plt.legend()
plt.show()
```

Output:
A plot showing the variation in the 'value' column over time.

Generally, time series analysis can be categorized into two main branches: time domain methods and frequency domain methods. Time domain methods analyze the temporal structure of the data, looking for patterns such as trends, cycles, and seasonal effects. Frequency domain methods, on the other hand, analyze the periodic relationships within the data by transforming the time series into the frequency domain using tools such as the Fourier Transform.

There are several key components of a time series that need to be considered:

- **Trend Component:** A trend exists when there is a long-term increase or decrease in the data. It is the component that indicates the overall direction of the time series data over a long period. Trends can be linear, exponential, or more complex forms.
- **Seasonal Component:** Seasonality refers to periodic fluctuations or regular patterns that repeat at consistent intervals, such as daily, monthly, yearly, etc. Examples include temperature changes throughout the year or sales peaks during holiday seasons.
- **Cyclical Component:** A cyclical component represents wavelike fluctuations around the trend with a duration of more than one year. These cycles are often tied to economic or business cycles, and their duration tends to be irregular.
- **Irregular Component:** Also known as the residual or noise component, the irregular component is the random variation in the

time series that cannot be attributed to the trend, seasonal, or cyclical components. This component is assumed to be a random variable with a mean of zero.

Mathematically, a time series can be described by the equation:

$$y_t = T_t + S_t + C_t + I_t$$

where y_t is the observed value at time t, T_t is the trend component, S_t is the seasonal component, C_t is the cyclical component, and I_t is the irregular component. Alternatively, a multiplicative model can be used:

$$y_t = T_t \times S_t \times C_t \times I_t$$

Time series analysis involves several preprocessing steps to transform the data into a form that can be effectively analyzed. Common preprocessing techniques include differencing to achieve stationarity, detrending, and decomposition to isolate and analyze the components discussed.

The stationarity of a time series is critical for most time series models. A stationary time series has consistent statistical properties over time, such as a constant mean and variance. Non-stationary data must often be transformed into a stationary form before analysis.

An essential task in time series analysis is to develop models that can describe the data accurately and make forecasts. Various models exist for time series data, such as Moving Average (MA), AutoRegressive (AR), AutoRegressive Integrated Moving Average (ARIMA), and Seasonal ARIMA (SARIMA).

```
from statsmodels.tsa.arima.model import ARIMA

# Fit an ARIMA model
model = ARIMA(data['value'], order=(5, 1, 0)) # ARIMA(p, d, q)
model_fit = model.fit()

print(model_fit.summary())
```

```
Output:
A summary of the ARIMA model fit, including coefficients and diagnostic statistics.
```

Proper evaluation of these models is crucial for ensuring their validity and accuracy in predicting future values. Techniques such as out-of-sample forecasting, cross-validation, and error metric calculations (e.g., Mean Absolute Error (MAE), Mean Squared Error (MSE), and Root Mean Squared Error (RMSE)) are employed to assess model performance.

Time series forecasting extends the analysis by using the fitted models to predict future data points. Forecasting methods are central to applications across various domains, such as finance, meteorology, economics, and more.

In summary, time series analysis is a powerful tool for examining data points collected over time. It provides insights into the importance of trends, seasonality, and cyclical patterns, offering significant value in various real-world applications.

9.2 Components of Time Series Data

Time series data, representing observations recorded sequentially over time, inherently possess various components. Understanding these components is essential for effective analysis and forecasting. While the nature and behavior of these components may vary depending on the context and domain in which the time series data is applied, the primary components we focus on include Trend, Seasonality, Cyclical Patterns, and Irregular/Random Components.

Trend refers to the long-term progression of the data, capturing the general direction in which the data points are moving over an extended period. A trend can be either upward or downward, indicating overall increases or decreases, respectively. In mathematical terms, this component can be modeled by functions such as linear regression or polynomial regression.

Seasonality encompasses regular and predictable patterns that repeat over a fixed time period such as days, months, or years. These patterns are often driven by external factors, such as weather conditions, holidays, or other recurring events, and must recur at regular intervals to be classified as seasonal. The period of the seasonality must be predetermined or inferred from data, and functions like Fourier series or trigonometric polynomials can be employed to model this component.

Cyclical Patterns denote fluctuations that occur over irregular intervals, often associated with business cycles, economic conditions, or other non-static processes. Unlike seasonal effects, cyclical variations do not have a fixed periodicity, making them harder to predict and model. Identifying cyclical patterns traditionally involves advanced statistical techniques such as Hodrick-Prescott filtering or spectral analysis.

Irregular/Random Components encapsulate the unpredictable and stochastic aspects of the data, often attributed to random noise or any deviations not captured by the other components. These components are typically modeled using probabilistic methods, ensuring that the noise characteristics (e.g., white noise, Gaussian noise) are well-understood and appropriately factored into the analysis.

The interplay and identification of these components are critical in the decomposition of time series data, providing clarity and facilitating better forecasting models. Analyzing and separating these components can be achieved through several methodologies, the most common being:

- **Additive Decomposition**: Assumes that the time series components additively combine to form the observed values. Mathematically, it is expressed as:

  $$Y(t) = T(t) + S(t) + C(t) + E(t)$$

  where $Y(t)$ is the observed time series value at time t, $T(t)$ is the trend component, $S(t)$ is the seasonal component, $C(t)$ is the cyclical component, and $E(t)$ represents the irregular component.

- **Multiplicative Decomposition**: Assumes that the components multiply to produce the observed data. This approach is useful when the magnitude of variations is proportional to the level of the time series. The mathematical representation is:

  $$Y(t) = T(t) \times S(t) \times C(t) \times E(t)$$

- **Log-Additive Decomposition**: Involves transforming the multiplicative model into an additive form by taking the logarithm, resulting in:

  $$\log Y(t) = \log T(t) + \log S(t) + \log C(t) + \log E(t)$$

  This transformation aids in stabilizing variance and making the components additive.

- **Classical Seasonal Decomposition (Census I and II, X-11)**: These methods involve iterative procedures to separate components efficiently, often including smoothing techniques to isolate intricate seasonal and cyclical patterns.

To give practical insights into the process of decomposing components, consider a simple example using Python's statsmodels library. This example demonstrates additive decomposition of a time series dataset:

```
import pandas as pd
import statsmodels.api as sm
import matplotlib.pyplot as plt

# Load the dataset
data = sm.datasets.co2.load_pandas().data
data = data.fillna(method='ffill') # Handle missing values

# Perform additive decomposition
decomposition = sm.tsa.seasonal_decompose(data['co2'], model='additive', period=12)
decomposition.plot()
plt.show()
```

The output generated by the above code visualizes the original time series, trend component, seasonal component, and residuals:

<Figure of the decomposed time series>

The decomposition output elucidates the respective contributions of each component, providing a clear, interpretable structure of the time series data. By isolating the trend, seasonal effects, and residuals, we ensure that each aspect of the data is analyzed independently, facilitating more robust forecasting models.

Throughout numerous domains, correctly identifying and modeling these components enables better data interpretation, enhanced forecasting precision, and insightful business or scientific decisions. Time series decomposition becomes particularly valuable in understanding historical data patterns and predicting future values, forming the foundation for more sophisticated analytical techniques in time series analysis.

9.3 Time Series Decomposition

Time series decomposition is a fundamental technique in time series analysis that involves breaking down a time series into its constituent components. This technique helps in understanding the underlying patterns and structures within the data, making it easier to interpret and forecast. The primary components that are often considered in time series decomposition are trend, seasonality, and residual (or noise). Decomposing a time series into these components allows for a more nuanced analysis and can improve the accuracy of predictive models.

The process of time series decomposition can be broadly categorized into two types: additive and multiplicative decomposition. The appropriate type of decomposition to use depends on the nature of the data and the relationships between its components.

Additive Decomposition

In additive decomposition, the components of a time series are assumed to add together to form the observed data. The additive model can be represented as:

$$Y_t = T_t + S_t + R_t$$

where Y_t represents the observed value at time t, T_t is the trend component, S_t is the seasonal component, and R_t is the residual component.

The trend component (T_t) captures the long-term progression in the data, indicating a general direction in which the data is moving over time, such as an upward or downward slope. The seasonal component (S_t) represents the repeating short-term cycle within the data, which could be daily, monthly, quarterly, or yearly. The residual component (R_t), or noise, captures the random variation in the data that cannot be attributed to either the trend or seasonality.

Multiplicative Decomposition

In multiplicative decomposition, the components are assumed to multiply together to form the observed data. The multiplicative model can be represented as:

$$Y_t = T_t \times S_t \times R_t$$

In this model, the relationships between the components are multiplicative. This type of decomposition is often used when the seasonal variations change proportionally with the level of the trend. For instance, if the seasonal variations become more pronounced as the overall level of the series increases or decreases, a multiplicative model might be more suitable.

Decomposition Techniques

There are several computational algorithms available for decomposing a time series into its components. The most common techniques include:

- **Classical Decomposition:** This method involves estimating the trend component using techniques like moving averages, extracting the seasonal component by averaging over the periods, and calculating the residual as the difference between the observed data and the sum of the estimated trend and seasonal components.

- **STL (Seasonal-Trend Decomposition using LOESS):** STL is a robust and versatile method that uses LOESS (locally estimated scatterplot smoothing) to separate the seasonal and trend components of a time series. This method is flexible and can handle data with complex seasonal patterns and varying trends.
- **X-12-ARIMA and X-13-ARIMA-SEATS:** Developed by the U.S. Census Bureau, these methods are sophisticated time series decomposition techniques that incorporate ARIMA modeling and seasonal adjustment procedures. They are particularly effective for handling seasonal adjustment in economic and financial data.

Example: Decomposing a Time Series Using STL

The STL decomposition method is widely used due to its flexibility. Let's illustrate the STL decomposition with a practical example using Python and the statsmodels library:

```
import numpy as np
import pandas as pd
import matplotlib.pyplot as plt
from statsmodels.tsa.seasonal import STL

# Sample time series data creation
np.random.seed(0)
times = pd.date_range('2020-01-01', periods=100, freq='M')
data = pd.Series(np.random.randn(100) + np.linspace(0, 10, 100), index=times)

# STL decomposition
stl = STL(data, seasonal=13)
result = stl.fit()

# Plotting the decomposed components
fig, (ax1, ax2, ax3, ax4) = plt.subplots(4, 1, sharex=True, figsize=(10, 8))

ax1.plot(data)
ax1.set_ylabel('Observed')

ax2.plot(result.trend)
ax2.set_ylabel('Trend')

ax3.plot(result.seasonal)
ax3.set_ylabel('Seasonal')

ax4.plot(result.resid)
ax4.set_ylabel('Residual')

plt.show()
```

The output of the above code would be four plots corresponding to the observed data, the trend component, the seasonal component, and the residual component, respectively.

```
plt.show()
```

By examining these plots, one can gain insights into the underlying structure of the time series, identify seasonal patterns, and detect any anomalies or irregularities present in the data. The decomposed components can then be used for further analysis, such as forecasting future values or understanding the impact of different factors influencing the time series.

Understanding time series decomposition is crucial for any data scientist or analyst working with temporal data. It not only aids in the initial exploratory data analysis but also improves the performance of time series forecasting models by isolating and modeling the different components separately.

9.4 Stationarity in Time Series

Stationarity is a fundamental concept in time series analysis, crucial for the application of various modeling techniques. A time series is said to be stationary if its statistical properties, such as mean, variance, and autocovariance, remain constant over time. Stationarity ensures the dependability of future predictions by assuming that the underlying process generating the time series does not change over time.

To formally define stationarity, a time series $\{Y_t\}$ is considered strictly stationary if the joint distribution of $(Y_{t_1}, Y_{t_2}, \ldots, Y_{t_k})$ is the same as the joint distribution of $(Y_{t_1+h}, Y_{t_2+h}, \ldots, Y_{t_k+h})$ for all time points t and time lag h, and for any choice of k. This strict criterion is often relaxed in practical applications to weak or second-order stationarity.

A time series $\{Y_t\}$ exhibits weak stationarity if:

- The mean $\mathbb{E}[Y_t]$ is constant for all t: $\mathbb{E}[Y_t] = \mu$.
- The variance $\text{Var}(Y_t)$ is constant for all t: $\text{Var}(Y_t) = \sigma^2 < \infty$.
- The autocovariance function $\gamma(k) = \text{Cov}(Y_t, Y_{t+k})$ depends only on the lag k and not on time t.

Understanding and testing for stationarity is paramount as many modeling techniques, such as ARIMA, require stationary data. There are several methods for checking stationarity, primarily through graphical analysis and statistical tests.

Graphical methods involve plotting the time series data to visually inspect any apparent trends or seasonal patterns. The Autocorrelation Function (ACF) and Partial Autocorrelation Function (PACF) plots can also provide insights. Specifically, in a non-stationary series, the ACF will decay slowly, indicative of long-term dependencies.

For statistical testing, the Augmented Dickey-Fuller (ADF) test, Kwiatkowski-Phillips-Schmidt-Shin (KPSS) test, and the Phillips-Perron (PP) test are commonly used. The ADF test's null hypothesis states that the series has a unit root (non-stationary), whereas the KPSS test has a null hypothesis that the data is stationary. The complementary use of these tests provides a robust approach to determining stationarity.

```
from statsmodels.tsa.stattools import adfuller

# Perform the ADF test
result = adfuller(time_series_data)
print('ADF Statistic: %f' % result[0])
print('p-value: %f' % result[1])
print('Critical Values:')
for key, value in result[4].items():
    print('\t%s: %.3f' % (key, value))
```

```
ADF Statistic: -3.678
p-value: 0.004
Critical Values:
    1%: -3.431
    5%: -2.862
    10%: -2.567
```

In practice, transforming non-stationary data into a stationary form is essential for effective modeling. Common techniques for achieving stationarity include differencing, detrending, and logarithmic transformations.

Differencing involves computing the differences between consecutive observations. First-order differencing is often sufficient to stabilize the mean of the series.

```
# First-order differencing
diff_series = time_series_data.diff().dropna()
```

Detrending removes a known trend component from the time series. This can be performed using regression techniques where the observed series is regressed on time.

```
from scipy.signal import detrend
```

```
detrended_series = detrend(time_series_data)
```

Logarithmic transformation can stabilize variance and is particularly useful when the series exhibits an exponential growth pattern.

```
import numpy as np

log_series = np.log(time_series_data)
```

Ensuring that the time series data is stationary simplifies the modeling process and enhances the reliability of forecasts. As the temporal structure remains consistent, the models can leverage the static properties of the data, yielding more accurate and interpretable results.

9.5 Autocorrelation and Partial Autocorrelation

Autocorrelation refers to the correlation of a time series with its own past and future values. It is a crucial aspect in the analysis of time series data, as it provides insights into the persistence of patterns over time. Autocorrelation, often represented as the autocorrelation function (ACF), helps in identifying the dependency between observations at different time lags.

Consider a time series $\{X_t\}$, where t represents time. The autocorrelation at lag k is denoted as ρ_k and is mathematically defined as:

$$\rho_k = \frac{\text{Cov}(X_t, X_{t+k})}{\sqrt{\text{Var}(X_t) \cdot \text{Var}(X_{t+k})}}$$

where $\text{Cov}(X_t, X_{t+k})$ is the covariance between the values of the time series at times t and $t+k$, and $\text{Var}(X_t)$ is the variance of the time series at time t.

The autocorrelation function (ACF) is a plot of ρ_k against k. This function is useful for identifying repeating patterns, such as seasonal effects, in the data. Significant autocorrelations at specific lags indicate that past values have a predictive influence on future values at those specific intervals.

Partial autocorrelation, on the other hand, measures the correlation between the time series and its lagged values, with the linear influence of the intervening values removed. This is particularly important for disentangling the direct effect of a lagged value from the indirect effects of other intermediate lags. The partial autocorrelation function (PACF) at lag k, ϕ_k, is obtained by regressing X_t on $X_{t-1}, X_{t-2}, \ldots, X_{t-(k-1)}$ and examining the residuals' correlation with X_{t-k}.

Mathematically, the PACF at lag k can be found through the following technique:

- Perform a regression of X_t on $X_{t-1}, X_{t-2}, \ldots, X_{t-(k-1)}$.
- Calculate residuals from this regression.
- Examine the correlation of these residuals with X_{t-k}.

By considering the partial autocorrelation, one can identify the order of an autoregressive model, which indicates how many lagged terms of the series are significant.

The following is an example of calculating and plotting the Autocorrelation Function (ACF) and Partial Autocorrelation Function (PACF) using Python and the 'statsmodels' library:

```
import numpy as np
import pandas as pd
import matplotlib.pyplot as plt
from statsmodels.graphics.tsaplots import plot_acf, plot_pacf

# Example time series data
data = np.random.randn(100)
time_series = pd.Series(data)

# Plotting ACF and PACF
fig, axes = plt.subplots(1, 2, figsize=(15, 5))

# Autocorrelation Function (ACF)
plot_acf(time_series, lags=30, ax=axes[0], title="Autocorrelation Function (ACF)")

# Partial Autocorrelation Function (PACF)
plot_pacf(time_series, lags=30, ax=axes[1], title="Partial Autocorrelation Function (
    PACF)")

plt.show()
```

```
# Output
ACF and PACF plots displaying correlation coefficients for lags 1 to 30.
```

In the ACF plot, each bar represents the autocorrelation coefficient at a specific lag. Bars extending beyond the significance threshold indicate statistically significant correlations at those lags. In the PACF plot, significant lags suggest the appropriacy of the corresponding autoregressive terms for modeling.

Both ACF and PACF are fundamental tools in the identification, estimation, and diagnostic checking of autoregressive integrated moving average (ARIMA) models. Properly interpreting these plots enables the selection of appropriate model parameters, contributing to more accurate forecasting and understanding of the underlying data structure.

9.6 Moving Averages and Smoothing Techniques

Moving averages and smoothing techniques are fundamental tools for analyzing time series data. These methods help in identifying trends by smoothing out noise and fluctuations that may conceal underlying patterns. Moving averages, in particular, are pivotal in reducing random variation and making the fundamental characteristics of the series more apparent.

The moving average of a time series is calculated by averaging the values of the series over a specified number of consecutive periods. The most commonly used types are the simple moving average (SMA) and the weighted moving average (WMA).

A **Simple Moving Average (SMA)** is computed by taking the arithmetic mean of a specified number of time series data points. If we denote the time series data as $x_1, x_2, \ldots, x_T$, the SMA at time t over a window of size n is given by:

$$\text{SMA}_t = \frac{1}{n} \sum_{i=0}^{n-1} x_{t-i}$$

where n is the number of periods over which the average is calculated. This formula smooths the data by filtering out random noise, ideally leading to a better understanding of the longer-term trends.

The **Weighted Moving Average (WMA)** addresses a limitation of the SMA by assigning different weights to the data points. More recent data points can be assigned higher weights to capture trends more effectively. The formula for WMA at time t is as follows:

$$\text{WMA}_t = \frac{\sum_{i=0}^{n-1} w_i x_{t-i}}{\sum_{i=0}^{n-1} w_i}$$

where w_i is the weight assigned to the i-th data point, and these weights typically sum up to one. The weighted approach allows recent observations to exert more influence on the average, making it more responsive to changes in the data.

Another powerful technique for smoothing time series data is **Exponential Smoothing**. This approach applies decreasing weights to past observations exponentially, ensuring that more recent observations have a more substantial impact. The simple exponential smoothing model is given by:

$$S_t = \alpha x_t + (1 - \alpha) S_{t-1}$$

where S_t is the smoothed value at time t, x_t is the actual value at time t, and α is the smoothing constant ($0 < \alpha < 1$). The parameter α determines the weight assigned to the most recent observation, with a higher α making the model more responsive to recent changes in the data.

Double Exponential Smoothing, or Holt's Method, extends simple exponential smoothing by including a trend component. This method is expressed with two equations:

$$S_t = \alpha x_t + (1 - \alpha)(S_{t-1} + T_{t-1})$$
$$T_t = \beta(S_t - S_{t-1}) + (1 - \beta) T_{t-1}$$

where T_t is the estimated trend at time t and β is a smoothing constant for the trend ($0 < \beta < 1$). This method is particularly useful for time series data with a trend that changes over time.

To further refine smoothing techniques, **Triple Exponential Smoothing**, or Holt-Winters Method, incorporates seasonal components. This model assumes that there are three aspects influencing the data: the level, trend, and seasonality, modeled as:

$$S_t = \alpha \frac{x_t}{I_{t-L}} + (1 - \alpha)(S_{t-1} + T_{t-1})$$
$$T_t = \beta(S_t - S_{t-1}) + (1 - \beta) T_{t-1}$$
$$I_t = \gamma \frac{x_t}{S_t} + (1 - \gamma) I_{t-L}$$

where L represents the length of the seasonal cycle and I_t is the seasonal component. The parameters α, β, and γ are the smoothing constants that govern the level, trend, and seasonal adjustments respectively.

To illustrate the efficacy of these techniques, consider a simulation in Python using real-world data. First, we import the necessary packages and load our time series data:

```
import pandas as pd
import numpy as np
import matplotlib.pyplot as plt

# Load sample time series data (e.g., stock prices)
data = pd.read_csv('timeseries_data.csv')
data['Date'] = pd.to_datetime(data['Date'])
data.set_index('Date', inplace=True)
```

Next, we compute and plot the SMA and WMA to visualize the smoothing effect:

```
# Define window size
window_size = 10

# Compute Simple Moving Average (SMA)
data['SMA'] = data['Close'].rolling(window=window_size).mean()

# Compute Weighted Moving Average (WMA)
weights = np.arange(1, window_size + 1)
data['WMA'] = data['Close'].rolling(window=window_size).apply(lambda prices: np.
    dot(prices, weights) / weights.sum(), raw=True)

# Plot the results
plt.figure(figsize=(12, 6))
plt.plot(data['Close'], label='Original Time Series')
plt.plot(data['SMA'], label='Simple Moving Average (SMA)')
plt.plot(data['WMA'], label='Weighted Moving Average (WMA)')
plt.legend()
plt.show()
```

For exponential smoothing, we utilize the statsmodels library to apply simple and Holt-Winters smoothing:

```
from statsmodels.tsa.holtwinters import SimpleExpSmoothing, ExponentialSmoothing

# Apply Simple Exponential Smoothing
ses_model = SimpleExpSmoothing(data['Close']).fit(smoothing_level=0.2)
data['SES'] = ses_model.fittedvalues

# Apply Holt-Winters Exponential Smoothing
holt_winters_model = ExponentialSmoothing(data['Close'], trend='add', seasonal='
    add', seasonal_periods=12).fit()
data['Holt_Winters'] = holt_winters_model.fittedvalues

# Plot the results
plt.figure(figsize=(12, 6))
plt.plot(data['Close'], label='Original Time Series')
plt.plot(data['SES'], label='Simple Exponential Smoothing (SES)')
plt.plot(data['Holt_Winters'], label='Holt-Winters Exponential Smoothing')
plt.legend()
plt.show()
```

These visualizations highlight how moving averages and smoothing techniques can be leveraged for trend analysis in time series data. The implementation of such methods allows practitioners to discern underlying patterns more effectively and prepare data for further predictive modeling.

9.7 ARIMA Models

The ARIMA (AutoRegressive Integrated Moving Average) model is a comprehensive and flexible class of models for univariate time series forecasting. An ARIMA model can be thought of as a combination of three components: autoregression (AR), differencing (I) to induce stationarity, and a moving average (MA). The model is formally denoted as ARIMA(p, d, q), where p, d, and q are non-negative integers.

Autoregressive (AR) Component: The autoregressive part of ARIMA (denoted as AR(p)) indicates that the evolving variable of interest is regressed on its own lagged values. Mathematically, it can be represented as follows:

$$y_t = c + \phi_1 y_{t-1} + \phi_2 y_{t-2} + \cdots + \phi_p y_{t-p} + \epsilon_t$$

where y_t is the actual value of the series at time t, c is a constant, ϕ_i (for $i = 1, 2, \ldots, p$) are the parameters of the AR model, and ϵ_t represents white noise.

Differencing (I) Component: The integration part (denoted as I(d)) involves differencing the time series data to achieve stationarity. Differencing is a process of computing the differences between consecutive observations to remove trends and seasonality. The differencing operation can be expressed as:

$$\Delta y_t = y_t - y_{t-1}$$

where Δy_t denotes the differenced time series. This operation can be iterated d times to induce stationarity.

Moving Average (MA) Component: The moving average part (denoted as MA(q)) models the error term as a linear combination of error terms occurring contemporaneously and at various times in the past. It is mathematically represented by:

$$y_t = c + \epsilon_t + \theta_1 \epsilon_{t-1} + \theta_2 \epsilon_{t-2} + \cdots + \theta_q \epsilon_{t-q}$$

where θ_j (for $j = 1, 2, \ldots, q$) are the parameters of the MA model and ϵ_t represents white noise.

Thus, an ARIMA(p, d, q) model can be conceptualized as:

$$\Delta^d y_t = c + \sum_{i=1}^{p} \phi_i y_{t-i} + \sum_{j=1}^{q} \theta_j \epsilon_{t-j} + \epsilon_t$$

where Δ^d indicates differencing d times.

Model Identification: The Box-Jenkins methodology outlines an iterative three-stage process to identify, estimate, and check an ARIMA model. These stages include:

- **Identification:** This involves determining the values of p, d, and q. The identification stage typically relies on tools such as the Autocorrelation Function (ACF) and Partial Autocorrelation Function (PACF) plots to diagnose the structures within the time series. For instance, an AR process is suggested if the PACF shows a cut-off after p lags, whereas an MA process is suggested if the ACF shows a cut-off after q lags.

- **Estimation:** Estimation refers to the process of fitting the model to the data and estimating the parameters. This can be accomplished through techniques such as maximum likelihood estimation (MLE) or least squares estimation.

- **Diagnostic Checking:** Once a model is estimated, diagnostic checking involves ensuring that the residuals of the fitted model are white noise. This could be verified by inspecting the ACF of the residuals or through statistical tests such as the Ljung-Box test.

Estimation Example Using Python: Below is an example of fitting an ARIMA model using the Python ‘statsmodels‘ library.

```
import pandas as pd
import numpy as np
from statsmodels.tsa.arima.model import ARIMA

# Load the time series data
data = pd.read_csv('time_series_data.csv')
time_series = data['value']

# Fit the ARIMA model
model = ARIMA(time_series, order=(p, d, q))
model_fit = model.fit()

# Summary of the model
print(model_fit.summary())
```

The output of the above code, assuming the data is correctly preprocessed and the time_series_data.csv file is available, may look like:

```
                    SARIMAX Results
==============================================================================
Dep. Variable:                  y   No. Observations:              100
Model:             ARIMA(p, d, q)   Log Likelihood             -123.456
Date:            Mon, 01 Jan 2023   AIC                         250.912
Time:                    00:00:00   BIC                        260.710
Sample:                         0   HQIC                       254.001
                          - 100
Covariance Type:              opg
==============================================================================
coefficients    std err     z     P>|z|      [0.025      0.975]
-------------------------------------------------------------------
const        0.1234    0.056    2.205    0.028    0.013     0.234
ar.L1        0.5674    0.078    7.279    0.000    0.415     0.719
ma.L1       -0.3123    0.091   -3.433    0.001   -0.491    -0.133
sigma2       0.9876    0.123    8.028    0.000    0.746     1.229
...
```

Test results such as the AIC (Akaike Information Criterion) and BIC (Bayesian Information Criterion) as well as the parameter estimates allow us to evaluate the fit quality and determine if model improvements are necessary.

In forecasting future values, the fitted ARIMA model can be used to generate out-of-sample predictions. An example in Python is:

```
forecasts = model_fit.forecast(steps=10)
print(forecasts)
```

The predictive power of ARIMA models hinges on the proper selection of parameters and robust diagnostic checking, ensuring that residuals do not exhibit autocorrelation or any hidden patterns. When correctly specified, ARIMA models have proven to be powerful tools for time series forecasting in diverse domains ranging from economics and finance to environmental science and engineering.

9.8 Seasonal ARIMA (SARIMA) Models

Seasonal ARIMA (SARIMA) models are an extension of the ARIMA (AutoRegressive Integrated Moving Average) models that specifically address the challenges posed by time series data exhibiting seasonality. Seasonality refers to patterns that repeat at regular intervals due to seasonal effects. SARIMA models incorporate both non-seasonal and seasonal components, making them highly effective for time series forecasting in scenarios where periodic patterns are present.

SARIMA models are denoted as $SARIMA(p, d, q)(P, D, Q)_s$, where:

- p: Order of the non-seasonal autoregressive (AR) part
- d: Degree of non-seasonal differencing

- q: Order of the non-seasonal moving average (MA) part
- P: Order of the seasonal autoregressive (AR) part
- D: Degree of seasonal differencing
- Q: Order of the seasonal moving average (MA) part
- s: Length of the seasonal cycle

The process of building a SARIMA model involves several key steps:

Step 1: Identifying Seasonality and Differencing

Seasonal differencing is vital for removing seasonal trends. If the time series data show a clear periodic pattern, seasonal differencing (D) is applied. The seasonal differencing operator is $\Delta_s = (1 - L^s)$, where L is the lag operator and s is the seasonal period.

```
# Python code for seasonal differencing
import pandas as pd
data = pd.Series(Data) # Data is the time series
diff_seasonal = data.diff(s)
```

```
Output:
0    NaN
1    NaN
2    NaN
3    NaN
4    NaN
...
```

Non-seasonal differencing (d) might also be necessary to achieve stationarity. Non-seasonal differencing is performed using the operator $\Delta = (1 - L)$.

Step 2: Identifying Model Orders p, q, P, Q

The orders of the AR and MA components are determined by analyzing autocorrelation functions (ACF) and partial autocorrelation functions (PACF). The seasonal components P and Q are selected by examining the ACF and PACF plots at lags that are multiples of the seasonal period s.

```
# Python code to plot ACF and PACF
from statsmodels.graphics.tsaplots import plot_acf, plot_pacf
plot_acf(data)
plot_pacf(data)
```

Step 3: Model Estimation

Once the orders are identified, the SARIMA model is estimated using maximum likelihood estimation (MLE). The statsmodels library in

Python is commonly used for this purpose.

```
# Python code to fit SARIMA model
from statsmodels.tsa.statespace.sarimax import SARIMAX
model = SARIMAX(data, order=(p, d, q), seasonal_order=(P, D, Q, s))
result = model.fit()
```

```
Output:
                    SARIMAX Results
==============================================================================
Dep. Variable:                  y   No. Observations:                  200
Model:          SARIMAX(1, 1, 1)x(1, 1, 1, 12)   Log Likelihood          ...
Date:                           Time:
...
```

Step 4: Model Diagnostics

Diagnostic checks are performed to validate the adequacy of the model. Residuals analysis involves plotting residuals and conducting statistical tests like the Ljung-Box test to check for any autocorrelation.

```
# Python code for residual diagnostic
residuals = result.resid
plot_acf(residuals)

from statsmodels.stats.diagnostic import acorr_ljungbox
ljung_box = acorr_ljungbox(residuals, lags=[10, 20], return_df=True)
```

```
Output:
Ljung-Box Q (10)  0.523
Ljung-Box Q (20)  0.489
```

Step 5: Forecasting

With a validated model, forecasts can be produced, often with confidence intervals. The prediction and forecasting steps allow for projecting future values and understanding the associated uncertainties.

```
# Python code for forecasting
forecast = result.get_forecast(steps=12)
forecast_ci = forecast.conf_int()
```

```
Output:
       mean   mean_ci_lower  mean_ci_upper
200    10.5        10.0          11.0
201    10.6        10.1          11.1
...
```

SARIMA models are robust tools for analyzing time series data with both seasonal and non-seasonal components. Their strength lies in their ability to handle complex patterns by integrating differencing, autoregressive, and moving average components tailored to capture both short-term and seasonal dependencies. Properly selecting the model parameters through rigorous statistical analysis ensures the model's effectiveness in forecasting and provides valuable insights into the temporal dynamics of the data.

9.9 Exponential Smoothing and Holt-Winters

Exponential smoothing is a time series forecasting method that applies weighted averages of past observations where the weights decrease exponentially as the observations get older. This technique is versatile and can be adapted to handle a variety of time series types, including those with trends and seasonality.

Exponential smoothing methods are categorized into three types:

- Single Exponential Smoothing
- Double Exponential Smoothing
- Triple Exponential Smoothing (Holt-Winters)

Single Exponential Smoothing

The simplest form, Single Exponential Smoothing (SES), is suitable for univariate time series without trend or seasonality. The smoothed value S_t at time t is given by:

$$S_t = \alpha Y_t + (1 - \alpha) S_{t-1}$$

where Y_t is the actual value at time t, S_{t-1} is the previous smoothed value, and α is the smoothing parameter, $0 < \alpha < 1$. The parameter α determines the rate at which the influence of the observations at prior time steps declines exponentially. Choosing an appropriate α is crucial, as a higher α places more emphasis on recent observations, making the model more reactive to changes in data.

Double Exponential Smoothing

To handle data with trends, Double Exponential Smoothing, also known as Holt's Linear Trend Model, extends SES by adding another smoothing equation for the trend component. This method involves two equations: one for the level L_t and another for the trend T_t.

$$L_t = \alpha Y_t + (1 - \alpha)(L_{t-1} + T_{t-1})$$
$$T_t = \beta(L_t - L_{t-1}) + (1 - \beta) T_{t-1}$$

where α and β are smoothing parameters for the level and trend, respectively. Forecasting a future value at time $t + m$ is done using:

$$F_{t+m} = L_t + mT_t$$

Triple Exponential Smoothing (Holt-Winters)

For time series data exhibiting both trend and seasonal components, the Triple Exponential Smoothing method, known as the Holt-Winters method, is applied. There are two versions of this method: the additive and the multiplicative models. The choice between them depends on the nature of the seasonality in the data.

In the additive model, the seasonality is added to the trend and level components, suitable for data with roughly constant seasonal variations:

$$\begin{aligned}
L_t &= \alpha(Y_t - S_{t-s}) + (1 - \alpha)(L_{t-1} + T_{t-1}) \\
T_t &= \beta(L_t - L_{t-1}) + (1 - \beta)T_{t-1} \\
S_t &= \gamma(Y_t - L_t) + (1 - \gamma)S_{t-s}
\end{aligned}$$

Forecasting m periods ahead:

$$F_{t+m} = L_t + mT_t + S_{t-s+m}$$

In these equations, S_{t-s} is the seasonal component at $t - s$. The smoothing parameters α, β, and γ control the updating process for the level, trend, and seasonal components, respectively.

For multiplicative seasonality, the seasonal component modifies the level and trend multiplicatively:

$$\begin{aligned}
L_t &= \alpha\frac{Y_t}{S_{t-s}} + (1 - \alpha)(L_{t-1} + T_{t-1}) \\
T_t &= \beta(L_t - L_{t-1}) + (1 - \beta)T_{t-1} \\
S_t &= \gamma\frac{Y_t}{L_t} + (1 - \gamma)S_{t-s}
\end{aligned}$$

Forecasting is given by:

$$F_{t+m} = (L_t + mT_t) \cdot S_{t-s+m}$$

The multiplicative model is suitable for time series data where the seasonal variations change proportionally with the level of the series.

```
import numpy as np
import pandas as pd
from statsmodels.tsa.holtwinters import ExponentialSmoothing

# Load your data
data = pd.read_csv('path_to_your_data.csv')
time_series = data['TimeSeriesColumn']

# Fit the Holt-Winters Model
model = ExponentialSmoothing(time_series, seasonal='mul', seasonal_periods=12).fit
    ()

# Generate forecast
forecast = model.forecast(steps=12)

print(forecast)
```

```
Output:
12    123.456
13    130.789
14    135.987
15    140.654
...   .......
23    189.345
24    195.678
dtype: float64
```

Choosing appropriate values for α, β, and γ is vital, and these parameters can be optimized using various techniques, such as grid search or through the minimization of prediction error metrics like Mean Squared Error (MSE) and Mean Absolute Error (MAE). Advanced packages like statsmodels in Python provide built-in functions for these calculations.

Holt-Winters method handles complexities in time series data efficiently, making it a robust choice for forecasting in varied applications. Its adaptability and resilience in modelling trends and seasonality are critical for accurate long-term forecasting.

9.10 Machine Learning Approaches for Time Series

Machine Learning (ML) approaches have become indispensable tools for time series analysis, offering robust methods to handle complex temporal data patterns that traditional statistical techniques sometimes fail to capture. This section reviews several machine learning methods commonly applied to time series data, highlighting their mechanisms, strengths, and applications. We will delve into methods like regression models, decision trees, ensemble methods, and neural networks.

The application of machine learning to time series data necessitates careful preparation of the data and tuning of models to account for the temporal dependencies inherent in the data. Traditional machine learning algorithms often assume independence between observations, a condition rarely met in time series datasets. Thus, preprocessing steps such as feature engineering, scaling, and splitting must be adapted to honor the sequential nature of the data.

Feature Engineering for Time Series

Effective machine learning models rely heavily on the quality and relevance of input features. For time series data, this often involves the creation of additional time-related features. Common techniques include:

- **Lag features**: The creation of lagged versions of the time series data, which act as predictor variables. For example, for a time series y_t, lag features could be $y_{t-1}, y_{t-2}, \ldots, y_{t-n}$.
- **Rolling statistics**: Computation of rolling mean, rolling standard deviation, rolling minimum, and maximum values, providing smoothed features that help capture local trends.
- **Date-time features**: Extraction of components such as hour, day, week, month, and year. This helps the model recognize seasonal patterns and other temporal characteristics.
- **Special calendar events**: Adding features to account for holidays, weekends, and other special events can significantly enhance model performance in forecasting tasks.

Regression Models

Regression models predict future values based on historical data and engineered features. Linear regression is the simplest form, assuming a linear relationship between the dependent and independent variables. However, for time series data, this relationship is often non-linear, requiring more complex models:

- **Linear Regression**: Despite its simplicity, linear regression can provide baseline results and insights into the nature of temporal relationships.

- **Regularized Regression Models**: Techniques like Ridge Regression and Lasso Regression introduce penalties for large coefficients, which help in preventing overfitting by shrinking the coefficients towards zero.

Examples of Python code for Ridge Regression applied to a time series dataset are shown below:

```
from sklearn.linear_model import Ridge
import pandas as pd

# Assume df is a pandas DataFrame with time series data

# Create lag features
df['y_lag_1'] = df['y'].shift(1)
df = df.dropna()

# Split data into training and test sets
train_size = int(len(df) * 0.8)
train, test = df[:train_size], df[train_size:]

# Prepare features and target
X_train, y_train = train[['y_lag_1']], train['y']
X_test, y_test = test[['y_lag_1']], test['y']

# Fit the Ridge Regression model
ridge = Ridge(alpha=1.0)
ridge.fit(X_train, y_train)

# Predict and evaluate
y_pred = ridge.predict(X_test)
```

Decision Trees and Ensemble Methods

Decision trees and their ensemble extensions, such as Random Forests and Gradient Boosting Machines (GBMs), can capture non-linear relationships and interactions between variables effectively, often performing better than simple regressions:

- **Decision Trees**: Build a model in the form of a tree structure, partitioning the data into subsets based on feature thresholds.
- **Random Forests**: An ensemble technique that builds multiple decision trees and merges them to get a more accurate and stable prediction.
- **Gradient Boosting Machines (GBMs)**: Combine several weak models (usually decision trees) to create a strong predictive model, focusing on correcting the errors of previous models.

Sample code for a Random Forest applied to time series data is as follows:

```
from sklearn.ensemble import RandomForestRegressor

# Create lag features as in the previous example, then split the data

# Fit the Random Forest model
rf = RandomForestRegressor(n_estimators=100, random_state=42)
rf.fit(X_train, y_train)

# Predict and evaluate
y_pred = rf.predict(X_test)
```

Neural Networks

Neural networks, especially recurrent architectures such as Long Short-Term Memory (LSTM) and Gated Recurrent Units (GRU), are particularly well-suited for time series forecasting due to their ability to retain memory over time steps.

- **Feedforward Neural Networks (FNNs)**: Can be used for time series forecasting by feeding lagged values as input features.
- **Recurrent Neural Networks (RNNs)**: Specifically designed for sequential data, allowing information to persist.
- **Long Short-Term Memory (LSTM)**: An extension of RNN that can learn long dependencies by mitigating the vanishing gradient problem.
- **Gated Recurrent Units (GRU)**: Another variant of RNN that simplifies the LSTM architecture while retaining its benefits.

An example Keras implementation for an LSTM network:

```
from keras.models import Sequential
from keras.layers import LSTM, Dense
import numpy as np

# Assume X_train, y_train, X_test, y_test are NumPy arrays with lag features and
    targets

# Reshape data for LSTM layer [samples, time steps, features]
X_train_lstm = X_train.reshape((X_train.shape[0], 1, X_train.shape[1]))
X_test_lstm = X_test.reshape((X_test.shape[0], 1, X_test.shape[1]))

model = Sequential()
model.add(LSTM(50, activation='relu', input_shape=(X_train_lstm.shape[1],
    X_train_lstm.shape[2])))
model.add(Dense(1))
model.compile(optimizer='adam', loss='mse')
```

```
# Fit model
model.fit(X_train_lstm, y_train, epochs=200, batch_size=32, verbose=0)

# Predict and evaluate
y_pred = model.predict(X_test_lstm)
```

The data preprocessing step preceding the model training is critical in ensuring that time series characteristics are adequately captured. These neural network architectures, when tuned correctly, can outperform conventional methods in capturing the intricacies of temporal dependencies.

Machine learning approaches for time series data offer powerful alternatives to classical methods, with the potential for better predictive performance and flexibility. Proper feature engineering, model selection, and tuning are imperative to harnessing these benefits effectively.

9.11 Evaluating Time Series Models

Evaluating the performance of time series models is essential for validating model efficacy and ensuring accurate forecasting. Various metrics and techniques are employed to assess the predictive accuracy, robustness, and reliability of these models. This section delves into the methods and performance measures used for model evaluation, offering a detailed discourse on how to execute and interpret these evaluations effectively.

Performance Metrics

Several performance metrics are commonly utilized to assess the accuracy of time series forecasts. These metrics provide quantitative measures of the discrepancies between the actual values and the values predicted by the model.

- **Mean Absolute Error (MAE)**: MAE quantifies the average absolute errors between the predicted and actual values.

  $$MAE = \frac{1}{n}\sum_{t=1}^{n} |y_t - \hat{y_t}|$$

  where y_t represents the actual value, $\hat{y_t}$ denotes the predicted value, and n is the number of observations.

- **Mean Squared Error (MSE)**: MSE measures the average squared difference between actual and predicted values, emphasizing larger errors.

$$MSE = \frac{1}{n}\sum_{t=1}^{n}(y_t - \hat{y}_t)^2$$

- **Root Mean Squared Error (RMSE)**: RMSE is the square root of MSE and provides an error metric in the same units as the original data.

$$RMSE = \sqrt{MSE}$$

- **Mean Absolute Percentage Error (MAPE)**: MAPE measures the accuracy as a percentage.

$$MAPE = \frac{100\%}{n}\sum_{t=1}^{n}\left|\frac{y_t - \hat{y}_t}{y_t}\right|$$

- **Symmetric Mean Absolute Percentage Error (sMAPE)**: sMAPE addresses the potential issues of infinite or undefined MAPE when the actual values are zero.

$$sMAPE = \frac{100\%}{n}\sum_{t=1}^{n}\frac{|y_t - \hat{y}_t|}{(|y_t| + |\hat{y}_t|)/2}$$

- **Theil's U Statistic**: Theil's U compares the forecasted values with a naive baseline model.

$$U = \frac{\sqrt{\frac{1}{n}\sum_{t=1}^{n}(y_t - \hat{y}_t)^2}}{\sqrt{\frac{1}{n}\sum_{t=1}^{n}y_t^2}}$$

The choice of metric may depend on the specific context and nature of the data being analyzed. It is often useful to consider multiple metrics to obtain a comprehensive view of model performance.

Train-Test Split

A fundamental aspect of evaluating time series models is the proper division of the dataset into training and testing sets. Ensuring that the model is validated on unseen data is crucial for assessing its generalizability. Typically, the dataset is divided chronologically, where earlier portions of the data are used for training the model while later portions are reserved for testing.

An example train-test split:

```
# Assumed packages: pandas for data manipulation and train_test_split from sklearn
      for splitting data.
import pandas as pd
from sklearn.model_selection import train_test_split

data = pd.read_csv('time_series_data.csv')
train_size = int(len(data) * 0.8)
train, test = data[:train_size], data[train_size:]
```

This approach ensures that temporal dependencies are preserved, and the model is evaluated on its ability to forecast future values.

Cross-Validation

Cross-validation in time series analysis differs from traditional machine learning cross-validation due to the ordered nature of the data. A commonly used method is Time Series Cross-Validation or rolling window cross-validation. It involves using expanding or rolling windows to create multiple training and validation sets.

For example, using an expanding window approach:

```
# Pseudocode illustration of expanding window cross-validation
n_splits = 5
for i in range(n_splits):
    train_set = data[:train_size + i*window_size]
    validation_set = data[train_size + i*window_size: train_size + (i+1)*
          window_size]
    # Fit model and evaluate on validation set
```

This method helps in assessing the model's performance over various splits and ensures robustness against different segments of the data.

Residual Analysis

Analyzing residuals, which are the differences between actual and predicted values, is vital for diagnosing model performance. Ideally, residuals should be randomly distributed without patterns, indicating that the model has captured all the underlying structures of the data.

Procedures for residual analysis:

```
import matplotlib.pyplot as plt
import statsmodels.api as sm

# Assuming 'residuals' is a series of the residuals obtained from the model
plt.figure(figsize=(10, 6))
plt.plot(residuals)
plt.title('Residuals over Time')
plt.show()

sm.graphics.tsa.plot_acf(residuals, lags=40)
plt.title('Residuals Autocorrelation')
plt.show()
```

If residuals exhibit autocorrelation, it may suggest that the model has overlooked some temporal patterns, prompting further model refinement.

Benchmarking Against Naive Models

To ascertain the effectiveness of a time series model, it is beneficial to compare it against simple naive models. Common naive benchmarks include:

- **Naive Forecast**: The forecast is simply the last observed value.

$$\hat{y}_{t+1} = y_t$$

- **Seasonal Naive Forecast**: The forecast repeats the value from the same season in the previous year (or cycle).

$$\hat{y}_{t+s} = y_t$$

  where s is the seasonal period.

Comparing the advanced model's performance metrics against these naive models helps determine if the additional complexity is warranted by significantly better performance.

Model Robustness and Stability

Robustness refers to a model's performance under different conditions, while stability pertains to consistency across various subsets of the data. Evaluating these characteristics involves several techniques:

- **Backtesting**: Running the model in a simulated real-time environment where forecasts are made iteratively over various points in history.
- **Stress Testing**: Assessing model performance under extreme variations in the data to determine its resilience.

Developing a robust and stable forecasting model is crucial, particularly when dealing with volatile or non-stationary time series.

These comprehensive evaluation techniques ensure that time series models are both accurate and reliable, ultimately leading to more informed data-driven decisions.

9.12 Time Series Forecasting

Time series forecasting is a crucial aspect in the realm of data science, where the goal is to predict future values based on previously observed data points. The process involves the utilization of various statistical and machine learning techniques to capture the underlying patterns within the data. Forecasting can be categorized into univariate and multivariate time series, where univariate involves a single variable and multivariate includes multiple variables.

Classical Forecasting Methods

Classical methods for forecasting primarily include ARIMA (AutoRegressive Integrated Moving Average) models, Seasonal ARIMA (SARIMA), and exponential smoothing techniques such as Holt-Winters. These methods are well-established and have been extensively used for time series forecasting.

ARIMA Models

ARIMA models are a popular class of models used to forecast time series data. They combine three components: Autoregression (AR), where the forecast variable depends linearly on its own previous values; Differencing (I), which involves differencing the series to make it stationary; and a Moving Average (MA) model, where the forecast error is a linear combination of past errors. The general form of an ARIMA model can be represented as:

$$ARIMA(p, d, q) : \phi(B)(1 - B)^d X_t = \theta(B)\epsilon_t$$

Where:

- p is the number of lag observations included in the model (lag order).
- d is the number of times that the raw observations are differenced.
- q is the size of the moving average window.
- $\phi(B)$ is the autoregressive polynomial.
- $\theta(B)$ is the moving average polynomial.
- ϵ_t is the white noise error term.

Seasonal ARIMA (SARIMA)

For time series data with seasonality, SARIMA models extend ARIMA by incorporating seasonal components. SARIMA takes into account both non-seasonal and seasonal patterns in the data, adding seasonal differencing and seasonal order parameters to the model. The SARIMA model can be represented as:

$$SARIMA(p, d, q)(P, D, Q)_s$$

Where:

- P is the number of seasonal autoregressive terms.
- D is the number of seasonal differences.
- Q is the number of seasonal moving average terms.
- s is the length of the seasonal cycle.

Exponential Smoothing and Holt-Winters

Exponential smoothing methods provide another approach to forecasting. These methods apply weighted averages of past observations, with the weights decaying exponentially as the observations get older. The Holt-Winters method is an enhancement of exponential smoothing that considers both trend and seasonality.

The basic form of exponential smoothing can be written as:

$$y_t = \alpha y_{t-1} + (1 - \alpha) y_{t-2}$$

Where α is the smoothing parameter.

Holt-Winters extends this basic model by adding equations for trend and seasonality, resulting in additive or multiplicative models for seasonal data. The equations for the Holt-Winters additive method are:

$$\begin{aligned}
l_t &= \alpha(y_t - s_{t-s}) + (1 - \alpha)(l_{t-1} + b_{t-1}) \\
b_t &= \beta(l_t - l_{t-1}) + (1 - \beta) b_{t-1} \\
s_t &= \gamma(y_t - l_t) + (1 - \gamma) s_{t-s} \\
\hat{y}_{t+h|t} &= l_t + h b_t + s_{t-s+h}
\end{aligned}$$

Where:

- l_t is the level component.
- b_t is the trend component.
- s_t is the seasonal component.
- α, β, and γ are the smoothing parameters.

Machine Learning Approaches for Forecasting

Recent advances in machine learning have introduced powerful tools for time series forecasting. Algorithms such as Random Forests, Gradient Boosting Machines, and Long Short-Term Memory (LSTM) networks are capable of capturing complex, non-linear dependencies in time series data.

Long Short-Term Memory (LSTM)

LSTM networks are a special kind of Recurrent Neural Network (RNN) capable of learning long-term dependencies. The structure of an LSTM cell includes three main gates: input gate, forget gate, and output gate, which control the flow of information. An example implementation of an LSTM model in Python using Keras could be:

```
from keras.models import Sequential
from keras.layers import LSTM, Dense

model = Sequential()
model.add(LSTM(50, return_sequences=True, input_shape=(timesteps, features)))
model.add(LSTM(50))
model.add(Dense(1))
model.compile(optimizer='adam', loss='mse')
model.fit(X_train, y_train, epochs=50, batch_size=72, validation_data=(X_test,
    y_test), verbose=0, shuffle=False)
```

The model's performance can be evaluated using standard metrics such as Mean Squared Error (MSE) or Mean Absolute Error (MAE). The output of the prediction could look like:

```
Epoch 1/50
Train on 800 samples, validate on 200 samples
800/800 [==============================] - 2s - loss: 0.0023 - val_loss: 0.0015
Epoch 2/50
800/800 [==============================] - 1s - loss: 0.0012 - val_loss: 0.0011
...
```

The comprehensive use of both classical and modern machine learning techniques for time series forecasting enables a robust approach to predict future values, considering various patterns and dependencies within the data. Understanding the principles and implementations of these methods equips practitioners with the necessary tools to handle a wide range of forecasting tasks.

9.13 Case Studies in Time Series Analysis

This section delves into practical applications of time series analysis through detailed case studies, demonstrating the techniques previously discussed. Each case study outlines a specific problem, the methodology applied, the analysis process, and the interpretation of results.

Case Study 1: Forecasting Stock Prices

Stock prices exhibit significant temporal dependencies, making them a perfect candidate for time series analysis. This case study focuses on predicting the stock price of a public company using the ARIMA model.

Problem: Predict the closing price of Company XYZ's stock for the next 30 trading days using past data.

Methodology: We employ the ARIMA (AutoRegressive Integrated Moving Average) model for this task. The ARIMA model is defined by three parameters: p, d, and q. Here:

- p represents the number of lag observations included in the model (lag order).
- d is the number of times that the raw observations are differenced.
- q is the size of the moving average window.

Analysis Process: We start by visualizing the stock price data to understand its trend and seasonality.

```
import pandas as pd
import matplotlib.pyplot as plt
from statsmodels.tsa.seasonal import seasonal_decompose

# Load dataset
data = pd.read_csv('XYZ_stock_prices.csv', index_col='Date', parse_dates=True)
stock_prices = data['Closing Price']

# Plot the time series
plt.figure(figsize=(10, 6))
plt.plot(stock_prices)
plt.title('Company XYZ Stock Prices')
plt.show()
```

Next, we check for stationarity using the Augmented Dickey-Fuller (ADF) test.

```
from statsmodels.tsa.stattools import adfuller

# Perform ADF test
adf_test = adfuller(stock_prices)
```

```
print(f'ADF Statistic: {adf_test[0]}')
print(f'p-value: {adf_test[1]}')
```

We find that the series is non-stationary (p-value > 0.05), and differencing is necessary.

```
# Differencing the series
stock_prices_diff = stock_prices.diff().dropna()

# Plot differenced series
plt.figure(figsize=(10, 6))
plt.plot(stock_prices_diff)
plt.title('Differenced Stock Prices')
plt.show()
```

Post differencing, we reapply the ADF test and determine stationarity. We then use the autocorrelation function (ACF) and partial autocorrelation function (PACF) plots to identify the values of p and q.

```
from statsmodels.graphics.tsaplots import plot_acf, plot_pacf

plot_acf(stock_prices_diff, lags=30)
plt.show()

plot_pacf(stock_prices_diff, lags=30)
plt.show()
```

Based on the ACF and PACF plots, we choose appropriate p and q.

```
from statsmodels.tsa.arima_model import ARIMA

# Fit ARIMA model
model = ARIMA(stock_prices, order=(p, d, q))
model_fit = model.fit(disp=0)
print(model_fit.summary())
```

Finally, we forecast future values and plot the results.

```
# Forecasting
forecast, stderr, conf_int = model_fit.forecast(steps=30)

# Plot forecast
plt.figure(figsize=(10, 6))
plt.plot(stock_prices, label='Observed')
plt.plot(pd.date_range(start=stock_prices.index[-1], periods=30, freq='D'), forecast,
    label='Forecast')
plt.fill_between(pd.date_range(start=stock_prices.index[-1], periods=30, freq='D'),
    conf_int[:, 0], conf_int[:, 1], color='k', alpha=0.15)
plt.title('Stock Price Forecast')
plt.legend()
plt.show()
```

The results show the forecasted stock prices for the next 30 days along with confidence intervals.

Case Study 2: Electricity Consumption Forecasting

Accurate forecasting of electricity consumption is crucial for energy management and planning. This case study demonstrates the use of Seasonal ARIMA (SARIMA) to forecast monthly electricity consumption.

Problem: Forecast the monthly electricity consumption of a city for the next 12 months.

Methodology: We apply the Seasonal ARIMA (SARIMA) model, which includes additional seasonal parameters P, D, and Q to account for seasonality:

- P is the seasonal autoregressive order.
- D is the seasonal differencing order.
- Q is the seasonal moving average order.

The SARIMA model is denoted as $(p, d, q) \times (P, D, Q, s)$, where s is the length of the seasonal cycle.

Analysis Process: We begin by plotting the historical electricity consumption data.

```
# Load dataset
data = pd.read_csv('city_electricity_consumption.csv', index_col='Month',
    parse_dates=True)
electricity_consumption = data['Consumption']

# Plot the time series
plt.figure(figsize=(12, 7))
plt.plot(electricity_consumption)
plt.title('Monthly Electricity Consumption')
plt.show()
```

We decompose the data to analyze trend, seasonality, and residuals.

```
decomposition = seasonal_decompose(electricity_consumption, model='additive')
decomposition.plot()
plt.show()
```

Next, we check for stationarity and perform seasonal differencing if necessary.

```
# Seasonal differencing
electricity_consumption_diff = electricity_consumption.diff(12).dropna()

# Plot differenced series
plt.figure(figsize=(12, 7))
plt.plot(electricity_consumption_diff)
plt.title('Seasonally Differenced Electricity Consumption')
plt.show()
```

```
# Reapply ADF test
adf_test = adfuller(electricity_consumption_diff)
print(f'ADF Statistic: {adf_test[0]}')
print(f'p-value: {adf_test[1]}')
```

Based on ACF and PACF plots, we identify values for p, d, q, P, D, and Q.

```
plot_acf(electricity_consumption_diff, lags=30)
plt.show()

plot_pacf(electricity_consumption_diff, lags=30)
plt.show()
```

We fit the SARIMA model and summarize the results.

```
from statsmodels.tsa.statespace.sarimax import SARIMAX

# Fit SARIMA model
sarima_model = SARIMAX(electricity_consumption, order=(p, d, q), seasonal_order
    =(P, D, Q, 12))
sarima_fit = sarima_model.fit(disp=0)
print(sarima_fit.summary())
```

Finally, we predict future consumption and visualize it.

```
# Forecasting
forecast = sarima_fit.get_forecast(steps=12)
confidence_intervals = forecast.conf_int()

# Plot forecast
plt.figure(figsize=(12, 7))
plt.plot(electricity_consumption, label='Observed')
forecast_index = pd.date_range(start=electricity_consumption.index[-1], periods=12,
    freq='M')
plt.plot(forecast_index, forecast.predicted_mean, label='Forecast')
plt.fill_between(forecast_index, confidence_intervals.iloc[:, 0], confidence_intervals.iloc
    [:, 1], color='k', alpha=0.15)
plt.title('Electricity Consumption Forecast')
plt.legend()
plt.show()
```

The results provide the predicted electricity consumption for the next 12 months with associated confidence intervals.

Case Study 3: Website Traffic Forecasting

Predicting website traffic helps in capacity planning and optimizing resource allocation. This case study uses exponential smoothing methods to model and forecast website traffic.

Problem: Forecast daily visits to a website for the next 60 days.

Methodology: We employ the Holt-Winters exponential smoothing method, which accounts for trend and seasonality. This method has three smoothing parameters: α (level), β (trend), and γ (seasonality).

Analysis Process: First, we visualize the website traffic data.

```
# Load dataset
data = pd.read_csv('website_traffic.csv', index_col='Date', parse_dates=True)
website_traffic = data['Visits']

# Plot the time series
plt.figure(figsize=(12, 7))
plt.plot(website_traffic)
plt.title('Daily Website Traffic')
plt.show()
```

We apply the Holt-Winters method and summarize the model.

```
from statsmodels.tsa.holtwinters import ExponentialSmoothing

# Fit Holt-Winters model
hw_model = ExponentialSmoothing(website_traffic, trend='add', seasonal='add',
    seasonal_periods=7)
hw_fit = hw_model.fit()
print(hw_fit.summary())
```

We use the model to forecast future visits and plot the forecast.

```
# Forecasting
forecast = hw_fit.forecast(steps=60)

# Plot forecast
plt.figure(figsize=(12, 7))
plt.plot(website_traffic, label='Observed')
plt.plot(pd.date_range(start=website_traffic.index[-1], periods=60, freq='D'), forecast,
    label='Forecast')
plt.title('Website Traffic Forecast')
plt.legend()
plt.show()
```

This provides a visual and numerical forecast of daily website traffic for the next 60 days, allowing for better resource management and strategic planning.

Chapter 10

Big Data Technologies and Tools

This chapter explores big data technologies and tools, starting with the characteristics of big data. It provides an overview of the Hadoop ecosystem and the MapReduce programming model. Key platforms and databases such as Apache Spark, MongoDB, and Cassandra are discussed. The chapter covers data warehousing solutions like Hive and HBase, big data storage, and processing with Apache Flink. It also addresses real-time streaming technologies like Kafka and Storm, the concept of data lakes, and big data solutions in the cloud, supplemented by relevant case studies.

10.1 Introduction to Big Data

The term *Big Data* encompasses an extensive range of data sets that are characterized by their significant volume, velocity, and variety. These attributes, often referred to as the three Vs, demand advanced techniques and technologies for efficient processing, analysis, and storage. As conventional data processing tools fall short in handling such massive and diverse data efficiently, the advent of big data technologies provides new frameworks and methodologies for dealing with these challenges.

The **volume** aspect of big data pertains to the enormous amount of data generated every second. Sources such as social media platforms, sensor data, transactional records, and more contribute to the exponential growth of data. This volume necessitates scalable storage and processing solutions capable of handling petabytes and exabytes of information.

Velocity refers to the speed at which new data is generated and needs to be processed. Applications that require near real-time data processing, such as fraud detection systems, online recommendation engines, and Internet of Things (IoT) infrastructure, exemplify the high-velocity nature of data. This requires technologies that can rapidly ingest and process streaming data.

Variety denotes the different types of data—structured, unstructured, and semi-structured. While structured data fits well into traditional databases, unstructured data like text, images, and videos pose significant challenges. Big data technologies must adapt to these diverse data formats and ensure efficient processing and analysis.

Another important concept to consider is **veracity**, which deals with the uncertainty of data. Data sources can introduce biases, noise, and abnormalities, making data veracity crucial in ensuring the correctness and quality of data being analyzed. Effective big data solutions must incorporate robust mechanisms for data validation, cleaning, and consistency checks.

Big data's **value** is a key driving force behind its adoption. The primary goal of big data analytics is to extract valuable insights that can inform decision-making processes. By analyzing extensive data sets, organizations can uncover hidden patterns, predict future trends, and gain a competitive edge in their respective fields.

To better understand the significance of big data, consider the following Python code snippet that demonstrates the creation of a large dataset and its basic manipulation:

```
import numpy as np
import pandas as pd

# Generating a large dataset
data = np.random.randn(1000000, 10)
columns = [f"Feature_{i}" for i in range(10)]
data_frame = pd.DataFrame(data, columns=columns)

# Displaying the first few rows of the dataset
print(data_frame.head())

# Statistical summary of the dataset
summary = data_frame.describe()
print(summary)
```

Upon executing the above code, a dataset with one million rows and ten columns of normally distributed random numbers is created. The first few rows and the statistical summary are then displayed, which might look like:

```
   Feature_0  Feature_1  Feature_2  Feature_3  Feature_4  Feature_5  Feature_6  Feature_7  Feature_8  Feature_9
0   0.123456   0.654321   0.234567  -0.123456   0.987654   0.345678  -0.456789   0.231456  -0.654321   0.145678
1  -0.876543  -0.567890   0.123456   0.567890  -0.234567  -0.678954  -0.123457   0.567890   0.345678  -0.145678
2   0.234567   0.876543  -0.234567   0.876543  -0.567890   0.456789  -0.234567  -0.567890  -0.345678   0.234567
3  -0.987654  -0.789012   0.345678   0.789012   0.234567   0.678954   0.987654  -0.789012   0.456789  -0.987654
4   0.345678   0.987654  -0.123456   0.987654  -0.678954  -0.890123  -0.567890  -0.678954  -0.567890   0.345678

            Feature_0       Feature_1  ...      Feature_8       Feature_9
count  1000000.000000  1000000.000000  ...  1000000.000000  1000000.000000
mean         0.000123        0.000456  ...        0.000321        0.000234
std          1.000234        1.000567  ...        1.000678        1.000123
min         -4.567234       -4.789034  ...       -4.890123       -4.567890
25%         -0.678901       -0.789012  ...       -0.678954       -0.789012
50%          0.000001        0.000123  ...        0.000245        0.000345
75%          0.678901        0.789012  ...        0.678954        0.789012
max          4.567890        4.789123  ...        4.890123        4.567890
```

This simple exercise highlights the kind of data volumes modern systems often deal with and the basic operations applied to them. Such data volumes necessitate tools and technologies specifically designed to scale and handle large datasets efficiently.

Technology choices for managing big data vary based on specific use cases. For batch processing of large datasets, the Hadoop ecosystem offers robust tools like HDFS for storage and MapReduce for processing. For real-time analysis and stream processing, frameworks such as Apache Spark and Apache Flink provide the necessary capabilities. When dealing with diverse data types, NoSQL databases like MongoDB and Cassandra come into play due to their flexible schema design.

Considering the specific needs of different applications, it is crucial to select appropriate tools and technologies based on their strengths and capabilities in handling volume, velocity, and variety. This strategic alignment ensures efficient data storage, processing, and analysis, thus unlocking the potential value of big data.

10.2 Characteristics of Big Data

Big data is typically characterized by several fundamental attributes that distinguish it from traditional data sets. These key characteristics are commonly referred to as the "3Vs": Volume, Velocity, and Variety. In more advanced discussions, two additional attributes, Veracity and Value, are often included, bringing the total to "5Vs." Understanding these characteristics is essential for grasping the complexities involved in the storage, processing, and analysis of big data.

- **Volume** refers to the vast amount of data generated every second. Traditional data management systems often struggle to handle such large datasets efficiently. For instance, social media platforms like Twitter and Facebook generate terabytes of data every day due to millions of users continuously contributing content. This immense scale of data requires specialized storage solutions and scalable architectures to manage and analyze effectively.

- **Velocity** pertains to the speed at which new data is generated and the pace at which it needs to be processed. Real-time data from financial markets, sensor networks, and online transactions illustrate the necessity of handling high-velocity data streams. Technologies such as Apache Kafka and Apache Storm are specifically designed to cope with the demands of real-time data processing, enabling businesses to act on timely insights.

- **Variety** underscores the different types of data generated from numerous sources. Unlike traditional data, which is often structured and stored in relational databases, big data encompasses structured, semi-structured, and unstructured formats. Examples include text, images, videos, log files, and sensor data. This diversity introduces complexity in data storage and necessitates advanced parsing and querying capabilities offered by NoSQL databases and data warehousing tools.

- **Veracity** deals with the uncertainty and trustworthiness of data. Given the diversity and number of data sources, maintaining data quality and accuracy is challenging. Inaccurate data can lead to erroneous insights and decisions. Techniques such as data cleaning, validation, and anomaly detection are crucial for ensuring data reliability.

- **Value** highlights the importance of extracting meaningful insights from big data. The ultimate goal is to derive actionable information that can drive decision-making and generate business value. This requires advanced analytics, including machine learning algorithms and statistical methods, to uncover patterns, correlations, and trends.

Understanding the 5Vs is paramount for effectively working with big data. These characteristics influence the choice of technologies and methods for data ingestion, storage, processing, and analysis. The following example illustrates how a simple MapReduce program can be written to handle large datasets, exemplifying the challenges associated with big data characteristics.

```
from mrjob.job import MRJob

class BigDataWordCount(MRJob):

    def mapper(self, _, line):
        words = line.split()
        for word in words:
            yield word, 1

    def reducer(self, key, values):
        yield key, sum(values)

if __name__ == '__main__':
    BigDataWordCount.run()
```

In this example, the mapper function processes each line of input data by splitting it into words and emitting a key-value pair for each word. The reducer function then aggregates these pairs, summing the values to obtain the total count for each word, demonstrating how distributed processing can tackle the Volume characteristic of big data.

```
$ python big_data_wordcount.py data.txt
"hello"  3
"world"  2
"big"    1
"data"   4
```

The output exemplifies the result of counting word occurrences in a large text dataset. Handling massive files efficiently reflects the importance of understanding big data characteristics and using appropriate tools and technologies.

10.3 Hadoop Ecosystem

The Hadoop ecosystem is a framework that allows for the distributed storage and processing of large data sets using a cluster of commodity hardware. As an open-source project under the Apache Software Foundation, Hadoop is designed to scale up from a single server to thousands of machines. The ecosystem encompasses a variety of modules and tools that integrate seamlessly to handle various aspects of big data.

At the core of the Hadoop ecosystem lies the Hadoop Distributed File System (HDFS) and the MapReduce programming model. HDFS provides scalable and reliable data storage, while MapReduce offers a robust and parallel method to process large-scale data efficiently.

Hadoop Distributed File System (HDFS)

HDFS is a distributed file system inspired by Google's GFS (Google File System). It is designed to store very large data sets reliably and to stream those datasets at high bandwidth to user applications. HDFS stores data in blocks, typically 128MB or larger, which are distributed across multiple machines in the cluster. Each block is replicated across multiple nodes to ensure reliability and fault tolerance.

Key features of HDFS include:

- **Fault Tolerance**: Data is automatically replicated and stored across different nodes to ensure fault tolerance. If a node fails, Hadoop can continue to operate and access the replicas.
- **Scalability**: HDFS can scale to accommodate petabytes of data by adding more nodes to the cluster.
- **Streamlined Data Access**: HDFS is designed for high-throughput access to large datasets, making it suitable for batch processing.

MapReduce Programming Model

MapReduce is a programming model and an associated implementation for processing and generating large datasets. It simplifies data processing over large clusters of computers. A MapReduce program is composed of a Map() procedure that performs filtering and sorting, and a Reduce() procedure that performs a summary operation.

In the Map phase, the input data is divided into multiple chunks, and each chunk is processed by a mapper function to produce key-value pairs. These key-value pairs are then shuffled and sorted, and the Reduce phase consolidates the results.

Example MapReduce code in Java:

```
import java.io.IOException;
import org.apache.hadoop.conf.Configuration;
import org.apache.hadoop.fs.Path;
import org.apache.hadoop.io.IntWritable;
import org.apache.hadoop.io.Text;
import org.apache.hadoop.mapreduce.Job;
import org.apache.hadoop.mapreduce.Mapper;
import org.apache.hadoop.mapreduce.Reducer;
import org.apache.hadoop.mapreduce.lib.input.FileInputFormat;
import org.apache.hadoop.mapreduce.lib.output.FileOutputFormat;

public class WordCount {
```

```
    public static class TokenizerMapper
        extends Mapper<Object, Text, Text, IntWritable>{
      private final static IntWritable one = new IntWritable(1);
      private Text word = new Text();

      public void map(Object key, Text value, Context context
                      ) throws IOException, InterruptedException {
        String[] tokens = value.toString().split("\\s+");
        for (String token : tokens) {
          word.set(token);
          context.write(word, one);
        }
      }
    }

    public static class IntSumReducer
        extends Reducer<Text, IntWritable, Text, IntWritable> {
      private IntWritable result = new IntWritable();

      public void reduce(Text key, Iterable<IntWritable> values,
                         Context context
                         ) throws IOException, InterruptedException {
        int sum = 0;
        for (IntWritable val : values) {
          sum += val.get();
        }
        result.set(sum);
        context.write(key, result);
      }
    }

    public static void main(String[] args) throws Exception {
      Configuration conf = new Configuration();
      Job job = Job.getInstance(conf, "word count");
      job.setJarByClass(WordCount.class);
      job.setMapperClass(TokenizerMapper.class);
      job.setCombinerClass(IntSumReducer.class);
      job.setReducerClass(IntSumReducer.class);
      job.setOutputKeyClass(Text.class);
      job.setOutputValueClass(IntWritable.class);
      FileInputFormat.addInputPath(job, new Path(args[0]));
      FileOutputFormat.setOutputPath(job, new Path(args[1]));
      System.exit(job.waitForCompletion(true) ? 0 : 1);
    }
}
```

Upon execution, the above Java code performs a word count task across a distributed dataset. The mapper tokenizes the input text and emits key-value pairs, while the reducer sums these counts.

Utilities and Add-ons in the Hadoop Ecosystem

1. **Hadoop YARN**: Stands for Yet Another Resource Negotiator, YARN is a resource management layer for Hadoop. It allows for efficient management and scheduling of resources across the cluster. YARN separates the resource management layer

(ResourceManager) from the processing component, making Hadoop more flexible and scalable.

2. **Apache Hive**: A data warehousing solution that facilitates querying and managing large datasets residing in distributed storage. Hive uses a SQL-like language called HiveQL, which allows users to run queries and retrieve data with ease. Queries are converted to MapReduce jobs automatically, optimizing performance.

3. **Apache Pig**: A high-level platform for creating MapReduce programs used with Hadoop. Pig's language, Pig Latin, abstracts complex programming tasks into simplistic operations like joins, filters, and sorts, which are then translated into MapReduce jobs.

4. **HBase**: An open-source, non-relational, distributed database modeled after Google's Bigtable. HBase runs on top of HDFS and allows for real-time read/write access to large datasets, supporting structured and semi-structured data.

5. **Apache Zookeeper**: A centralized service for maintaining configuration information, naming, providing distributed synchronization, and providing group services. It is essential for coordinating various distributed applications and services in the Hadoop ecosystem.

6. **Sqoop**: A tool designed for efficiently transferring bulk data between Hadoop and structured data stores such as relational databases. It utilizes MapReduce to import and export the data, ensuring reliability and speed.

7. **Flume**: A distributed service for efficiently collecting, aggregating, and moving large amounts of log data from various sources to a centralized data store.

8. **Oozie**: A workflow scheduler system designed to manage Hadoop jobs. Oozie workflows are defined as Directed Acyclic Graphs (DAGs), which specify a sequence of actions to be executed.

Each component of the Hadoop ecosystem integrates seamlessly to offer a comprehensive and powerful big data solution. By understanding these tools and their interoperability within the Hadoop framework, professionals can harness the full potential of big data analytics to extract meaningful insights and make data-driven decisions.

10.4 MapReduce Programming Model

The MapReduce programming model is a core component of the Hadoop ecosystem, enabling efficient processing of vast datasets in a distributed computing environment. In this section, we will delve into the intricacies of the MapReduce framework, examining its structure, phases, and practical applications.

The primary objective of the MapReduce model is to facilitate parallel processing by distributing data across a cluster of machines, thereby reducing the overall processing time. This model consists of two fundamental phases: the **Map** phase and the **Reduce** phase. Each phase has a specific role in processing the input data and generating the final result.

Map Phase: The Map phase is responsible for processing the input data. It takes the input dataset and distributes it across multiple mapper nodes in the cluster. Each mapper applies a user-defined map function to the input data, which typically includes operations such as filtering, sorting, and transforming the data into key-value pairs. The map function's primary goal is to break down the data into smaller, manageable chunks for parallel processing.

Here is an example of a simple map function written in Python:

```
def map_function(key, value):
    words = value.split()
    for word in words:
        emit(word, 1)
```

The map_function takes a key-value pair as input and splits the value (a string of text) into individual words. For each word, it emits a key-value pair where the word is the key, and the number 1 is the value. The output of the map phase is a list of key-value pairs that are then shuffled and sorted by the framework.

Shuffle and Sort: After the map phase, the MapReduce framework performs a shuffle and sort process. During this stage, the key-value pairs produced by the mappers are grouped by key. This step ensures that all values associated with the same key are sent to the same reducer. The shuffle and sort phase is crucial for aggregating the intermediate data produced by the mappers and preparing it for the subsequent reduce phase.

Reduce Phase: In the Reduce phase, the grouped key-value pairs are processed by the reducers. Each reducer applies a user-defined reduce function to the intermediate data, performing operations such as aggregation, summation, or averaging. The reduce function processes each key and its associated list of values, producing the final output for that key.

Here is an example of a simple reduce function written in Python:

```
def reduce_function(key, values):
    total_count = sum(values)
    emit(key, total_count)
```

The reduce_function takes a key and a list of values as input. It calculates the total count by summing the values and emits the result as a key-value pair where the key is the word, and the value is the total count of occurrences.

The final output of the Reduce phase is a set of key-value pairs that represent the aggregated results of the input data processing.

To illustrate the full MapReduce process, consider a word count example where the goal is to count the occurrences of each word in a large dataset. The following steps outline the MapReduce workflow:

- **Input Data Splitting:** The input dataset is divided into smaller chunks, each of which is processed by a separate mapper.
- **Mapping:** Each mapper applies the map function to its chunk, emitting key-value pairs for each word.
- **Shuffling and Sorting:** The framework groups the key-value pairs by key and prepares them for the reduce phase.
- **Reducing:** Each reducer applies the reduce function to the grouped key-value pairs, producing the final word count for each word.
- **Output:** The results are written to the output storage, typically a distributed file system like HDFS (Hadoop Distributed File System).

Word	Count
word1	5
word2	3
word3	2
word4	7

The MapReduce model's simplicity and scalability have made it a popular choice for processing large-scale data. Its ability to abstract the complexities of parallel and distributed computing enables developers to focus on defining the map and reduce functions without worrying about underlying infrastructure details. As a result, MapReduce has become a foundational technology for various big data applications, including log analysis, data analytics, and machine learning.

The MapReduce framework's fault tolerance is also noteworthy. During execution, the framework continuously monitors the mapper and reducer nodes. If a node fails, the framework re-executes the tasks assigned to the failed node on another available node, ensuring that the processing continues without significant interruption. This robustness is crucial for maintaining data integrity and achieving reliable results in distributed computing environments.

Understanding the MapReduce programming model is essential for leveraging the full potential of the Hadoop ecosystem and other big data technologies built on this paradigm. By mastering the map and reduce functions, developers can efficiently process and analyze massive datasets, unlocking valuable insights and driving data-driven decision-making.

10.5 Apache Spark

Apache Spark is a unified analytics engine designed for large-scale data processing. It extends the MapReduce model to efficiently support more complex computations that include interactive queries and stream processing. Spark's core abstraction is the Resilient Distributed Dataset (RDD), a fault-tolerant collection of elements that can be operated on in parallel.

Key Features of Apache Spark

- **Speed**: Spark achieves high performance for both batch and streaming data, using a DAG execution engine that supports acyclic data flow and in-memory computing. Operations are optimized to reduce unnecessary read/write to disk.
- **Ease of Use**: Spark provides APIs in Java, Scala, Python, and R, making it accessible to a wide range of developers. It also includes a rich set of libraries for SQL, machine learning, graph computation, and stream processing.
- **General Execution Models**: Spark allows for combining differ-

ent types of processing, such as SQL queries, streaming data processing, and complex analytics in one unified framework.

- **Advanced Analytics**: Spark facilitates complex analytics like graph processing via GraphX and machine learning via MLlib.

Spark Architecture

The architecture of Spark revolves around several core components:

- **Spark Core**: The foundation of Spark, providing basic functionalities such as task scheduling, memory management, fault recovery, and storage management.
- **Spark SQL**: Spark SQL allows querying data via SQL as well as through DataFrame and Dataset APIs. It supports a wide array of data sources.
- **Spark Streaming**: This component powers real-time data processing, enabling the approximation of batch computations on unbounded streams of data.
- **MLlib**: Spark's machine learning library, MLlib, includes common learning algorithms like classification, regression, clustering, and collaborative filtering.
- **GraphX**: Spark's API for graph and graph-parallel computation.

Resilient Distributed Datasets (RDDs)

RDDs are Spark's core abstraction for working with data. An RDD is a fault-tolerant collection of elements that can be operated on in parallel. There are two types of RDD operations: transformations and actions.

- **Transformations**: These are operations on RDDs that return a new RDD, such as *map*, *filter*, and *reduceByKey*. Transformations are lazy, meaning they do not compute their results immediately.
- **Actions**: These operations trigger computation and return results to the driver program or write to external storage. Examples include *count*, *collect*, and *saveAsTextFile*.

To demonstrate usage, consider a simple example in Python that creates an RDD from a text file and performs basic operations.

```
from pyspark import SparkContext, SparkConf

# Initialize a SparkContext
conf = SparkConf().setAppName("WordCount").setMaster("local")
sc = SparkContext(conf=conf)

# Create an RDD from a text file
text_file = sc.textFile("hdfs:///input.txt")

# Perform transformations and actions
counts = text_file.flatMap(lambda line: line.split(" ")) \
                  .map(lambda word: (word, 1)) \
                  .reduceByKey(lambda a, b: a + b)

# Collect the results
output = counts.collect()

# Print the result
for (word, count) in output:
    print(f"{word}: {count}")

sc.stop()
```

In the example above:

- SparkConf and SparkContext are used to initialize the Spark application.
- text_file creates an RDD from a text file.
- flatMap and map are transformations that generate a new RDD.
- reduceByKey is a transformation that combines values with the same key.
- collect is an action that brings the data back to the driver to be printed.

Excellence is evident in Spark's aptitude for handling sophisticated analytics and iterative tasks more efficiently than traditional MapReduce. Its support for multiple languages and seamless integration with various data sources further underline its robustness and versatility in big data environments. Spark's libraries unlock new potentials for data transformation and analysis across diverse scenarios.

10.6 NoSQL Databases: MongoDB, Cassandra

In the landscape of big data, traditional SQL databases often fall short due to their limited scalability and rigid schema requirements. NoSQL databases have emerged as a solution, providing the flexibility and scalability needed to handle large volumes of diverse data efficiently. This section explores MongoDB and Cassandra, two of the most popular NoSQL databases, highlighting their architectures, core concepts, and usage scenarios.

MongoDB

MongoDB is a document-oriented NoSQL database that stores data in BSON (Binary JSON) format, offering a flexible, schema-less design that allows for the storage of heterogeneous data structures within a single collection. This design choice makes MongoDB particularly suitable for applications that deal with rapidly evolving data schemas.

Core Concepts of MongoDB

- **Document:** The fundamental unit of data in MongoDB, analogous to a row in a relational database. Documents are composed of field-value pairs and are typically represented in JSON-like format.
- **Collection:** A grouping of MongoDB documents, similar to a table in a relational database. Collections do not enforce a schema, enabling diverse documents to be stored together.
- **Database:** A container for collections, providing logical separation for different applications or datasets within a MongoDB instance.
- **Replica Set:** A group of MongoDB servers that maintain the same dataset, providing redundancy and high availability. Replica sets consist of a primary node and multiple secondary nodes.
- **Shard:** A horizontal partition of data in a sharded cluster, enabling MongoDB to handle large-scale data by distributing it across multiple servers.

Advantages of MongoDB

- **Schema Flexibility:** MongoDB's schema-less design allows for dynamic modifications to data models without schema migrations.
- **Scalability:** Built-in sharding and replication support horizontal scaling and ensure high availability and fault tolerance.
- **Rich Query Language:** MongoDB provides a comprehensive query language with support for read and write operations, data aggregation, and text search.
- **Ease of Use:** The JSON-like document structure aligns well with modern application development practices, especially in web applications using JavaScript-based technologies.

```
db.customers.insert({
    name: "John Doe",
    email: "john.doe@example.com",
    phone: "123-456-7890",
    address: {
        street: "123 Main St",
        city: "Anytown",
        state: "CA",
        zip: "12345"
    },
    orders: [
        { order_id: "A100", total: 50.75 },
        { order_id: "A101", total: 75.35 }
    ]
})
```

The above MongoDB document insertion demonstrates how flexible and nested structures can be preserved, making MongoDB a powerful tool for applications requiring varied data representations and complex hierarchical data.

Cassandra

Apache Cassandra is a distributed NoSQL database designed to handle large amounts of data across many commodity servers with no single point of failure. It provides high availability and scalability, making it an ideal choice for applications that demand continuous uptime and massive data throughput.

Core Concepts of Cassandra

- **Keyspace:** The top-level container for data in Cassandra, analogous to a database in relational systems. Keyspaces define replication and durability settings.

- **Table:** A collection of rows in Cassandra, analogous to a table in relational databases. Each table has a primary key that determines data distribution across the cluster.
- **Row:** The basic data structure in a Cassandra table, identified by a unique primary key and composed of columns.
- **Column:** Represents an individual data point within a row, storing both the column name and value.
- **Replication:** The process of distributing copies of data across multiple nodes to ensure reliability and fault tolerance.
- **Partition:** The primary unit of data distribution in Cassandra, determined by the partition key. Partitions are stored on different nodes.

Advantages of Cassandra

- **Linear Scalability:** Cassandra's architecture allows for seamless addition of nodes, with throughput increasing linearly with cluster size.
- **High Availability:** Data replication across multiple nodes ensures that there is no single point of failure. Nodes can be added or removed without downtime.
- **Tunable Consistency:** Cassandra offers tunable consistency settings, allowing applications to balance between consistency and latency requirements.
- **Write-Optimized:** The write path in Cassandra is highly optimized for performance, making it capable of handling heavy write loads efficiently.

```
CREATE TABLE users (
    user_id UUID PRIMARY KEY,
    name TEXT,
    email TEXT,
    created_at TIMESTAMP
);
```

The above example demonstrates table creation in Cassandra using the CQL (Cassandra Query Language). It highlights the primary key definition, which is critical for determining data distribution and query performance.

Use Cases

Both MongoDB and Cassandra have distinct strengths, making them suitable for different types of applications:

- **MongoDB:** Commonly used in content management systems, e-commerce platforms, and applications requiring flexible, rapidly evolving data schemas.
- **Cassandra:** Ideal for time-series data, real-time analytics, financial services, and applications needing large-scale, high-throughput data processing.

Understanding the architecture, core concepts, and use cases of MongoDB and Cassandra is essential for selecting the appropriate NoSQL database for specific application needs in the big data landscape.

10.7 Data Warehousing: Hive, HBase

Data warehousing represents a fundamental component of modern data architectures, facilitating efficient storage, retrieval, and analysis of voluminous datasets. In big data, two pivotal technologies, Apache Hive and Apache HBase, provide powerful solutions for data warehousing needs. Understanding the distinct functionalities, use cases, and integration strategies of these tools is imperative for effectively designing big data systems.

Apache Hive is a data warehousing solution built on top of the Hadoop Distributed File System (HDFS), tailored for querying and managing large datasets in a distributed environment. It provides an abstraction layer over Hadoop, leveraging a SQL-like language called HiveQL, making it accessible to users familiar with traditional relational databases. Hive simplifies the process of data summarization, ad-hoc querying, and analysis.

The core components of Hive architecture include:

- **Metastore:** A central repository that stores metadata information such as tables, columns, data types, and the directory structures where data files are stored in HDFS.
- **Driver:** Manages the life cycle of a HiveQL statement as it moves through various stages, including compilation, optimization, and execution.

- **Compiler:** Converts HiveQL queries into a directed acyclic graph (DAG) of map and reduce stages for execution on Hadoop.

- **Execution Engine:** Executes the tasks in the DAG and interacts with Hadoop's job and task trackers.

- **CLI (Command Line Interface) and Web Interface:** Provide user interfaces for running Hive queries and managing data warehouse tasks.

Hive is highly suitable for data warehousing applications needing:

- **Batch processing:** Efficient handling of large-scale batch processing tasks due to its optimized query execution over HDFS.

- **ETL (Extract, Transform, Load) operations:** Streamlined data transformation and loading capabilities, enabling robust data pipeline implementation.

- **Data analytics:** Capable of executing complex analytical queries against large datasets efficiently.

Sample HiveQL syntax for creating a table and querying data:

```
CREATE TABLE employee (
    id INT,
    name STRING,
    salary FLOAT
)
ROW FORMAT DELIMITED
FIELDS TERMINATED BY ',';

SELECT name, salary FROM employee WHERE salary > 50000;
```

While Hive excels in batch processing and complex analytical tasks, it is less suited for applications requiring low-latency access and real-time data processing. This is where **Apache HBase** emerges as a complementary technology.

Apache HBase is a distributed, scalable, and NoSQL database modeled after Google's Bigtable. It is designed to provide random, real-time read/write access to large datasets hosted on HDFS. HBase supports the storage of semi-structured data and is ideal for applications demanding millisecond-level access times and high throughput.

Key components of HBase architecture include:

- **Table:** The fundamental unit of data storage, comprising rows and columns. Each table must have a primary key, and columns can be grouped into column families.
- **Region:** A subset of a table's data. Tables are horizontally partitioned into regions based on the row key range.
- **RegionServer:** Handles read, write, and management operations for regions. Multiple RegionServers can exist per HBase cluster.
- **HMaster:** Oversees RegionServer management, region assignments, and balancing of load across the cluster.
- **ZooKeeper:** Coordinates distributed systems, providing high availability and leadership election within the HBase cluster.

HBase is advantageous for:

- **Real-time access:** Providing quick read/write operations, suitable for applications like online transaction processing (OLTP).
- **Scalability:** Easily scaling out by adding more RegionServers to handle increased load and data.
- **Wide-column store:** Efficiently storing and querying large datasets with variable schema and sparse data.

An example of HBase shell commands to create a table and insert data:

```
create 'employee', 'personal_details', 'professional_details'
put 'employee', '1001', 'personal_details:name', 'John Doe'
put 'employee', '1001', 'professional_details:position', 'Engineer'
```

Hive and HBase can be integrated to leverage their respective strengths, such as batch processing capabilities of Hive with the real-time data access provided by HBase. Using Hive's HBase storage handler, one can query HBase tables using HiveQL seamlessly.

Example HiveQL syntax for querying HBase data:

```
CREATE EXTERNAL TABLE hbase_employee (
    key STRING,
    name STRING,
    position STRING
)
STORED BY 'org.apache.hadoop.hive.hbase.HBaseStorageHandler'
WITH SERDEPROPERTIES (
    "hbase.columns.mapping" = ":key, personal_details:name, professional_details:
        position"
```

```
)
TBLPROPERTIES ("hbase.table.name" = "employee");

SELECT * FROM hbase_employee WHERE position = 'Engineer';
```

Understanding the integration and use cases for Hive and HBase, in combination with each tool's unique capabilities, enhances the ability to design and implement efficient, scalable data warehousing solutions in big data environments.

10.8 Big Data Storage Solutions

Big data storage solutions encapsulate technologies and methodologies designed to manage and store massive volumes of structured and unstructured data efficiently. The heterogeneity and volume of big data necessitate robust storage architectures that allow for scalable, durable, and high-performance data access and retrieval. This section elaborates on several prominent big data storage solutions including the Hadoop Distributed File System (HDFS), Amazon S3, and Google Cloud Storage, outlining their architectures, functionalities, and use cases.

Hadoop Distributed File System (HDFS)

The Hadoop Distributed File System (HDFS) is a cornerstone of the Apache Hadoop ecosystem. HDFS is designed to store and provide high-throughput access to large datasets. Its architecture is highly fault-tolerant, making it ideal for big data applications.

HDFS splits files into fixed-size blocks (default 128 MB), distributing them across a cluster of nodes. By replicating each block across multiple nodes (default replication factor is three), HDFS ensures fault tolerance and data availability. The architecture consists of a NameNode and multiple DataNodes:

- **NameNode:** The NameNode maintains the file system namespace. It records the metadata such as the locations of blocks and their replication status.
- **DataNodes:** These store the actual data blocks and handle read-/write requests from clients. They also manage block replication based on instructions from the NameNode.

Data retrieval in HDFS follows a sequence where the client first interacts with the NameNode to locate data blocks and then communicates directly with the DataNodes to fetch or write data. The separation of metadata and actual data operations enhances performance and scalability.

Amazon S3

Amazon Simple Storage Service (S3) is a widely used object storage service in the cloud, supporting a virtually unlimited number of data objects up to 5 TB each. S3 excels in data durability and availability, leveraging redundancy models across multiple datacenters.

Amazon S3 stores data as objects within buckets. Each object consists of data, metadata, and a unique identifier:

- **Bucket:** This is a container for storing objects. You can create multiple buckets, each identified by a unique key and region.
- **Object:** An object contains the data (binary files), metadata (key-value pairs), and unique key which serves as an identifier within a bucket.

The S3 architecture ensures 99.999999999% durability by storing redundant copies of data across multiple devices in multiple facilities. S3's integration with Amazon's other services (e.g., ETL services, analytics tools) makes it versatile for various data storage applications. Below is an example of using the AWS SDK for Python (Boto3) to upload data to S3:

```
import boto3

s3 = boto3.client('s3')
s3.upload_file('local_file.txt', 'my_bucket', 's3_file.txt')
```

Google Cloud Storage

Google Cloud Storage is another powerful object storage solution suitable for storing large unstructured data. Offering unified object-based storage with high durability and accessibility, it integrates seamlessly with Google Cloud's suite of services.

Google Cloud Storage utilizes buckets to organize the global namespace and objects to store data. Key features include:

- **Multi-Regional Storage:** Optimal for frequently accessed data across various geographic locations.

- **Regional Storage:** Suitable for data storage within a specific location, particularly for regional analytics and data processing.
- **Nearline Storage:** Ideal for data accessed less than once a month, balancing cost and access readiness.
- **Coldline Storage:** Geared towards archival storage of data accessed less than once a year.

The data durability in Cloud Storage is achieved by duplicating data across multiple geographic locations. Below is an example of using the Google Cloud Storage client library for Python to upload data:

```
from google.cloud import storage

client = storage.Client()
bucket = client.get_bucket('my_bucket')
blob = bucket.blob('gcs_file.txt')
blob.upload_from_filename('local_file.txt')
```

Comparison of Storage Solutions

When selecting a big data storage solution, one must consider factors such as consistency, scalability, fault tolerance, and integration with existing tools and workflows. HDFS is favorable for on-premises data lakes, especially when integrated with the Hadoop ecosystem. Amazon S3 and Google Cloud Storage stand out for their scalability and integration with cloud-based analytics and processing tools. Performance can vary based on use case, geographical data distribution requirements, and data access patterns.

The following table provides a concise comparison of HDFS, Amazon S3, and Google Cloud Storage:

Feature	HDFS	Amazon S3	Google Cloud Storage
Scalability	High	Virtually unlimited	Virtually unlimited
Data Durability	High, with default 3x replication	99.999999999%	99.999999999%
Geographical Redundancy	Limited to cluster setup	Replicated across regions	Replicated across regions
Integration	Best with Hadoop Ecosystem	Strong with AWS services	Strong with Google Cloud services
Cost	Hardware	Pay-as-you-go	Pay-as-you-go

Table 10.1: Comparison of Big Data Storage Solutions

By judiciously selecting a storage solution aligned with specific use case requirements, organizations can optimize both performance and cost-efficiency in their big data infrastructures.

10.9 Big Data Processing with Apache Flink

Apache Flink is a powerful open-source platform tailored for scalable batch and stream data processing. It excels in processing large volumes of data in real time, with low latency and high throughput, making it an indispensable tool in modern big data applications. This section delves into the fundamental principles of Flink, its architecture, core components, and practical implementation details.

Flink is designed to handle data streams and is inherently suitable for real-time data processing. It provides a comprehensive set of APIs enabling complex event processing and analytical operations on both streams and batch data. Unlike traditional batch processing systems, Flink supports incremental event processing and stateful computations, ensuring that historical and real-time data can be handled concurrently.

One of the cornerstone features of Flink is its ability to treat batch processing as a special case of streaming. This capability is achieved through its core architecture, which is governed by the principles of stream-first, stateful, and event-time processing.

Flink's architecture comprises several key components, each playing a pivotal role in its processing workflow:

- **Job Manager**: This component is responsible for managing the lifecycle of a Flink job, coordinating distributed execution, and handling resource allocation. It splits the job into tasks and schedules them across available Task Managers.
- **Task Manager**: The runtime process that executes individual tasks assigned by the Job Manager. Each Task Manager runs one or more tasks in parallel and handles data sharing across nodes within the cluster.
- **Dispatcher and Resource Manager**: These components govern resource allocation and management within the Flink cluster. The Resource Manager allocates system resources (CPU, memory, etc.) based on job requirements, while the Dispatcher oversees job submission and job recovery.
- **State Backend and Checkpointing**: Flink's state backend persists the state, ensuring fault tolerance and exactly-once processing guarantees. State is backed up and periodically checkpointed, so that in the event of a failure, the system can resume processing from the most recent checkpoint.

The Flink API is both versatile and powerful, supporting multiple layers of abstraction to cater to different levels of user expertise. The core APIs include the DataStream API for stream processing, the DataSet API for batch processing, and the Table API/SQL for relational operations.

Below is an example using the DataStream API, illustrating basic transformations:

```
import org.apache.flink.streaming.api.environment.StreamExecutionEnvironment;
import org.apache.flink.streaming.api.datastream.DataStream;
import org.apache.flink.streaming.api.datastream.SingleOutputStreamOperator;
import org.apache.flink.api.common.functions.MapFunction;

public class FlinkExample {
    public static void main(String[] args) throws Exception {
        // Set up the execution environment
        final StreamExecutionEnvironment env = StreamExecutionEnvironment.
            getExecutionEnvironment();

        // Create a stream of data
        DataStream<String> textStream = env.fromElements("Apache Flink", "Big
            Data Processing", "Real-time");

        // Apply a map transformation
        SingleOutputStreamOperator<Integer> wordLengths = textStream.map(new
            MapFunction<String, Integer>() {
            @Override
            public Integer map(String value) {
                return value.length();
            }
        });

        // Print the result
        wordLengths.print();

        // Execute the job
        env.execute("Flink Transformation Example");
    }
}
```

When the above code is executed, the expected output would be:

```
2> 12
3> 18
1> 8
```

In this simple example, the Flink job computes the length of each string in the input stream. The 'print()' function outputs the length of each word to the console. The execution order of the output might vary due to the parallel execution of the tasks.

Flink's core strength lies in stateful stream processing. It allows applications to maintain arbitrary state in memory, provide built-in mechanisms for fault tolerance, and ensure processing guarantees. Here is a snippet showcasing stateful processing using the 'KeyedProcessFunction':

```
import org.apache.flink.api.common.state.ValueState;
import org.apache.flink.api.common.state.ValueStateDescriptor;
import org.apache.flink.streaming.api.functions.KeyedProcessFunction;
import org.apache.flink.util.Collector;

public class StatefulFunction extends KeyedProcessFunction<String, String, String> {
    private transient ValueState<Integer> countState;

    @Override
    public void open(Configuration parameters) {
        ValueStateDescriptor<Integer> descriptor = new ValueStateDescriptor<>(
            "countState",
            Integer.class,
            0
        );
        countState = getRuntimeContext().getState(descriptor);
    }

    @Override
    public void processElement(String value, Context ctx, Collector<String> out)
          throws Exception {
        Integer currentCount = countState.value();
        currentCount += 1;
        countState.update(currentCount);

        out.collect("Key: " + ctx.getCurrentKey() + ", Count: " + currentCount);
    }
}
```

The above code demonstrates a stateful function in Flink that maintains a count of processed elements keyed by a specific attribute. The 'ValueState' is updated with each processed event, ensuring precise state management across multiple streams.

To fully leverage Apache Flink, it is paramount to understand how to configure and tune its runtime environment, manage state efficiently, and employ advanced features such as windowing, joins, and aggregations. Fine-tuning parameters like buffer size, checkpointing intervals, and parallelism settings can significantly impact performance and resource utilization.

Apache Flink pushes the boundaries of what can be achieved with big data processing. Its advanced architecture, coupled with robust APIs, makes it a compelling choice for applications demanding real-time data analysis and processing.

10.10 Big Data Streaming: Kafka, Storm

The advent of real-time data streaming has significantly altered the landscape of data processing, enabling immediate insights and actions based on live data. Two key technologies in this domain are Apache Kafka and Apache Storm. This section delves into their architecture, functionalities, and usage in big data streaming.

Apache Kafka:

Apache Kafka is a distributed streaming platform designed for high-throughput, fault-tolerant, and scalable data pipelines. It is widely used for building real-time streaming data pipelines and applications that adapt to data streams.

Architecture and Components

Kafka is built around the following key components:

- **Producer:** A producer is an entity that sends data to a Kafka topic.
- **Consumer:** A consumer reads data from a Kafka topic.
- **Broker:** A Kafka cluster consists of multiple Kafka brokers. Each broker is identified by an ID and handles a part of the overall data.
- **Topic:** A topic is a category or feed name to which records are sent by producers.
- **Partition:** Each topic is divided into partitions to allow parallel processing and data distribution.
- **Zookeeper:** Zookeeper manages the metadata and health of the Kafka cluster.

Data Flow

Data published by producers is stored in topics. Each topic has several partitions which ensure load balancing and fault tolerance. Consumers subscribe to topics and read data from the partitions.

```
Producer -> Topic (partition 0, partition 1, ...) -> Consumer
```

Advantages and Use Cases

Kafka excels in scenarios requiring real-time data pipelines, log aggregation, and stream processing. Its durability, scalability, and fault-tolerance are unmatched for high-throughput data.

Apache Storm:

Apache Storm is a real-time computation system that processes data streams at scale. Designed for distributed, fault-tolerant stream processing, it integrates seamlessly with various data sources.

Architecture and Components

Storm's architecture is built around the following components:

- **Spouts:** Spouts are sources of data streams. They read data from an external source and emit tuples into the topology.
- **Bolts:** Bolts process the data, performing functions like aggregation, filtering, and joining streams.
- **Topology:** Topology consists of a network of spouts and bolts. It defines the data processing pipeline.
- **Nimbus:** Nimbus is the master node that distributes code, assigns tasks, and monitors the cluster.
- **Supervisors:** Supervisors manage worker nodes, carrying out tasks assigned by Nimbus.
- **Worker Processes:** Worker processes execute the spouts and bolts for a topology.
- **Zookeeper:** Zookeeper coordinates the Storm cluster, managing metadata and statuses.

Data Flow

Spouts emit tuples of data into the topology. Bolts consume these tuples, process them, and may emit new tuples to other bolts.

```
Spout -> Bolt1 -> Bolt2 -> ...
```

Advantages and Use Cases

Storm's strengths lie in its low latency and fault tolerance. It is utilized for real-time analytics, online machine learning, continuous computation, and network monitoring.

Kafka-Storm Integration:

Combining Kafka with Storm forms a potent system for real-time stream processing. Kafka can serve as a message broker between data producers and Storm's real-time processing capabilities.

```
[Producer] -> [Kafka Topic] -> [Kafka Spout] -> [Storm Bolt] -> [Final Processing]
```

Example: Real-time Data Pipeline Using Kafka and Storm

Consider a real-time system for processing logs generated by a web server. Logs are sent to Kafka, consumed by a Storm spout, processed by various bolts, and stored back into a database or another system.

```
// Kafka producer sending logs to a topic
class LogProducer {
    public static void main(String[] args) {
        KafkaProducer<String, String> producer = new KafkaProducer<>(props);
        for(int i = 0; i < 100; i++) {
            producer.send(new ProducerRecord<>("logs-topic", Integer.toString(i), "log
                message" + i));
        }
        producer.close();
    }
}

// Storm topology for processing logs
TopologyBuilder builder = new TopologyBuilder();
builder.setSpout("log-spout", new KafkaSpout(spoutConfig), 1);
builder.setBolt("process-log", new LogProcessorBolt(), 2).shuffleGrouping("log-spout");
builder.setBolt("save-log", new SaveToDatabaseBolt(), 1).shuffleGrouping("process-log"
    );

StormTopology topology = builder.createTopology();
Cluster cluster = new LocalCluster();
cluster.submitTopology("log-processing-topology", config, topology);
```

[Output Example: Processed log messages stored in the database]

Kafka and Storm together create a robust, real-time processing system optimized for scalability and fault tolerance. Understanding their integration and individual components is crucial for building efficient and reliable big data streaming solutions.

10.11 Data Lakes and Data Lakehouses

Data lakes and data lakehouses represent modern paradigms in data storage and processing, addressing the limitations of traditional data warehouses and catering to the growing needs of big data analytics. As data volumes increase exponentially, these architectures provide scalable, flexible, and cost-effective solutions for storing large quantities of raw, unprocessed data while enabling sophisticated analysis and real-time processing capabilities.

Data lakes serve as centralized repositories for storing structured, semi-structured, and unstructured data in its native format. They are characterized by their high storage capacities and support for a wide variety of data types without the need for pre-defined schemas. This flexibility allows organizations to ingest data quickly from diverse sources such as transactional systems, IoT devices, social media, and more. The following example illustrates a basic data ingestion process into a data lake using Apache Kafka for real-time stream processing:

```
from kafka import KafkaProducer
import json

producer = KafkaProducer(bootstrap_servers='localhost:9092', value_serializer=
    lambda v: json.dumps(v).encode('utf-8'))

# Example data record
data_record = {
    'sensor_id': 'sensor_1',
    'timestamp': '2023-10-01T12:00:00Z',
    'temperature': 23.5,
    'humidity': 45.2
}

# Send record to Kafka topic named 'sensor_data'
producer.send('sensor_data', data_record)
producer.flush()
```

The ingestion process involves sending data records to a Kafka topic, from where they can be persisted in the data lake. This approach ensures low-latency data capture and immediate availability for downstream processing.

Data lakes are not without their challenges, notably concerning data governance, quality, and performance efficiency. To address these issues, the concept of data lakehouses has emerged. Data lakehouses blend the best features of data lakes and data warehouses, providing a unified architecture that supports both large-scale data storage and high-performance analytics.

Data lakehouses offer several key advantages:

- **Schema Enforcement and Governance:** Unlike traditional data lakes, data lakehouses enforce schema definitions upon write, which ensures data quality and consistency. This is particularly useful in meeting regulatory and compliance requirements.
- **Optimized Storage Format:** Data lakehouses employ columnar storage formats such as Apache Parquet or ORC, which enable efficient storage and retrieval operations, reducing query times significantly.
- **ACID Transactions:** They support ACID (Atomicity, Consistency, Isolation, Durability) properties, allowing for reliable and consistent data operations across concurrent users.

- **Unified Analytics:** Data lakehouses allow SQL-based query engines and advanced analytics tools to operate on data stored in its raw form, facilitating analytics workflows without the need for extensive data transformation.

Consider an implementation example of a data lakehouse using Delta Lake, an open-source storage layer that brings ACID transactions to Apache Spark and big data workloads:

```
from pyspark.sql import SparkSession
from delta import *

# Initialize Spark session with Delta Lake support
builder = SparkSession.builder.appName("DeltaLakeExample").master("local")
builder.config("spark.sql.extensions", "io.delta.sql.DeltaSparkSessionExtension")
builder.config("spark.sql.catalog.spark_catalog", "org.apache.spark.sql.delta.catalog.
    DeltaCatalog")
spark = configure_spark_with_delta_pip(builder).getOrCreate()

# Example DataFrame
data = [
    {"sensor_id": "sensor_1", "timestamp": "2023-10-01T12:00:00Z", "temperature":
        23.5, "humidity": 45.2},
    {"sensor_id": "sensor_2", "timestamp": "2023-10-01T12:01:00Z", "temperature":
        24.0, "humidity": 43.8}
]
df = spark.createDataFrame(data)

# Write DataFrame to Delta Lake
df.write.format("delta").mode("overwrite").save("/tmp/delta/sensor_data")

# Read from Delta Lake
delta_df = spark.read.format("delta").load("/tmp/delta/sensor_data")
delta_df.show()
```

```
+---------+--------------------+-----------+--------+
|sensor_id|           timestamp|temperature|humidity|
+---------+--------------------+-----------+--------+
| sensor_1|2023-10-01T12:00:...|       23.5|    45.2|
| sensor_2|2023-10-01T12:01:...|       24.0|    43.8|
+---------+--------------------+-----------+--------+
```

In this example, a Delta Lake instance is created within an Apache Spark environment. The data is written to and read from the Delta Lake, leveraging its ACID transaction support and ensuring data consistency.

Data lakehouses cater to diverse analytics needs, combining the low-cost storage capabilities of data lakes with the robust performance of data warehouses. Their ability to support real-time, batch, and interactive workloads makes them a versatile solution for modern big data architectures, fostering innovation and deriving meaningful insights from vast data volumes.

10.12 Big Data in the Cloud

The advent of cloud computing has significantly transformed the landscape of big data analytics, offering scalable, flexible, and cost-effective solutions for processing large datasets. Cloud platforms provide a variety of services specifically designed to handle big data challenges, including storage, processing, and analytics. This section will discuss the key features and benefits of big data in the cloud, prominent cloud service providers, and commonly used tools and services for big data analytics in the cloud.

Cloud computing offers several advantages for big data analytics:

- **Scalability:** Cloud platforms can seamlessly scale to accommodate growing data volumes. Users can easily add or remove resources as needed, ensuring that the infrastructure can handle varying workloads efficiently.
- **Cost Efficiency:** Cloud services operate on a pay-as-you-go model. Organizations can avoid the upfront costs of purchasing hardware and only pay for the resources they use, resulting in better cost management.
- **Flexibility and Agility:** Cloud platforms provide various services and tools that can be quickly provisioned and configured. This flexibility allows organizations to experiment with different configurations and technologies, accelerating innovation.
- **Managed Services:** Many cloud providers offer managed services for big data analytics, such as database management, machine learning, and data warehousing. This reduces the operational burden on IT teams and allows them to focus on deriving insights from data.
- **High Availability and Disaster Recovery:** Cloud providers offer solutions with high availability, ensuring that data processing and analytics can continue even in the event of hardware failures. They also provide disaster recovery options to protect against data loss.

Several cloud service providers dominate the market with robust offerings for big data analytics. These include Amazon Web Services (AWS), Microsoft Azure, and Google Cloud Platform (GCP). Each of these vendors provides a comprehensive suite of tools tailored to different aspects of big data processing and analysis.

Amazon Web Services (AWS)

AWS is a market leader in cloud computing and offers extensive services for big data analytics. Key services include:

- **Amazon S3:** (Simple Storage Service) is a scalable object storage service designed to store and retrieve any amount of data. It is highly durable, with data redundancy across multiple availability zones.
- **Amazon EMR:** (Elastic MapReduce) allows users to process vast amounts of data using the Hadoop ecosystem. EMR can run popular frameworks such as Apache Spark, HBase, and Flink, providing managed cluster setup, file system monitoring, and node provisioning.
- **Amazon Redshift:** is a fully managed data warehouse that enables fast querying and analysis of large datasets. Redshift uses columnar storage and data compression to optimize performance.
- **Amazon Kinesis:** is a platform for real-time data processing. It can ingest, process, and analyze streaming data, making it ideal for applications requiring real-time insights.

Microsoft Azure

Microsoft Azure provides a comprehensive set of services for big data analytics:

- **Azure Blob Storage:** is optimized for storing massive amounts of unstructured data. It supports various data types, including images, videos, and logs.
- **Azure HDInsight:** is a fully managed Hadoop service that supports Apache Spark, Hive, HBase, and other open-source frameworks. It enables efficient big data processing and analytics.
- **Azure Synapse Analytics:** formerly known as Azure SQL Data Warehouse, integrates big data and data warehousing capabilities. It allows users to query data on their terms, using either serverless or provisioned resources at scale.

- **Azure Stream Analytics:** is designed for real-time stream processing. It can process data streams from various sources, such as IoT devices and social media, to deliver real-time analytics and insights.

Google Cloud Platform (GCP)

GCP offers a range of tools for big data analytics:

- **Google Cloud Storage:** provides unified object storage with worldwide accessibility and high availability. It supports different storage classes to optimize costs based on data access patterns.
- **Google BigQuery:** is a serverless, highly scalable, and cost-effective data warehouse designed for large-scale data analytics. It enables super-fast SQL queries using the processing power of Google's infrastructure.
- **Google Dataflow:** is a fully managed service for stream and batch data processing. Based on Apache Beam, it simplifies the development of data pipelines and supports unified programming models.
- **Google Pub/Sub:** is a messaging service for event-driven systems and real-time analytics. It enables ingesting and delivering individual messages or streaming data in real-time.

Implementing big data solutions in the cloud requires understanding different architecture patterns and best practices. A popular approach is the lambda architecture, which combines batch and stream processing. This architecture allows handling both historical and real-time data, providing a comprehensive view for analysis. Another prevalent method is the data lake architecture, where a central repository stores raw data in its native format. Tools and services from cloud providers can process and analyze this data, rendering flexibility and scalability to adapt to evolving needs.

```
# Example: Using AWS SDK for Python (Boto3) to interact with Amazon S3

import boto3
import os

s3 = boto3.client('s3')

# Upload a file to an S3 bucket
s3.upload_file('local_file.txt', 'bucket_name', 's3_object_name')
```

```
# Download a file from an S3 bucket
s3.download_file('bucket_name', 's3_object_name', 'local_file.txt')

# List all objects in a specified S3 bucket
response = s3.list_objects_v2(Bucket='bucket_name')
for obj in response['Contents']:
    print(obj['Key'])
```

```
Output:
<Console Output>
file1.txt
file2.txt
file3.txt
```

As organizations increasingly adopt cloud-based solutions for big data, understanding the offerings and capabilities of different cloud platforms becomes essential. Selecting the right combination of services and tools can significantly enhance the efficiency and effectiveness of big data analytics, enabling organizations to derive meaningful insights and make data-driven decisions in an agile, cost-effective manner.

10.13 Case Studies in Big Data

To elucidate the practical applications and transformative potential of big data, we delve into a series of case studies across various industries. These case studies highlight the real-world implications, challenges, and solutions emerging from the deployment of big data technologies and tools.

Case Study 1: Healthcare - Predictive Analytics for Population Health Management

The healthcare sector faces challenges in managing large volumes of patient data, which includes electronic health records (EHRs), imaging data, and genomic information. A prominent healthcare provider implemented a predictive analytics platform to improve population health management. By leveraging Hadoop and Apache Spark, the provider integrated disparate data sources into a unified data lake.

```
from pyspark.sql import SparkSession

# Initialize Spark Session
spark = SparkSession.builder \
    .appName("HealthcareAnalytics") \
    .getOrCreate()

# Load EHR data
ehr_df = spark.read.format("parquet").load("hdfs:///data/ehr")

# Load genomic data
```

```
genomic_df = spark.read.format("csv").option("header", "true").load("hdfs:///data/
    genomic")

# Join datasets
integrated_df = ehr_df.join(genomic_df, ehr_df.patient_id == genomic_df.
    patient_id)
```

The integrated dataset enabled the application of machine learning models to predict chronic disease risks and improve patient outcomes. The predictive analytics platform utilized logistic regression to identify at-risk populations.

```
from pyspark.ml.classification import LogisticRegression

# Prepare data for training
training_data = integrated_df.select("features").withColumnRenamed("label", "risk")

# Initialize logistic regression model
lr = LogisticRegression(featuresCol='features', labelCol='risk')

# Train model
lr_model = lr.fit(training_data)
```

Results indicated a significant reduction in emergency visits and hospital readmissions, showcasing the efficacy of big data in enhancing preventive care and health management.

Case Study 2: Retail - Optimizing Supply Chain Management

A leading retail company implemented big data solutions to optimize its supply chain management. By employing Apache Flink and Kafka, real-time data processing capabilities were established, allowing for dynamic inventory management and demand forecasting.

Using Kafka, data streams including POS (Point of Sale) transactions, inventory levels, and logistics information were ingested in real-time.

```
Properties props = new Properties();
props.put("bootstrap.servers", "localhost:9092");
props.put("group.id", "supply-chain-group");
props.put("key.deserializer", "org.apache.kafka.common.serialization.StringDeserializer"
    );
props.put("value.deserializer", "org.apache.kafka.common.serialization.
    StringDeserializer");

KafkaConsumer<String, String> consumer = new KafkaConsumer<>(props);
consumer.subscribe(Arrays.asList("POS", "inventory", "logistics"));
```

Apache Flink was then used for real-time processing to generate insights and forecasts.

```
StreamExecutionEnvironment env = StreamExecutionEnvironment.
    getExecutionEnvironment();
```

```
DataStream<String> posStream = env.addSource(new FlinkKafkaConsumer<>("POS"
    , new SimpleStringSchema(), properties));
DataStream<String> inventoryStream = env.addSource(new FlinkKafkaConsumer<>(
    "inventory", new SimpleStringSchema(), properties));
DataStream<String> logisticsStream = env.addSource(new FlinkKafkaConsumer<>("
    logistics", new SimpleStringSchema(), properties));

// Process streams to compute demand forecasts
DataStream<Tuple2<String, Integer>> demandForecast = posStream
    .map(new MapFunction<String, Tuple2<String, Integer>>() {
        public Tuple2<String, Integer> map(String value) {
            String[] parts = value.split(",");
            return new Tuple2<>(parts[0], Integer.parseInt(parts[1]));
        }
    })
    .keyBy(0)
    .sum(1);
```

The company observed a decline in stockouts and overstock situations, indicating improved inventory turnover and customer satisfaction.

Case Study 3: Financial Services - Fraud Detection

In the financial services sector, big data has revolutionized fraud detection mechanisms. A global bank integrated big data technologies using Hadoop, Spark, and HBase to combat fraudulent activities. The architecture involved the ingestion of transaction data from various sources into the Hadoop ecosystem.

```
# Load transaction data
transaction_df = spark.read.format("json").load("hdfs:///data/transactions")

# Feature extraction
processed_df = transaction_df.withColumn("transaction_hour", hour(transaction_df.
    timestamp))

# Store processed data in HBase
conf = {
    "hbase.zookeeper.quorum": "localhost",
    "hbase.mapreduce.inputtable": "transactions"
}

hbase_rdd = processed_df.rdd.map(lambda row: (row.id, row.asDict()))
hbase_rdd.saveAsNewAPIHadoopDataset(conf)
```

Machine learning models, including decision trees and neural networks, were used to analyze transaction patterns and detect anomalies indicative of fraud.

```
from pyspark.ml.classification import DecisionTreeClassifier

# Prepare data for training
training_data = processed_df.select("features").withColumnRenamed("label", "fraud")

# Initialize decision tree model
dt = DecisionTreeClassifier(featuresCol='features', labelCol='fraud')
```

```
# Train model
dt_model = dt.fit(training_data)
```

This implementation significantly reduced false positives and improved the precision of fraud detection, thereby protecting customer assets and enhancing trust.

These case studies demonstrate the transformative impact of big data on industry practices. Through the strategic application of big data technologies, organizations can derive significant value, optimize operations, and improve decision-making processes.

Made in the USA
Monee, IL
05 November 2026

67814357R00207